REALMS
OF THE
RUSSIAN
BEAR

A NATURAL HISTORY OF RUSSIA
AND THE CENTRAL ASIAN REPUBLICS

REALMS
OF THE
RUSSIAN
BEAR

JOHN SPARKS

LITTLE, BROWN AND COMPANY

BOSTON   TORONTO   LONDON

First American Edition
ISBN 0–316–80494–0
Library of Congress Cataloging-in-Publication information is available.

10 9 8 7 6 5 4 3 2 1

Designed by Harry Green
Map by Don Parry

Published simultaneously in Canada by Little, Brown & Company (Canada) Limited

Printed in Great Britain

Frontispiece: Coming in from the cold – the Brown Bear, magnificent symbol of the great wildernesses of Russia.

PICTURE CREDITS

JAN ALDENHOVEN pages 38, 44–5, 48–54 *all* & 64–5; PELHAM ALDRICH-BLAKE pages 18, 86 *both bottom*, 93, 199, 209 & 227; B. & C. ALEXANDER page 165; ARDEA pages 47 (J. A. Bailey), 56 (Peter Steyn), 186 (Ian Beames), 204 (Edgar T. Jones), 251 (Kenneth W. Fink), 254 (François Gohier), 257 *left* (Kenneth W. Fink) & 273 *both bottom* (Kenneth W. Fink); ASPECT PICTURE LIBRARY page 145 (Jan Vsetecka); BBC page 30; OLEG BELYALOV pages 15, 86 *top right*, 106–7, 128, 132 & 153; MARK BRAZIL page 264; FRED BRUEMMER pages 118 & 201; GLEN CARRUTHERS page 58; MARTYN COLBECK pages 80–1, 91, 96–7, 98, 148–9, 236 & 258; BRUCE COLEMAN pages 2 (Johnny Johnson), 130 (J. Zwaenepoel), 168 *bottom* (Uwe Walz), 193 (Jeff Foott), 207 (Wayne Lankinen), 252 (Eckart Pott), 275 (Orion Press) & 278 (Hans Reinhard); COLORIFIC! page 36 (David Turnley); RICHARD COTTLE pages 113, 115 & 123; ROBERT HARDING PICTURE LIBRARY page 135 (Chris Rennie); RODGER JACKMAN pages 40, 67, 68 & 69; RICHARD KIRBY pages 25, 221, 223, 229, 230, 234, 235 & 270 *top*; ALGIRDAS KNYSTAUTAS pages 88 *top right* (Oleg Belyalov) and 101 *top*; FRANK LANE PICTURE AGENCY pages 9 (Hannu Hautala), 203 *left* (Hannu Hautala), 205 (Silvestris) & 214 (Hannu Hautala); ANTTI LEINONEN page 29; RICK MCINTYRE page 27; NIGEL MARVEN pages 134, 138, 139, 244, 246, 248, 257 *right* & 269; ARNE NÆVRE pages 101 *bottom*, 161, 181 & 238; NATURE PRODUCTION, TOKYO page 210 (Seiichi Meguro); NHPA pages 42 (John Hartley), 61 (John Hartley), 87 (David Tomlinson), 168 *top right* (Melvin Grey), 173 (Brian Hawkes) & 226 (John Hartley); N. OBSYANNIKOV pages 155 & 194–5; OSF pages 105 (David C. Fritts), 218 (David C. Fritts), 224 (Doug Allan), 232–3 (Tony Bomford), 260–1 (Frank Huber) & 262 (David C. Fritts); EUGENE POTAPOV pages 88 *top left* (E. Golovanova), 117 (V. Tanaysitchuk), 125 (N. A. Orlov), 129 (N. Sablin), 147 (E. Golovanova), 160, 162, 177 & 191; MICHAEL R. RICHARDS pages 158–9, 182 & 183; G. RUSANOV page 71; YURI SHIBNEV pages 267, 268 *all*, 270 *both bottom*, 273 *both top & centre*, 274 & 280–1; JOHN SPARKS pages 20–1, 33, 66, 75, 77, 111, 112, 137, 141, 175, 179 & 241; JOHN MASSEY STEWART page 122; SURVIVAL ANGLIA pages 23 (K. Wothe), 73 (Bomford & Borrill) & 203 *right* (K. Wothe); GAVIN THURSTON pages 121 & 282; NIGEL TUCKER pages 83 & 88 *bottom*; JAN VAN DE KAM pages 168 *top left*, 169, 171 *all*, 189 & 190; WILDTYPE PRODUCTIONS page 131; ZEFA PICTURE LIBRARY pages 102 (Wisniewski), 142 & 215.

CONTENTS

Acknowledgements *6*

Foreword by *Dr Nikolai Drozdov* *8*

Map *12*

1   The Bear's Domain *14*

2   The Inland Seas and the Volga Delta *32*

3   The Celestial Mountains *76*

4 The Great Central Asian Deserts and Steppes *110*

5   The Arctic Frontier *154*

6 Siberia: The Frozen Forest *198*

7 The Far East of Russia – Born of Fire *240*

Bibliography *284*

Index *285*

ACKNOWLEDGEMENTS

Realms of the Russian Bear was conceived and completed during the period when the Soviet Union was disintegrating. Although it no longer exists as a political reality, the area formerly embraced by the USSR is still meaningful from the perspective of natural history because it is a geographical entity. The vast swathe of the Euroasian continent that was governed by Moscow was delineated on three sides by natural frontiers, the Arctic and Pacific oceans to the north and east respectively, and rugged mountains along its southern boundary.

Realms of the Russian Bear was written to accompany the BBC Natural History Unit TV series, but covers more ground than the programmes. The text gives a much fuller account of the landscape of Russia and the Central Asian republics, and of the characteristic creatures that inhabit them.

Information about the former Soviet Union is still relatively inaccessible to us in the west. Both the language barrier and the lamentable state of Soviet science conspired to make the task of researching the project somewhat difficult. Also, the absence of a thriving amateur naturalist movement was a hindrance. Obtaining the facts to plan the series and the book was not easy. I have therefore drawn not only upon my personal observations, but also upon other literature, both Soviet and non-Soviet, and information gleaned by myself and the other members of the production team on our numerous journeys across the former USSR. I am particularly indebted to Fergus Beeley, an Assistant Producer on the TV series, who ferreted out a great deal of information about the vast sub-continent. My fellow Producers, Pelham Aldrich-Blake and Nigel Marven, also willingly gave their advice, for which I am truly grateful, and Duncan Balfour Thomson was always on hand to translate obscure Russian texts.

Foremost among those who advised us in the Soviet Union was Dr Nikolai Drozdov, who not only introduces and narrates the BBC version of *Realms of the Russian Bear,* but also hosts the popular wildlife series on Russian television, *V Mirye Zhivotnikh* (*In the World of Animals*). His enthusiasm, charm and good humour did much to mitigate the grimmer aspects of working in his country. The time spent in his company elucidated both the natural history of the sub-continent and its bureaucratic systems, which achieve the heights of Byzantine complexity. Both he and Alexei Mackeyev, the Editor of *V Mirye Zhivotnikh,* were a source of great encouragement during the years before *perestroika,* when my preliminary attempts to talk about the possibility of making the series were invariably met by an implacable '*niet*'!

Among those who helped us with the filming and shared their experiences and knowledge with us were Dr Alexandr Alexeyev, Dr Alexandr Ananin, Dr Alexandr Andreyev, Dr Ernar Auezov, Alexandr Burduk, Dr Vladimir Burkanov, Dr Valeri Darkin, Professor Vladimir Flint, Dr Nikolai Formosov, Dr Vadim Fyalkov, Dr Edward Gavrilov, Vladimir Glasovsky,

Dr Gennady Karpov, Dr Alexandr Kondratiev, Dr Alexandr Konechny, Dr Igor Kostin, Dr Anatolie Kovshar, Professor Nikolai Kurzenko, Dr Yevgeny Lobkov, Dr Lena Muchina, Dr Rustam Muratov, Dr Vittaly Ostroumov, Dr Nikita Ovsyannikov, Anatolie Petrov, Dr Artyom Polkanov, Eugene Potapov, Igor Rivienko, Dr German Rusanov, Yuri Shibnev, Dr Leonid Simakin, Dr Vladimir Spitzen, Boris Studenin, Dr Pavel Tompkovich, Professor Nikolai Vorontsov, Professor Vadim Yevsikov and Dr Vladimir Zubakin.

I should also like to pay tribute to the long-suffering Soviet people whom we met during the course of our travels into remote places. Sometimes, we were the first foreigners that our hosts had met. What we saw and experienced made us very aware of our relative affluence in a country that was crumbling before our very eyes. And yet, despite the problems of daily survival, the endemic and shameful shortages of food, and often desperate poverty, many people invited us into their homes. These varied from small, crowded flats to tents made of skins erected on the Siberian tundra, in the valleys of the Tien Shan, or in the deserts of Turkmenia. In such places, we always experienced touching and unsparing hospitality. More than seventy years of Communism had deprived these people of almost everything that we have come to regard as essential in the West, but had not suppressed their generosity and desire for friendship.

Westerners working in the Soviet Union, especially on a project as complex as this, require an army of fixers and interpreters who can obtain the different layers of permissions, make contacts, extort seats out of Aeroflot, and spirit transport and accommodation out of nowhere! This was the role of the East–West Creative Association, a joint venture formed between Central Television (UK), Goskino and Ogonyok. Richard Creasey, its chairman, and Stepan Pojenian, its Production Executive in Moscow, vowed that the Association would move bureaucratic mountains to get us into some of the 'closed' frontier regions, and I am indeed grateful to them and their team for doing so. My special thanks go to our Moscow Production Manager, Igor Nosov, whose flamboyant style and sheer panache in the face of obdurate petty officialdom was a joy to behold. Pamela Bagshaw, David South, John Raymond, Caroline McManus, Olga Nosova, Tanya Karavaeva, Lena Smolina and Marat Transkii deserve a special mention for their assistance. In my own Bristol office of the BBC, I am grateful to Cynthia Connolly, Diana Richards, Jon Cox, Fiona Marsh and Isabel Pritchard for managing the comings and goings of camera crews and orchestrating without a hitch the ever more complex business of post-production.

The lenses of an international team of cameramen brought the beauty of the Soviet countryside and its wildlife to the TV screen, and, through their photographs, to the pages of this book. They were Martin Saunders, Hugh Maynard, Rodger Jackman, Richard Kirby, Jeff Goodman, Glen Carruthers, Jan Aldenhoven, Robert Brown, Michael Richards, Ian McCarthy, Gavin Thurston, Arne Naevre, Martyn Colbeck, Rick Price and Vyacheslav Belyalov. Martyn Kiszko's wonderfully evocative music enhanced their images.

Finally, I should like to record my thanks to Sheila Ableman, Martha Caute, Frances Abraham and Harry Green who masterminded the editing and design of this book. I am especially grateful to Jonathan Elphick, a fellow ornithologist with an interest in the Soviet Union, who took my text and moulded it so sensitively into shape. And lastly, to Sara, my wife, who kept Nikolai Drozdov supplied with delicious home-made muesli on location, and gave me daily support while I pored over the word processor.

JOHN SPARKS
BRISTOL 1992

FOREWORD

WHEN I FIRST met Dr John Sparks in 1983, when he was Head of the BBC's Natural History Unit, little did I realize that just seven years later I would be travelling with him across the vastness of my country, from the desert of Badkhyz and the mighty Tien Shan Mountains on our southern borders, to Yakutia deep in the cold heart of Siberia, and to Kamchatka, with its geysers, fumaroles and great volcanoes, on the edge of the Pacific Ocean.

John came to the Gosteleradio (State Broadcasting System) TV studios in Ostankino, Moscow, where he took part in *V Mirye Zhivotnikh (In the World of Animals)*, a television series that I host, which is watched by up to 200 million people; we have a very big country! His frequent visits enabled John to make friends with many Russian scientists and conservationists. In time, he became convinced of the need for a series of films that documented the magnificent scenery and wildlife of what was then the Soviet Union, harnessing the expertise of the BBC's world-famous Natural History Unit. Teams from its base in Bristol, England, had already travelled to most parts of the world and made outstanding programmes. But, hitherto, all attempts to work inside the Soviet Union had come to nothing.

For several years, great obstacles to John's plan presented themselves in the form of bureaucratic objections, and many less determined producers would have despaired and gone elsewhere to places where wildlife film-makers are openly welcomed. Luckily for us,

Looking like some fantastic sculpture, these snow-covered
ranks of trees form part of the vast belt of conifer
forest, or taiga, that extends from the shores of
the Baltic to the far east of Russia, forming the
world's largest forest.

John was immensely stubborn, and the difficulties seemed only to harden his resolve.

There were a number of eminent Soviet scientists who approved of the project, such as Professor Nikolai Vorontsov, then Chairman of the State Committee for Nature Conservation, and the well-known zoologists Academician Vladimir Sokolov and Professor Vladimir Flint. I also used my own influence to persuade the authorities of the desirability of allowing the experts from the BBC to film in our remote, wild places. However, despite such an encouragement, the plans might have foundered had it not been for the policy of *perestroika*, which gave our country opportunities and relationships with the West beyond our wildest dreams.

One result of this dramatic change in outlook was the creation of many joint ventures enabling the West to conduct business with the Soviet Union. One such organization was the Soviet-British Creative Association, headed by Richard Creasey, a distinguished British television executive. He saw the potential of John's plan, and harnessed the newly created Association and its officers to put the project into motion.

Finally, in the autumn of 1989, the programme of filming got underway, and from then until early 1992, John and his teams of talented producers, cameramen and sound recordists travelled to the most exciting wildlife areas of the Soviet Union. The crews came not only from Great Britain, but also from Norway, the USA, and even from as far away as Australia and New Zealand. When the shooting was in full swing, as many as six separate teams were filming simultaneously in different corners of this vast country.

I learned a lot from John and his colleagues, who shared with me some of the secrets of making the finest natural history films in the world. Foremost among these was their insistence that only the very best shots would do, even if it meant a great deal of extra effort on all our parts.

During the course of filming my introductions to the six episodes, I became enthused with the staggering beauty of the remote regions of my country. We climbed the great Inylchek Glacier in the mighty Tien Shan Mountains on our border with China. Here, the icy peak of Khan Tengri looms to a height of almost 7,000 metres (23,000 ft).

Our next adventure was to plunge far beneath the surface of Lake Baikal, the world's deepest lake at over a kilometre and a half (a mile) deep. We used the submersible *Pisces* to explore its depths and film the creatures that dwell in this mysterious world of eternal cold and darkness.

Then we journeyed to the southernmost point of the country, in Turkmenistan, on the border with Afghanistan. Here we shot some sequences in an ancient rift valley, where the landscape, with its remains of ancient volcanoes, (aptly named *kazany*, or 'hotpots') resembles the surface of the moon. With the air temperature rising to an unbearable 50°C (122°F) and the ground baked to a staggering 80°C (176°F), John insisted that we climb to the tallest and most difficult butte. When asked by one of the Russian members of the team why we could not content ourselves with reaching a nearer, much more accessible slope, John explained that, whereas another film crew might be satisfied with this, the BBC Natural History Unit never accepts second best.

The location for the next stage of our Soviet safari could not have been more different – the very heart of Siberia, where we visited the Verkhoyansk Mountains, the location of the coldest place in the northern hemisphere. Of course this sequence had to be filmed in the depths of the cruel Siberian winter, when the temperature occasionally plummets to almost −70°C (−94°F). It was comparatively 'warm' when we were there; it was only −45°C (−49°F)! But this was not warm enough to prevent me from discovering that even the famous Russian sheep *tulup* (fur coat) could not keep out the numbing cold.

My last expedition was to the Kamchatka Peninsula, part of the Pacific 'Ring of Fire' – a wilderness of volcanic cones in the far east of Russia. John persuaded our intrepid helicopter pilot to land inside the throat of the active volcano Mytnovsky. It was an awesome experience, talking to camera amid choking sulphurous fumes, with steam rising from the ground and great pools of boiling water heated by red-hot lava somewhere beneath my feet. It was a fitting climax to my journey across the subcontinent, and made me realize that, despite our difficulties, we have much to cherish.

I will be eternally grateful for the opportunity to make this odyssey through the *Realms of the Russian Bear*, and to visit places I had never seen and marvelled at in my thirty-odd years of travelling the length and breadth of my vast country. But just as important to me was making so many good friends among what I came to regard as the most professional team of wildlife film-makers ever to focus their attention on the Soviet Union.

It is my earnest hope that you will enjoy reading about the unique landscapes and wildlife of my wonderful country and that this book, and the BBC TV film series it accompanies, will help to ensure that these incomparable riches can be preserved, despite the great problems our environment faces, for future generations to marvel at.

DR NIKOLAI DROZDOV
Moscow State University, 1992

GERMANY

DENMARK

NORWAY

SWEDEN

BALTIC SEA

FINLAND

Spitsbergen

Franz Josef Land

ARCTIC

BARENTS SEA

Kola Peninsula

CZECHOSLOVAKIA

POLAND

LATVIA

•Tallinn

ESTONIA

Riga•

LITHUANIA

•Vilnius

Lake Ladoga

WHITE SEA

Novaya Zemlya

KARA SEA

ROMANIA

Carpathian Mtns

BYELORUSSIA

•Minsk

•St Petersburg

Lake Onega

Yamal Peninsula

Gydan Peninsula

UKRAINE

Dnepr

Rybinsk Reservoir

R   U   S   S   I   A   N

Pechora

MOLDAVIA

•Kiev

•Moscow

Ural Mountains

Ob

ARCTIC

•Nizhni Novgorod

•Kharkov

Don

Crimean Mtns

SEA OF AZOV

Volga

Volga-Don Canal

Tsimlyansk Reservoir

•Volgograd

•Sverdlovsk

Ob

BLACK SEA

Kuban

Caucasus Mountains

KALMYKIA

Ural

K   A   Z   A   K   H   S   T   A   N

Ishim

•Omsk

•Tomsk

Mt Elbrus ▲

Batumi•

GEORGIA

Kura

•Astrakhan

Terek

Irtysh

•Novosibirsk

TURKEY

ARMENIA

Volga Delta

CASPIAN SEA

AZERBAIJAN

○Kyzyl-Agach Nature Reserve

Ustyurt Plateau

ARAL SEA

Lake Tengiz

Altai Mounte

IRAQ

KARA BOGAZ GOL

Syr Darya

Betpakdala Desert

Lake Balkhash

Lake Alakol

Karakum

Kyzylkum Desert

Kopet-Dag

Karakum Desert

Amu Darya

TURKMENISTAN Canal

UZBEKISTAN

Ashkhabad•

IRAN

Repetek Biosphere Reserve ○

•Tashkent

Lake Issyk-Kul

Tien Shan Mtns

•Khan Tengri

KIRGHIZIA

Badkhyz Nature Reserve ○

•Samarkand

TADZHIKISTAN

Alai Mountains

Lake Kara-Kul

Pik Pobeda

CHI

Murgab

Pamir Mtns

▲*Pik Kommunisma*

AFGHANISTAN

Rudol

| 0 | 200 | 400 | 1000 | 2000 | METRES |
| 0 | 600 | 1200 | 3000 | 6000 | FEET |

OCEAN

BERING STRAITS ALASKA

Gerald Island

CHUKCHI SEA

Uelen

Wrangel Island

Chukotka Peninsula

EAST SIBERIAN SEA

New Siberian Islands

Chukot Mountains

Severnaya Zemlya

LAPTEV SEA

Omolon

BERING SEA

Byrranga Mountains

Lake Taimyr

Indigirka

Kolyma

Anadyr

Koryak Mountains

Gulf of Karaginsky

Karaginsky I

aimyr Peninsula

Khatanga

Yana

Kolyma Mountains

Penzhinskaya Bay

KAMCHATKA

Medny I

Bering I

Komandor Islands

Lena

Verkhoyansk

Chersky Mountains

Kamchatka

Klyuchevskaya Volcanoes

CIRCLE

Mountains

Oymyakon

Petropavlovsk-Kamchatsky

YAKUTIA

R E P U B L I C A

Yakutsk

Lake Kurilsky

Shumshu Island

SEA OF OKHOTSK

Angara

Lena

Stanovoy Mountains

Lake Udyl

Sakhalin Island

Islands

Broughton I

E R

Krasnoyarsk

Bratsk Reservoir

Barguzin

Yablonovy Mountains

Amur

Sikhote-Alin

Bikin Mountains

Kuril

Kunashir I

Mountains

Lake Baikal

BURYATIA

Irkutsk

Ulan-Ude

Lake Barun-Torei

Ussuri

USSURILAND

Hokkaido

Baikalsk

Selenga

Biki

Z

Kedrovaya Pad Nature Reserve

Lake Khanka

Vladivostok

MONGOLIA

CHINA

SEA OF JAPAN

NORTH KOREA

A

P

A

N

| 0 | 100 | 200 | 300 | 400 | 500 | 600 | MILES |
| 0 | 200 | 400 | 600 | 800 | 1000 | | KILOMETRES |

SOUTH KOREA

CHAPTER ONE

THE BEAR'S DOMAIN

THE SOVIET UNION was regarded as being as formidable as the Brown Bears that roam the length and breadth of this immense subcontinent. With our perceptions conditioned by a generation of the 'cold war', many people in the West came to regard this great land as a foe personified by the Russian bear – without doubt big, unquestionably powerful, and irascible enough to make it dangerous.

Fortunately, the enlightened policies of *perestroika* and *glasnost* initated by Mikhail Gorbachev in 1985 have brought about an unexpected and recently dramatic series of changes in the public face of the former Soviet Union. Previously, our view of it had been dim and distorted because much of the country was placed out of bounds and beyond the ken of people from abroad – indeed, most of its citizens were and still are discouraged from visiting areas in which they have no business or dwelling rights. Accordingly, the images that filtered across the Iron Curtain were largely those needed to embellish news stories about the USSR's military might and of political machinations within the sturdy walls of the Kremlin. But that was to change; the countenance of this huge, once monolithic country was to become transformed with astonishing speed, culminating in the formation of the Commonwealth of Independent States.

As part of the 'new thinking', a veil was lifted from the Russian empire, and swathes of her landscape were opened to inspection by foreigners, revealing great splendours that hitherto had been witnessed by only a few of her own people. And yet, despite the ever

Although a popular image of the former USSR is one of rolling
steppes and gloomy conifer forests, this vast region also contains great
areas of baking desert in the south-west, in the Central Asian republics.
At night, heat is lost to the clear skies, and the temperature plummets
to as low as $-31°C$ ($-23.8°F$) in winter.

increasing clarity of its image, this huge country remains a daunting challenge for the mind to embrace, where only superlatives suffice to give power to the descriptions.

The sheer size of this new Commonwealth beggars the imagination. Its boundary encloses almost one-sixth of the entire land surface of our planet; in area it is equivalent to twice the size of North America, and the British Isles would fit seventy times over inside its borders.

Over the ages, travellers have certainly had to master the scale of the place first hand. Before the age of the train, a trek across the continent to the wild Pacific coast could be achieved only by a combination of horses, carriages, sledges, and boats. Accordingly, progress was slow. It took anything from six months to two years to traverse the territory of Imperial Russia, with its fast-flowing rivers, mountain barriers, quagmires infested with infernos of biting insects, and immense, almost impenetrable coniferous forests. However, when the Trans-Siberian Railway – a monumental feat of engineering – was eventually completed in 1905, these impediments were mercifully by-passed, and the long-distance traveller had a sporting chance of finishing the journey in two weeks.

Today, the *Rossiya,* Russia's celebrated modern Trans-Siberian Express, completes the 9,500 km (5,900 mile) rail journey from Moscow to Vladivostok in six days. Of course, such distant places are effectively brought even closer together by jet airliners streaking through the stratosphere at nearly the speed of sound, and yet the cross-continent journey can still take eleven muscle numbing hours – the time it takes to fly from London to Singapore.

A Land of Superlatives

Although the majority of the former Soviet Union's 280 million or so citizens are of European extraction, in all, some 130 different nationalities and ethnic groups, and as many different languages, are represented within its boundaries. Although both China and India can boast larger populations, Russia and the other countries of the Commonwealth of Independent States have so much space and huge uninhabited expanses that the average population density is merely 12.5 people per square kilometre ($7\frac{3}{4}$ people per square mile). By contrast, the USA has a population density of about 23 per square kilometre (14 per square mile) and the United Kingdom is positively crowded, at nearly 600 to the square kilometre (nearly 375 to the square mile).

Like all statistics – and Russians revel in facts and figures – these need to be interpreted so as not to give the impression that humanity is thinly spread across the whole of the country. Far from it – much of the population is highly urbanized and packed into rambling cities, where large concentrations of people are housed in high-rise tenement blocks.

Not surprisingly, the former Soviet Union has the biggest area of any of the world's nations – 22,402,200 sq km (8,648,500 sq miles). It straddles both Europe and Asia; indeed, many Europeans are ignorant of the fact that the eastern border of their own continent extends way beyond Moscow to the Urals, that chain of ancient mountains that runs north-south from the Arctic almost to the Caspian Sea. From here, the frontier between Asia and Europe turns west along the watershed of the Caucasus Mountains, leaving the republics of Georgia, Armenia and Azerbaijan in Asia, but passing just south of the tallest peak in the Caucasus, Mount Elbrus, thus conferring on it the distinction of being the highest point in Europe. At 5,642 m (18,510 ft), this glaciated mountain comfortably exceeds the height of Mont Blanc in the French Alps by 835 m (2,740 ft).

A glance at a globe will reveal that Russia and her allied republics dominate the northern hemisphere. Furthermore, they stretch nearly halfway round the top of the planet. This means that a journey along the Arctic Circle from the westernmost border of Russia, on the edge of the Barents Sea, to the Bering Straits, within sight of Alaska, involves crossing no less than eleven time zones. Thus, when the inhabitants of St Petersburg are sitting down to breakfast, the thoughts of their compatriots on the Chukotka Peninsula are turning towards sleep. Even in winter, the sun hardly sets on Russian soil!

Landscapes, Climate and Vegetation

Despite its almost unimaginable size, the Commonwealth of Independent States is not as rich in variety of landscapes as one might expect. One reason for this impoverishment is purely geographical. Most of its vast area lies at a latitude north of the Canadian border. Moscow is at virtually the same latitude as Edinburgh, Scotland, or Halifax, Nova Scotia. Even Badkhyz, a spectacular nature reserve on the Afghan and Iranian borders and the most southerly point in the former Soviet Union, is equivalent in latitude only to Gibraltar or Chesapeake Bay. Because of their generally northerly position, the realms of the Russian bear contain no tropical rain forests, mangrove swamps or coral reefs.

The country's physical geography has had a profound effect upon both its climate and the natural distribution of vegetation and wildlife. Much of it is an extensive, relatively flat plain, that reaches only a few hundred metres (a few hundred feet) above sea level in the central and western parts. In the south and east, this vast, almost featureless area is rimmed by chains of mighty mountains and rugged plateaus.

These highlands run in a great arc from the Carpathians in the west through the Caucasus, Pamir, Tien Shan, Altai and Sayan mountains, along the Chinese and Mongolian borders, to the Sikhote-Alin Mountains in the Far East, opposite northern Japan. They act as a barrier to animals and plants from adjacent countries to the south. True, some birds manage to breach these formidable ramparts by migrating at great heights – the Bar-headed Goose, for example, crosses the Pamir and Tien Shan mountains every spring to nest in Tadzhikistan and Kirghizia – but these are remarkable exceptions.

The great mountains act as a climatic barrier, too. Warm, moisture-laden air from the tropics fails to penetrate beyond these and other obstructions, leaving much of the interior of the subcontinent somewhat dry and dominated by the Arctic and the cold blasts of air that emanate from it. In addition, much of the land is so far from the oceans that their ameliorating influence upon seasonal extremes is absent. In summer, the sun is sufficiently powerful for its heat to roast the landscape. But when its warmth wanes with the approach of winter, the temperature of nearly the whole of this enormous landmass plunges below freezing point. The Verkhoyansk region of north-eastern Siberia is famous as the northern 'pole of cold', with temperatures occasionally sinking to a numbing −68°C (−90.4°F). By contrast, in summer, the thermometer reading can soar to 38°C (100°F), resulting in the greatest temperature swing recorded anywhere on earth – an amazing 106°C (190.8°F)!

The mountains and high plateaus along the southern borders of the Central Asian republics are responsible for generating the moisture that irrigates much of their land. The high peaks catch as much as 1,000 mm (40 in) of precipitation each year on their wind-ward slopes, usually in the form of snow. This is slowly released over the course of the summer months into rivers such as the Syr Darya and Amu Darya which flow through otherwise arid lowlands, where the water is needed by both the natural and cultivated vegetation.

The lie of the land is also responsible for causing many of the great Russian rivers, such as the Ob, Lena, and Yenisei, to flow northwards. Arising in the mountainous border areas,

Left: Glinting in the distance like silver braid, frozen rivers thread narrow ravines in this winter view of part of the mighty Pamir Mountains, justly named 'the roof of the world'. There are an estimated 10,000 to 12,000 rivers and streams in the Central Asian Mountains.

Overleaf: Here, in the grim, frozen wastes of the Verkhoyansk Mountains, in north-eastern Siberia, the February temperature averages only −49°C (−56°F) and, in some winters, has dropped to −68°C (−90.4°F). Together with Oymyakon, in the valley of the Indigirka River, this is the coldest place on Earth outside Antarctica.

they flow across the continent for thousands of kilometres until they meet the Arctic Ocean. In winter, they freeze over, but in spring, the upper reaches thaw before the northerly stretches, causing great volumes of water to back up and flood extensive areas on either side of the rivers.

To the west of the Ural Mountains, the major rivers flow to the south, the Dnepr and Don feeding the Black Sea which ultimately spills into the Mediterranean via the Bosporus, and the Volga and Ural entering the Caspian Sea – the largest inland sea in the world. The surge of water that accompanies the spring thaw in the north also causes extensive annual flooding, especially along the upper Volga and its tributaries, where many animals are forced to seek high ground or drown.

Much of the moisture that falls on Russia and the Ukraine comes on weather fronts that sweep in from the Atlantic and to a lesser extent, the Mediterranean. After they have tracked across the European plain, they have lost much of their capacity for precipitation. Even so, Moscow receives an average of 685 mm (27 in) of rain and snow each year. But the interior of the continent is relatively less well endowed with rainfall. In winter, a large area of high pressure, the Siberian Anticyclone, becomes established over the centre of Siberia, and this blocks the passage of the rain-bearing fronts from the west, and deflects them northwards to become dissipated on the Arctic coast of western Siberia. The amount of rain and snow from these pulses of warm, humid air therefore diminishes south-eastwards, resulting in the semi-arid steppes and parched deserts of the Central Asian republics. This is one reason why the major vegetation zones lie in broad bands running diagonally from north-west to south-east across the Soviet union; the distribution of permanently frozen ground (permafrost) is another.

The Inhospitable North

The conditions in the far north of Russia are very severe, with the average temperature rising above freezing point for only two and a half months in the middle of the summer. The northernmost part of this northern fringe is an Arctic desert where few plants grow and much of the landscape is snow, ice and rock. This is the kingdom of the great white bear – the Polar Bear.

To the south of this polar desert, it is still too inhospitable for proper trees to grow and much of the land is open *tundra*, where a sward of mosses, lichens, hardy grasses, rushes, and herbaceous flowers, sometimes mixed with low-growing dwarf conifers, birches and willows, survives by tucking in close to the ground. Beneath the surface, the soil has been permanently frozen for tens of thousands of years. In places in the tundra, this permafrost layer is up to 600 m (2,000 ft) deep. Well over half the land area of Russia lies above a layer of permafrost. Tundra covers some 15 per cent of the entire land area of the former Soviet Union.

The Greatest Forest

To their south, the bleak northern landscapes merge with the *taiga*, the largest area of forest in the world. This, together with the steppe, is the kind of landscape that we all associate with Russia, especially when it is covered with a blanket of pristine snow, and the sun emerges to glint off the ice crystals like so many diamonds. At this time, the stands of white-trunked birches loom stark and leafless, and the spruces display their elegant form, with snow clinging to their downward sweeping branches. The scene is completed by a

Here, in the Pechoro-Ilych nature reserve, in the western foothills of the northern Ural Mountains, the Pechora River winds its way through the boundless dense conifer forest, or taiga. This huge reserve, 7,213 sq km (2,785 sq miles) in area, was created in 1930 and protects over 200 species of birds and 43 species of mammals.

troika moving briskly through the frozen forest, transporting peasants well wrapped in furs against the bitter cold.

This vision of Russia is quite appropriate. Covering about 8 million sq km (3 million sq miles), the taiga accounts for almost two-thirds of the land surface. Indeed, it makes up about half of the world's total area of coniferous forest and about a quarter of the entire forested area of the world; the Siberian part alone is one-third larger than the whole of the USA!

In reality, the taiga is a gloomy, forbidding wilderness of pines, larches and spruce trees that runs unbroken for 10,000 km (6,000 miles) from the Atlantic coast of Norway to the Sea of Okhotsk. In the north, the forest sits above a layer of frozen subsoil (the permafrost layer extends to a depth of up to 1,400 m (4,600 ft) beneath the taiga of the Yakut region of Siberia). Also, the drainage is very poor, and the ground is often covered by a soft carpet of wet, spongy mosses. Even excluding the European part, the Soviet taiga is the largest area of forest in the world. Blanketing much of European Russia north of the 55th parallel, it widens eastwards beyond the Urals until it engulfs much of Siberia.

Further south, the alchemy wrought by a more generous rainfall and temperature enables aspen, birch and alder to invade the conifers; other broadleaved species become dominant at lower latitudes, where warm, moist conditions prevail during the summer.

The Black Sea is regarded as the Russian Riviera, although its eastern end has a virtually subtropical climate, and is one of the wettest places in the former USSR. The annual rainfall in the Colchis lowlands, near Batumi on Georgia's Turkish border, is over 2,290 mm (90 in). In summer, the heat and humidity generate frequent thunderstorms and drenching downpours, and in winter cyclonic storms move up from the Mediterranean, cross the Black Sea and deposit abundant snow on the western slopes of the Caucasus Mountains. This climate, together with the fact that this area was not devastated by glaciers during the last Ice Age, is responsible for its wealth of plant species. Here, one can find temperate rain forest, complete with ferns and tangled lianas.

Towards the centre of the continent, the broadleaved zone is outflanked by the encroaching taiga to the north and by dry steppes edging in from the south. However, broadleaved trees really come into their own again in the far east of Russia, where the monsoons sweep in from the Pacific Ocean and the Sea of Japan to soak Ussuriland. Here, there is a unique combination of plants and animals from the northern taiga and the Oriental subtropics to the south, including many exotic plants and creatures, from tree frogs to tigers.

Rhododendrons glow in the sun at the Lazo nature reserve in Ussuriland,
at the southern end of the Sikhote Alin mountain range, on the coast
of the Sea of Japan. More than 1,000 species of flowering plants grow in
this lush habitat, including many rare and endemic kinds.

The Russian forests are home to a number of impressive though rarely seen mammals. Despite relentless persecution, Grey Wolves have the space to hide in the vast wilderness. Here, a walk in the woods can result in an encounter with these splendid creatures. Lynx – tufted-eared, medium-sized cats – also pad through the forests, ever vigilant for signs of rodents and roe deer upon which they feed. Large herbivores are represented by Elk (known in North America as Moose), Red Deer and Wisent, or European Bison.

The magnificent European Bison, which are rather less burly than their North American cousins, were once distributed throughout the forests of Europe and Russia. By the end of World War I, the herds had dwindled and only a few individuals remained in the Bialowieza Forest on the Russian-Polish border and in the foothills of the Caucasus Mountains. By careful breeding of both captive and semi-wild stock in zoos and reserves worldwide, their numbers were slowly built up, and today there are about 1,000 wild European Bison in Russia, mostly in special forest reserves. But pride of place among the animals of the Russian forests must go to the Brown Bears, the largest and most powerful of all members of the Order Carnivora.

The Great Russian Bear

From time immemorial, the Russians have regarded the Brown Bear with a mixture of awe and endearment. Whereas its might and unpredictable temper have led people to respect it, its sad hazel eyes and the tender affection shown by the mother bear towards her cubs have made this burly, flat-footed creature one of the most popular animals in the Commonwealth of Independent States. The Russian word for the Brown Bear is *medved*, referring to its legendary love of honey, but in the many folk tales in which it features, it is given nicknames such as the male name Misha, Mishka (an affectionate diminutive) or Koslapy (referring to its turned-in toes). Though clearly strong, Misha is often a touch lazy and often outwitted by the wicked wolf or by Lisa Patrikeyevna, the cunning fox.

If taken as cubs, bears are easily tamed, and many are still pressed into service in city circuses, where they are often dressed up and made to dance, ride bicycles and juggle. Sadly, despite the love that the Russian people have for these great shaggy mammals, large numbers are killed by hunters, even during the winter, when their lairs are found with the help of courageous *laika* dogs; when the sleepy occupants emerge, they are shot.

Bears need space, preferring thick woodland with a mixture of coniferous and deciduous trees, and the territory of the former Soviet Union can still provide plenty of both. Nevertheless, they occur from the tundra's southern boundary to the great mountain ranges of the south, and from the forests bordering the Baltic Sea to the shores of the Pacific. What was the Soviet Union could justifiably be called the 'Realms of the Russian Bear'. The only regions that do not contain bears are the dry steppes and the deserts of Central Asia.

Russian zoologists reckon there are about 80,000 Brown Bears between the Baltic and Pacific coasts. About a quarter of them are found west of the Ural Mountains. However, bears feel most at ease in Siberia and the far east of Russia, where people are relatively scarce. An estimated 15,000 live in the Krasnoyarsk region, 8,000 in the Amur-Ussuri area, and about 9,000 on the Kamchatkan Peninsula.

The minimum size of forest suitable for Brown Bears is about 100 sq km (40 sq miles), free from logging or other forms of human disturbance. In such an ideal situation, bears can survive at a density of three to every 10 sq km (three to every 4 sq miles). However, even in Russia, completely undisturbed virgin forest is a rarity, so bears are usually much less densely distributed.

Brown Bears return to their dens during winter and consume internal stores of fat equivalent to one third of their body weight, which they laid down during the previous autumn by eating huge quantities of berries and other nutritious foods. Some individuals, either through sickness or lack of good food supplies, may fail to accumulate sufficient fat. These miserable *shatuny*, or 'wanderers', roam the forests throughout the winter looking for food, and their irritable nature may cause them to charge and attack people. Sometimes, a bear becomes a *shatun* when it is disturbed by, and escapes from, hunters, because it is then unable to settle down again.

Bear Breeding

The baby bears are born in January when the females are dozing inside their snug dens. Females breeding for the first time often deliver only a single cub, but their subsequent litters usually include two, and there may even be three, rarely four, and exceptionally five. However, most she-bears give birth only every other year, although their fertility depends

A devoted Brown Bear mother suckles her six-month-old cubs.
Although the young are weaned at about five months, and regularly
accompany their mother on feeding expeditions, they continue to
take milk, and do not become fully independent for several years.

somewhat on the abundance of food. Up to a third of them may breed only once every three years.

The cubs are blind at first and at a weight of only 500–700 g (18–25 oz) are very small in comparison to their mother's great bulk of around 150 kg (330 lb): weight for weight, they are less than one-tenth the size of a human baby. This has survival value because the tiny creatures do not tax their mother's energy resources at a time when she must rely entirely on her body fat. But once they come out into the open, the cubs' initial chances of survival are not high. During the first year, 65 per cent of them die, and 57 per cent of those that live to experience their first birthday succumb before their second.

However, the fortunate cubs stay with their mother at first, sometimes for two summers, sleeping with her in her den during the winter along with their younger brothers and sisters. If the female breeds every year, she may have three generations of cubs in tow, with the eldest looking after the younger ones – in Russian, they are called *pestuny*, which means 'nurses'.

Inevitably, when the offspring become sexually mature, the mother chases them away, and the females accept males during the midsummer rutting period. Whereas female bears reach their full stature when they are five years old, the males continue to grow until they are ten. Once adult, Brown Bears have few enemies except man, with a natural mortality rate of only 5 per cent (although the mortality rates are obviously higher in areas where the bears are hunted). This means that some may enjoy the prospect of a long life of up to 47 years, although 30 is a more likely maximum.

Variations on a Theme

The Brown Bear is a circumpolar species, mostly associated with the taiga, which itself girdles the northern hemisphere. Those from North America are traditionally known by the name given to them by the pioneering settlers, who called them 'Grizzlies' because of the silvery, or 'grizzled', tips to their hairs.

Brown Bears are extremely variable, occurring in all sizes and in several coat colours. These characteristics were once used as the basis for differentiating a plethora of species – with some justification. For instance, there is a tenfold weight difference between the Syrian Brown Bear – the kind usually seen in zoos – which tips the scales at 68 kg (150 lb), and a real bruiser from Alaska, rearing up to 3 m (10 ft) tall and weighing half a ton

Scattering Ravens before it, a Brown Bear romps along the edge
of a taiga lake on a misty autumn day.

or more! Neverthless, contemporary zoological wisdom divines that they are all variations on the same theme, no matter where they live, and that they all belong to one and the same species – *Ursus arctos*.

Being large and omnivorous, with a taste for flesh should the opportunity arise, bears have never been thick on the ground, except when a glut of food causes temporary gatherings. However, Brown Bears are nowhere near as widespread as they used to be. Once, bears roamed throughout the North American and Eurasian forests, and they even inhabited the British wildwood during the Dark Ages. But bears and people do not comfortably share the same living space, and so over the centuries these great creatures have been forced to retreat as their haunts were whittled away by the implacable advance of human civilization.

Today, healthy populations of Grizzlies exist only in Alaska, Canada and Yellowstone National Park. As far as the Eurasian race is concerned, although there are a few bears in Spain, Italy and Scandinavia, the largest population by far occurs in Russia, thanks to its vast tracts of virgin forest. Here the Brown Bear is found at low densities throughout the taiga and other forests.

In the eastern part of Siberia and in Kamchatka, the bears supplement their diet of fresh

The pale, Isabelline, race of the Brown Bear lives in the Pamir
and Tien Shan mountains.

grass and berries with oil-rich salmon upon which they gorge themselves during the fishes' spawning runs. Accordingly, the bears prosper and some grow into magnificent specimens that rival the giant Grizzlies that live in Alaska.

Two separate and distinctive populations of Brown Bears are found in both the Caucasus Mountains and the mountains of the Central Asian republics. In the seclusion of the forests that clothe the slopes of the Caucasus, a few bears of the small Syrian race survive, and in the Pamir and Tien Shan mountains in Central Asia, the population consists of shaggy, fawn coated individuals. These 'Isabelline' bears also possess long, pale claws from which they derive their Russian name – *bielokogotny medved*, 'the white-clawed bear'.

Steppes and Deserts

South and east of the great forests, where the climate is less wet, the trees lose their dominance over the landscape in favour of perennial grasses. This results in another quintessentially Russian habitat – the rolling steppe. The transition is gradual, and on the northern fringes, there is a zone of 'wooded steppe', so called because of the presence of a scattering of trees, especially along the water courses, where their roots can tap into moisture. The true steppes are completely open to the sky and are equivalent to the pampas and prairies of America, and the east African savannahs. In Eurasia, they run from the Danube delta in Romania, across the north of the Black and Caspian Seas, through northern Kazakhstan and into Manchuria. To the south, where rainfall is even more meagre, they merge into the semi-arid zones and baking hot deserts of Central Asia.

Land of Contrasts

But the Commonwealth of Independent States is not only a land of tundra, taiga, steppes and deserts. It includes great areas of the Arctic Ocean, and a huge total area of wetlands – probably greater than those of any other country. On the edge of the Pacific, the Kamchatkan Peninsula hangs like a scimitar from the far eastern end of the continent. It is born of fire, with 29 active volcanoes looming into the sky. This is also the hunting ground for the biggest of Russian bears.

Brown Bears are also found looking for food on the shores of the greatest and deepest freshwater lake in the world – Lake Baikal – which sits in southern Siberia and contains enough water to supply the world's needs for nearly half a century. Likewise, the world's biggest inland seas are situated in the Commonwealth of Independent States, and the greatest of all of these, the Caspian, is the subject of the next stage of this safari.

CHAPTER TWO

THE INLAND SEAS
AND THE VOLGA DELTA

The south-western flank of the Commonwealth of Independent States embraces three of the world's greatest inland seas – the Black Sea, the Caspian Sea and the Aral Sea. How did these huge bodies of water come into being? Their history is complex, but the essential events are as follows.

About a hundred million years ago, a vast sea called the Tethys, connected to the southern oceans, stretched right across much of what is now the Middle East and Central Asia. Evidence for this can be seen today in canyons in Kazakhstan and on the border between Turkmenistan and Afghanistan, which have cut deeply into marine deposits full of fossilized shells of marine oysters that once lived on the floor of the Tethys Sea. Then, beginning about 65 million years ago, events in distant parts of the Asian continent caused the sea to shrink.

A fragment of Gondwanaland, the giant super-continent that once dominated the southern hemisphere, collided with the underbelly of Asia to form India. This produced a massive crumpling of the surface, throwing up the Himalayas and other chains of lofty mountains, such as the Pamirs and Tien Shan, that radiate from them into the territory of the Central Asian republics. As titanic forces inched the land up and slowly tilted it to the west, the southern outlet of the Tethys was gradually closed off, causing the once great sea to shrink and retreat westwards. Further bouts of mountain building between 25 million

Great beds of reeds stretch into the distance along the edge of the Caspian
Sea. This is the world's largest inland sea, and the shallow, sedimentary northern
Caspian, with an average depth of only 6.2 m (20 ft), supports
a rich community of birds and other wildlife.

and 10 million years ago resulted in the appearance of the Caucasus and Kopet-Dag mountains. Now a great wall of mountains encircled the depressions into which the remains of the Tethys Sea drained, isolating what we now see as the Black, Caspian and Aral seas.

The Greatest Inland Seas

The Caspian Sea is the largest body of completely enclosed water in the world, with a surface area of 436,000 sq km (168,350 sq miles) – a little larger than California and over one and a half times the size of the United Kingdom. All five of North America's Great Lakes would fit into just two-thirds of its area. It is 1,204 km (748 miles) from the northern shore to the southern, which is in Iran, and varies in width from just over 200 km (124 miles) to 566 km (352 miles). Despite its great size, most of it is quite shallow. The northern part, which has a flat muddy bottom, has an average depth of only 6.2 m (20 ft), less than the height of a small house. Further south, the sea-bed drops abruptly into two deep basins, separated by an east-west underwater ridge. The southernmost of the two trenches is almost 1,000 m (3,280 ft) deep in places.

With no outlet to the oceans, the Caspian would soon become reduced to a vast expanse of salt by the drying winds and fierce summer heat of the surrounding desert were it not for the fresh water pouring into it from the Volga and other rivers. Where the Caspian meets the Volga delta, the water contains almost no salt and the salinity in most of the rest of the sea is only about 1.3 per cent. But in the Kara Bogaz Gol, a large, shallow gulf on the eastern side, evaporation was so vigorous that the water had a salt content of 35 per cent, ten times that of most water in the oceans, and it was at a lower level than in the main body of the Caspian. Water used to pour over the lip separating the gulf to make good the loss, forming the world's only known marine waterfall. This unique phenomenon was destroyed in 1978 when a barrage was built across the entrance of the gulf.

The westernmost of the three inland seas, the Black Sea, lying between Europe and Asia, is not completely isolated from the oceans: it retains an outlet to the Mediterranean via the Bosporus Strait, the Sea of Marmara, the Dardanelles Strait and the Aegean Sea. The Black Sea has an area of 420,300 sq km (162,290 sq miles). Its southern and eastern shores in particular are flanked by great mountains. The maximum depth is just over 2,210 m (7,250 ft), in the south-central part of the sea, and the average salinity of 10 per cent is slightly over half that of the world's oceans.

In the north, the Sea of Azov, about 38,000 sq km (14,670 sq miles) in area, is connected to the Black Sea by the Strait of Kerch. With a maximum depth of only about

14 m (46 ft), it is the world's shallowest sea. Being so shallow, its waters become uniformly mixed and warmed, and it receives a high input of nutrients from the great Don and Kuban rivers and various other, smaller, rivers that flow into it. This has enabled the development of one of the world's most productive communities of aquatic animals and plants, with over 80 species of fish (compared with 180 for the whole of the Black Sea). The average salinity is very low – normally only slightly over 1 per cent – but irrigation projects on the Don and Kuban rivers have reduced the inflow by about 25 per cent. The currents have become reversed and, recently, saltier Black Sea water has entered the Sea of Azov, killing some of the fish.

Lying to the east of the Caspian, the Aral Sea has experienced dramatic changes in area and volume in geologically recent times. About 3 million years ago, the Aral and Caspian seas were probably joined. Subsequent movements of the earth's crust separated them and water flowed into the Aral chiefly from the Syr Darya – one of two great rivers running down from the mountains of Central Asia through the deserts surrounding the Aral Sea. Later, the second river, the Amu Darya, altered its course and flowed into the Aral, raising its level even higher. There followed alternate periods of inundation and relative drought, when only the western part of the Aral depression was filled with water, before a high water level became established throughout the basin about the first century BC.

Death of a Sea

Recently, the Aral has undergone another profound change – this time, as a result not of natural forces but of ill-advised human activity. Until 1960, it was the world's fourth largest inland body of water, its surface area of 67,335 sq km (26,000 sq miles) making it larger than any of the Great Lakes except Superior. However, over the next two decades, the Amu Darya and Syr Darya rivers were reduced to relative trickles. Their waters were hijacked to irrigate the cotton fields of Uzbekistan, and diverted down the Kara Kum Canal to conjure crops from the arid lands of Turkmenistan.

The price for this productivity was high – the changes resulting from the massive irrigation project led to one of the world's greatest ecological catastrophes. Deprived of the water that had replaced that lost by evaporation, the level of the Aral Sea dropped by 13 m (43 ft), and it is still shrinking fast. In a single year, between 1986 and 1987, its salinity more than doubled. What was once a healthy marine environment, sustaining a rich fishery with some twenty species and an annual catch of 25,000 tonnes (24,600 tons), is now a shallow, salty brew. The fish have gone, and so has nearly half the sea.

35

The hulks of abandoned fishing boats litter a dried-up canal in the dying Aral Sea. Deprived of water by ill-fated irrigation schemes, over 28,500 sq km (11,000 sq miles) of the once productive Aral waters have been transformed into lifeless deserts. Until 1960 the world's fourth largest inland sea, the Aral may have vanished completely by the year 2020.

The effect upon the local people and wildlife has been catastrophic. Not only has the once-thriving fishing industry, which provided over 60,000 jobs, been wiped out, but also the climate has changed for the worse. As the sea has diminished, the air has become less humid. Accordingly, the summers are now scorchingly hot, and the winters colder. Once the air carried beneficial moisture, but now it transports a thick, corrosive mixture of sand and salt. Between 40 and 70 million tonnes (39 and 69 million tons) each year is whipped up by increasingly fierce winds from the 30,000 sq km (11,580 sq miles) of newly exposed sea-bed, and blown far and wide, destroying crops and people's health.

And this is not all. Agricultural malpractice on a monumental scale has added to the misery of those who still live in the Aral region. As with other cotton-producing areas in the Central Asian republics, the excessive use of pesticides such as DDT, herbicides (including Agent Orange, the notorious defoliant used by US forces during the Vietnam War) and fertilizers have poisoned great swathes of land. The residues of this poisonous cocktail pervade the swirling dust and contaminate what little drinking water is left, resulting in a high level of throat cancers, birth defects and child mortality. Wildlife, too, has been devastated. Of the 173 animal species that once lived around the Aral Sea, including Wild Boar, Muskrats and egrets, only 38 have survived, and these in greatly reduced numbers.

Changes in the Black and Caspian Seas

The Black Sea will never suffer the terrible fate of the Aral Sea because its opening through the Bosporus allows a constant supply of oceanic water to reach it via an underwater current from the Mediterranean – as well as the passage of fish and other marine creatures. However, it contains fewer species than the Mediterranean. This is related to the fact that its waters are stratified into distinct layers. Fresh water discharged into the Black Sea from the rivers floats on top of the heavier, more saline water. There are no currents causing upwelling of the deeper waters, because the Black Sea is too small and the Strait of Bosporus is too narrow. This tends to prevent the mixing and penetration of oxygen from the surface to any great depth. Almost all living creatures need oxygen, so they cannot survive more than 100-150 m (330-500 ft) below the surface.

In addition, there is a more sinister influence working in the depths of the Black Sea. Beyond the first hundred or two meters, there is a build-up of hydrogen sulphide – the poisonous gas that produces the foul smell of rotten eggs. This is generated by bacteria that thrive on the sea-bed in the absence of oxygen, and is also released in jets from submarine hot springs, called 'smokers' or submarine solfataras. Held in solution in the depths, the hydrogen sulphide forms a powerful barrier to fish and other creatures. In recent years, the boundary between the noxious deeper waters and the oxygenated upper layer has been coming closer to the surface. This change is most marked in the centre of the Black Sea and is due to the reduced flow of the rivers as their waters are dammed and diverted for irrigating crops.

The Caspian, too, is experiencing new changes. In 1977, it reached its lowest level for 500 years, leaving fishing villages, whose houses once had water lapping against their walls, high and dry and destroying important shallow-water fish spawning grounds. However, since then, the water level has risen by as much as 1.5 m (5 ft), and may increase by the same amount by the turn of the century. Like Venice, this leaves ports such as Astrakhan and Makhachkala with the prospect of being inundated; the seaward face of the Volga delta will also be eroded by the rising water level, and the extra depth might make it less satisfactory for many kinds of wildfowl.

Why the Caspian's level should fluctuate like this is a mystery, but climatic changes and the draining of too much water from the Volga for irrigating crops have been implicated. Another possible cause may lie beneath the sea itself, where earth movements might be altering the topography of the sea-bed, resulting in changes at the surface.

The Origin of the Caspian Fauna

With a total of about 850 species of animals, the Caspian Sea has a relatively poor fauna for a body of water of its great size, but its animals are very varied in their origins. Although now completely cut off from the Mediterranean, the Caspian was joined to it via the Sea of Azov and the Black Sea until about 12 million years ago, when movements of the earth's crust severed this link. The Mediterranean connection was re-established about $2\frac{1}{2}$ million years ago. These links allowed a host of animals from the Mediterranean to colonize the Caspian, including pipefish.

When father is mother: a male pipefish carries his mate's fertilized
eggs in a brood pouch on his belly. This species, photographed
in the Astrakhan nature reserve, is endemic to the
Caspian Sea region.

38

Related to sea horses, pipefish occur in the lower channels of the Volga delta. Like sea horses, they are encased in a coat of armour made up of bony plates, or scutes, and also share a remarkable breeding system in which the males become 'pregnant'. A female pipefish lays her clutch of eggs directly into a brood pouch on the male's belly. After a short incubation period, the eggs hatch and the father gives birth to a mass of tiny babies.

In modern times, the invasion from the west has continued, as such creatures as mullets, flounders and prawns have been deliberately introduced by man, while others, including barnacles and clams, have made the journey by hitching a ride on ships that sail from the Mediterranean into Caspian ports via the Volga-Don canal. Most of the Caspian's freshwater species, such as carp, arrived by way of the Volga and other rivers that flow into it.

Other invaders came from the far north. The Caspian was greatly affected by the Ice Ages of the last million years. As the glaciers advanced and retreated across the top of Russia, the Caspian rose and fell by 50 m (165 ft) above and below its present day level, according to the amount of water released into the Volga by the massive ice-caps. As recently as 28,000 years ago, the Caspian was twice its current area. During this period, temporary connections were made between the White and Baltic Sea basins and the Volga, and these provided a route for Arctic creatures to find their way south, only to be marooned when the climate went through one of its regular changes.

Among the invaders were whitefish (Stenodus). These are members of the salmon family, and the Caspian species are little changed from their Arctic relatives. Brown trout also probably arrived by way of the northern route, and used to ascend the Volga and its tributaries to breed. There are also cold-water crustaceans which must have been swept southwards in melt water from the great glaciers. The Caspian has a very small nesting population of three species of northern ducks, Smew, Velvet Scoter, and Goldeneye, that may be relics of former, colder times.

One of the most remarkable and attractive of the immigrants from the Arctic is the Caspian Seal. No-one is sure exactly when this beguiling mammal arrived in the Caspian, but it is probably derived from ancestors of the Ringed Seal, a species which lives on the pack ice all around the Arctic and also in the Baltic Sea. It is a small seal, about 1.25 m (4 ft) long and weighing some 55 kg (120 lb), with a greyish-yellow coat marked on the upper surface with darker spots and patches.

Caspian Seals, which may live as long as fifty years, are confiding creatures and, as adults, have little to fear. However, during February and early March, the species is vulnerable as about 100,000 females migrate from other parts of the Caspian into the cold,

The attractive Caspian Seal feeds on a wide range of small fishes and crustaceans. This is one of the world's smallest seals. Today, about 450,000 individuals live in the Caspian Sea.

shallow northern end of the sea, to give birth to their white-pelted pups on the ice. Here they are met by seal hunters, who take between 10,000 and 15,000 pups a year in a scientifically managed cull.

In March, males arrive at the nurseries and mate with the females. As the ice breaks up, the seals moult before travelling south to the deeper end of the Caspian. Here, although the climate is subtropical, currents upwelling from the depths ensure cool surface waters and abundant food throughout the summer. In this way, Caspian Seals can cope with the greatest range of climates experienced by any of the world's seals.

As well as the relatively recent influx of animals from the west and north, the Caspian also received a living legacy from the ancient Tethys Sea. This includes foraminifera (microscopic, single-celled, planktonic creatures that build beautiful, intricate shells of silica), various sponges, bristleworms, bryozoans, shrimps and cockles and also some species of fish, such as herrings and bullheads. These have had to adapt to the drop in salinity that occurred after the Caspian was isolated. Although some of the fish still spawn in the more brackish regions of the sea, others migrate into the rivers to spawn.

The Mighty Volga

The Caspian and its bountifully rich wetlands exist by virtue of the rivers that flow into it. These include the Kura, Terek, and Ural. But by far the most important is the Volga, which accounts for three-quarters of the fresh water which continually replenishes the Caspian, and helps to maintain its current level. The Russian people regard it with affection and refer to it in the diminutive as *Matushka*, or 'dear little mother'.

Although it is the longest river in Europe, the Volga is by no means the longest of Russian rivers, especially when compared with those that flow across Siberia. Like most rivers, the Volga arises as an insignificant spring. It bubbles to the surface at an altitude of merely 228 m (750 ft) above sea level in the Valday Hills, between Moscow and St Petersburg. The lie of the land denies it access to the nearby Baltic. Instead, the Volga turns first north-eastward through the huge Rybinsk reservoir, then west and south to flow through the very heart of Russia, gathering strength from over 200 tributaries, until it reaches the Caspian Sea, 3,685 km (2,290 miles) away.

The Extraordinary Desman

The floodplains of the upper Volga are the home of one of the world's most unusual creatures – the Russian Desman. A relative of the moles, the size of a kitten, it is truly a living fossil because millions of years ago it was found throughout Europe.

The Russian Desman is thoroughly adapted for an aquatic life. Its powerful hind feet are webbed and provide much of the thrust for swimming. The tail is also used for propulsion, being laterally flattened and made all the more effective as a rudder by a fringe of stiff hairs. Like its terrestrial cousins, the Russian Desman is covered in soft, lustrous fur, but this is designed to repel the chilly water by the addition of a layer of oily guard hairs which project beyond the dense velvet undercoat. When the animal submerges, this retains a silvery mantle of insulating air from which bubbles occasionally escape to the surface, thus betraying its whereabouts.

Unfortunately, the pelts of these enchanting little mammals were once eagerly sought by trappers, and this form of persecution almost led to the creature's demise. Luckily, protection came in time to save this fascinating species, and now over 50,000 live in certain river basins like that of the Volga and its tributaries. The Oka Reserve, situated about 480 km (300 miles) south-east of Moscow, has a population of between 700 and 1,400, which live in its 500 or so ox-bow ponds and small lakes. Here, a part of the reserve is landscaped and maintained especially for desmans.

The Russian Desman's most commanding feature is its face. Externally there is virtually no sign of ears — they are embedded deeply in the fur, and the eyes are reduced to mere black specks surrounded by pale skin. Nevertheless, the desman makes up for any shortfall in its sense of vision or hearing by the size, shape, and sensitivity of its snout. This greatly

Its long, prehensile snout whiffling inquisitively, a Russian Desman
pauses on the melting ice at the edge of a river. Fossils indicate that
this remarkable aquatic relative of the moles lived throughout Europe
in prehistoric times, occurring as far west as the British Isles.

bewhiskered organ is fashioned like an elephant's trunk and is just as mobile. Whether on land or in the water, the nose sweeps frenetically from side to side, testing the air or water and probing every nook and cranny in the quest for food. For much of the day-time, desmans while away the hours in their burrows, but as evening approaches, they take to the water. Here, they root along the muddy bottom among the aquatic vegetation, using their noses like vacuum cleaners as they attempt to discover and dislodge prey, such as dragonfly larvae, tadpoles, small frogs and water snails. The latter are taken to the surface where the rubbery, mobile lips winkle the snails out of their shells.

Shallow, stagnant ponds congested with vegetation along major river valleys are the desmans' favourite hunting areas. They tend to live in pairs with the male defending a feeding territory. Each summer, as the floods subside, the couples retire to the banks into which they tunnel. Here, the female produces a litter of 1–6 young in a special chamber the size of a flattened rugby ball. She suckles them for about a month, after which her mate takes over while she busies herself rearing another brood.

Should the water level drop too much, causing their own pond to dry out, the desmans move to other areas of standing water. When the frosts of winter start to bite, and the surface of their ponds begins to freeze over, they continue to make forays under the ice from their under-water exits, often leaving trails of bubbles wherever they have rooted for snails among the dying weed. They maintain this routine throughout the winter until the spring thaw and resulting floods force them to leave their subterranean homes and seek the safety of the temporary nests they built earlier among willow branches or other waterside vegetation.

The Green Jewel of the Caspian

Draining about 2.6 million sq km (one million sq miles) of land west of the Urals, the mighty Volga carries approximately 350 cu km (84 cu miles) of water a year. Nowadays, the flow is interrupted by a series of massive dams constructed across the Volga for generating electricity, which also divert some of the water for irrigation. Nevertheless, much of it still reaches the Caspian, where it has built a broad delta of immense importance to wildlife.

Deltas result from erosion. Rain falling on the Euro-Russian plain dislodges grains of soil and fragments of rock, which are carried in suspension by water trickling into streams. These eventually meet the Volga. But as the great river widens on its journey to the sea, it becomes sluggish. The water current is no longer powerful enough to hold in suspension the river's burden of silt, which settles on the bottom as sludge, blocking the channels and

Overleaf: Groups of cattle take refuge on the sinking remains of old haystacks in the floodplain of the Volga delta. However, the spring floods are not only a threat – they also bring a rich supply of nutrients from the mighty Volga that help create one of the world's greatest wetlands for wildlife.

forcing the river to seek new paths. This begins to happen shortly after it passes the industrial city of Volgograd.

Further downstream, where the Volga merges with the Caspian, the current is weakest and, over the ages, huge quantities of the finest sediment have settled out to form a great, sprawling delta. This has an area of 10,000 sq km (3,900 sq miles) and is 200 km (125 miles) across on its seaward edge. But it is sometimes difficult to determine where the land finishes and the sea begins, because the delta continually creeps into the extensive northern shallows, which, in places, are only a metre (3 ft) deep and extend for 50 km (30 miles). Here, the Volga divides repeatedly like the branches of a gigantic tree, to empty its waters into the Caspian via a maze of 800 or so channels, producing a lush landscape of verdant pastures, vast reedbeds, ox-bow lakes, and lagoons strewn with lotuses and lilies.

Born of the union between river and sea, this green jewel set in the semi-desert of the south-eastern corner of Europe and flanked to the east by the arid lands of the Central Asian republics is one of the world's greatest wetlands, with a wealth of wildlife.

The Nourishing Floods

The Volga is the lifeblood of the Caspian and the river delta. Both are nourished by nutrients and sediment carried in her waters. Much of this is delivered during the spring floods. Each year, snow melting in more northerly regions of Russia creates a great surge of water that passes down the Volga. Although this sudden influx is now managed by its controlled release through the Volga dams, between March and May the river steadily rises to about 1.3 m ($4\frac{1}{4}$ ft) above its winter level.

To begin with, the network of small ditches and creeks fills with water, which spills onto the land, and then, as the flood peaks, all the main channels overflow their banks and inundate great expanses of the delta. These sheets of water not only saturate the soil with sufficient moisture to last the dry summer and autumn months, but also bring fertile silt to the delta lowlands, which settles out to enrich the pastures and stimulate lush plant growth.

The floods are crucial to the natural economy of the Volga delta. Creatures normally

Their burnished bodies and glittering wings shimmering in the sun
like jewels, a pair of Banded Agrion damselflies (the male below the
female) bask briefly on a reed before darting off to hunt down insects
in mid-air. These mini-predators, in turn, form a vital link in the
food chain for other creatures in the Volga delta, such as the
Whiskered Tern illustrated on page 56.

confined to ponds and river courses now move inland. Where once cows grazed, frogs and fishes spawn in the flooded fields. Being only a few inches deep, the water is quickly warmed by the spring sunshine, and this greatly assists the development of invertebrate life and the maturation of eggs. Among the many animals that reap the rich harvest of invertebrate food, Marsh Frogs provide a ready indicator of the great richness of the delta at this time of the year. They swim and leap about everywhere, burping and croaking with their vocal sacs inflated. During the early hours of darkness, their chorus reaches a deafening climax as astronomical numbers of males desperately try and attract ripe females, bloated with eggs.

As spring progresses, a combination of warmth and nutrients in the water stimulates the vegetation into growth. Beds of reeds and bulrushes throw up serried ranks of sharp,

At the Astrakhan nature reserve, a Grass Snake swallows a frog – a
single drama among countless scenes in the struggle for existence
among the complex animal communities that inhabit the Volga delta.

green blades that will eventually carry aloft feathery seed heads and brown velvet maces 4 m (13 ft) into the air. In autumn, after the floods have subsided, farmers will cut and stack the leaves to provide winter fodder for their cattle. Yellow Flags and Marsh Marigolds add a welcome touch of colour to the boggy landscape.

By the middle of May, the water has warmed up enough to allow the fish to spawn. Fifty kinds of fish live in the delta channels – including tench, roach, perch, pike, minnows, gudgeon and sticklebacks – and many breed in the shallow areas on the fringe of the sea. Carp even come out onto the land. Some migrate from the brackish parts of the Caspian,

As spring comes to the Volga delta, the flowers of Yellow Flags, or Yellow
Irises, add their cheerful splashes of colour to the green sea of foliage.

Overleaf: Fixing the observer with a glassy stare, a freshwater turtle
cautiously surveys its home in the Astrakhan nature reserve. These
wary reptiles feed mainly on insect larvae, tadpoles and small fish.

up the Volga's tributaries, to reach the flooded fields. When the temperature is between 13° C (55°F) and 20°C (68°F), the mature females, accompanied by males, swim into the shallows, where each lays up to $1\frac{1}{2}$ million eggs which adhere to the sub-aquatic vegetation. In places, their spawning sites are only a few centimetres (inches) deep, so the backs of the writhing fish are exposed to the air. Soon, they head into deeper water, leaving the eggs to hatch within a few days.

A Wealth of Waterbirds

The phenomenal productivity of the flooded delta provides the food that drives the great bird economies. Of the 250 species of birds recorded there, 56 are wetland species. About 230,000 pairs of wildfowl (North American: waterfowl) nest in the foredelta, including 10,000 pairs of Greylag Geese and almost 3,000 pairs of Mute Swans. These graceful birds behave very differently from the tame, feral swans that adorn our parks and rivers. The Caspian swans are thoroughly wild, taking off at the slightest provocation, their great angel wings making the air sing. Half a century ago, there were only a handful of mute swans in the Caspian, but they responded well to strict protection. By the end of the breeding season, the number of nesting wildfowl and coots has swollen to 1.5 million.

Herons of various kinds abound in these vast wetlands. Most spectacular are the dazzling Great White Egrets, among the world's most cosmopolitan birds, ranging from the Americas to Australia. Up to 4,600 pairs nest in the delta. There are also thousands of pairs of equally white Little Egrets. As well as being smaller, these are distinguished from their relatives by their all-black beaks and yellow feet, which look as if they have been freshly dipped in paint, so vividly do they contrast with the black legs. During the spring, both species possess gorgeous plumes – or 'aigrettes' – which they erect over their backs like diaphanous fans during the excitement of courtship. In the past, human greed for these feathers nearly wiped out the egrets, but fortunately it resulted, too, in a remarkable personal protest that led not only to a reprieve for the egrets but also to the establishment of the Soviet system of state nature reserves.

A Great White Egret performs its dramatic courtship display in the
Astrakhan nature reserve. During the breeding season, as well as
developing the long erectable plumes on its back, the colours of the bill,
the bare skin between the eyes and bill, and the legs change or intensify
for a short period, but start to fade as soon as the eggs are laid.

During the nineteenth century and the early years of the present one, fashionable Russian women, like their counterparts elsewhere in western Europe and North America, wore hats adorned with egret plumes. Furthermore, every cossack officer rode into battle or onto the parade ground similarly adorned. The result was inevitable. Egrets were virtually exterminated on the Volga delta. Other natural resources were also being squandered; hunters were rapidly plundering the stocks of geese and ducks, and fishermen were emptying the waters with no thought for the future. Luckily, Nicolai Podyapolsky, a citizen of Astrakhan, became so concerned at the decimation of the local wildlife that, in 1919, he decided to bring the situation to the attention of Lenin. Although it was just after the October Revolution, when he was preoccupied with the establishment of the new Soviet state, Lenin was sufficiently concerned to sign a petition giving a measure of protection to 9,700 hectares (24,000 acres) of the delta. Furthermore, Lenin asked Podyapolsky to draft legislation for the setting up of a nationwide system of reserves, or *zapovedniki*, along with measures for guarding them from exploitation.

Avoiding Competition

Several other species of herons share the delta with the egrets. All have their own hunting techniques or food preferences which enable them to co-exist without competing too seriously with each other. The larger, longer-legged species can wade into relatively deep water where they can spear larger prey. Grey Herons and Great White Egrets use the stalk-and-stand technique, with the neck stretched stiffly forward like a ramrod so the birds can peer into the water. By contrast, Little Egrets are fidgety feeders, often running along the water's edge with a high-stepping gait, pursuing fleeing frogs or fishes. Sometimes they flap their wings to flush out small fishes from hiding, and both they and Great White Egrets also use their feet to stir up the water for the same purpose.

Squacco and Purple Herons are birds of the vast dense reedbeds, against which the smaller Squacco Heron's buff plumage and the Purple Heron's pattern of grey, purplish-brown, chestnut and white, with bold black vertical streaks on the breast, camouflages them superbly. Both are solitary stalk-and-stand feeders, most active in the early morning and evening.

One very common species of heron in the delta avoids the daytime competition by

Its long legs dangling beneath it, a Purple Heron flaps lazily
just above the surface of a reedbed in the Volga delta.

55

Resplendent in its dapper grey, black and white plumage, a Whiskered Tern
alights at its nest, a floating platform of vegetation. Large numbers of these
dainty, elegant birds, along with the two other marsh terns, the Black Tern
and White-winged Black Tern, breed in the Volga delta.

having evolved a largely nocturnal lifestyle. Appropriately named, the dumpy, short-necked Black-crowned Night Heron is found throughout much of the world, except in Australia where it is replaced by a very similar relative. More than 4,000 pairs nest in this part of the Caspian. As dusk turns to night, the grey-and-black birds leave their communal treetop roosts, their hoarse calls ringing through the darkness, to fly to their separate feeding territories in the wetlands. With their big ruby-coloured eyes, they can hunt throughout the night. Although they feed mainly on fish, amphibians and aquatic invertebrates, they will also pillage the nests of waterbirds, including other herons, if given a chance, devouring both eggs and young. By sunrise, they return to their roosts as their daytime cousins take over the wetlands in the relentless quest for food.

The numbers of all these herons fluctuate from year to year, depending upon whether the floods are extensive and whether the water remains throughout the period when the birds have nests full of hungry young. If the pastures remain covered with shallow water for much of the summer, then the bonanza of fish and amphibians ensures that many chicks are reared. By the end of the season, the delta will be alive with the activity of newly fledged birds. But in relatively dry years, when the Volga bestows the delta with less water, hunting is less successful. The herons, however, have evolved a strategy for coping with the lean times, involving the staggered hatching of their eggs. The little food that the adults can bring back to the nest is monopolized by the oldest and strongest chick. Rather than all the chicks starving, this one at least may live.

Other distinctive waterbirds that grace the delta in small numbers in summer include pristine White Spoonbills and burnished purple and green Glossy Ibises. Superficially, spoonbills resemble herons although, being members of the ibis family, they fly with their necks outstretched. They wade into the water, and with scything motions of their long, spatulate bills, strain small fish and crustaceans from the surface. Glossy Ibises feed by probing in the mud and shallows for invertebrates with their long, downcurved bills.

Magnificent Eagles

By far the most impressive predator of fish in this part of the former Soviet Union is the White-tailed Eagle. One of the sea eagles, more closely related to the Old World vultures and kites than to the true, or 'booted' eagles, such as the Golden Eagle, it is a huge bird, with great broad wings that span $2\frac{1}{2}$ m ($8\frac{1}{4}$ ft). The White-tailed Eagle is a versatile hunter, sometimes searching for food by soaring at heights of up to 300 m (1,000 ft), sometimes by watching from the vantage of a perch.

When catching fish, its usual hunting method is to swoop down and scoop the prey from the surface, swinging its legs forward at the last moment so that the deadly, sharp claws can hook into and clutch its struggling victim. Like the smaller, more agile Osprey, which catches fish in a more spectacular plunge into the water, the White-tailed Eagle has horny spikes on the soles of its feet that help it keep a tight grip on the slippery prey. Occasionally, these eagles wade into shallow water to grasp a stranded fish or piece of carrion.

The eagle's strategy for taking ducks and Coots can be a lengthy business. When surprised by a hungry eagle, these birds usually dive, only to find it above them when they resurface. White-tailed Eagles have been observed making as many as 60 consecutive attacks on Coots before successfully exhausting their prey, which may take a total of 45 minutes. They also plunder colonies of cormorants and herons and, if the chance arises,

A splendid White-tailed Eagle visits its two chicks at a nest in the
Astrakhan nature reserve. This is one of three species of sea eagles
that breed in the former Soviet Union – the others are Pallas's Sea
Eagle and Steller's Sea Eagle (see page 264).

add mammals, terrapins, frogs and snakes to their diet. But, like most birds of prey, they
will not turn up the opportunity of an easy meal by scavenging carcases or harrying other
fish-eating birds such as Ospreys and gulls to frighten them into dropping their own hard
won catches.

The White-tailed Eagle was virtually exterminated in much of western Europe during
the nineteenth century. Today, despite protection, it is still on the endangered list, with
many populations declining because of shooting, deliberate poisoning, egg collecting,
disturbance at breeding sites, collisions with overhead power lines, changes due to fisheries

or water management schemes, habitat destruction and the effects of pesticides. Extinct as a breeding bird in Britain by 1916, it has been reintroduced into Scotland since 1975 in a programme aimed at establishing a viable population.

In the former Soviet Union, this magnificent bird is still widely distributed near rivers, lake shores and wetlands with abundant fish and other prey. However, it is nowhere common – big birds of prey which are at the apex of food chains are never abundant except where they may gather to roost or are attracted by unusual concentrations of food. Nevertheless, encouraging numbers of White-tailed Eagles can be seen soaring over the Volga delta. About 100 pairs nest there, no less than 30 of them settling to breed within secure boundaries of the State nature reserves.

In the Volga delta, White-tailed Eagles build their nests high up in willow trees. These are usually huge rambling structures of twigs and branches that may have accumulated after many years of use, and are often so bulky that several bold pairs of Tree Sparrows may set up their homes in the base of the nest right beneath the eagles. By March, the hen is sitting on one or two (rarely three) chalky white eggs.

On hatching, the fluffy white eaglets are very vulnerable, especially from being chilled by rain, so the hen stands guard while her mate brings food, often in the form of a still-flapping fish. This she tears apart, offering small morsels held in her great hooked bill to her diminutive offspring with great tenderness. After about three weeks, the female joins the male in providing for the growing brood. By early July, when the young are between 70 and 75 days old, the eaglets are as big as their parents and ready to try out their wings for the first time. This corresponds to the period when drying pools and a falling water level yield plenty of stranded fish. However, they will be unable to fend completely for themselves for a further one or two months. The white tail is the badge of full adulthood, and is not acquired until the birds have reached their fifth or sixth year.

Pelicans and Cormorants

Out in the delta, beyond the reach of eagles and herons, live huge shoals of fish. These are exploited by birds that can swim in the deeper waters. Dalmatian Pelicans, now sadly rare, with only 160 pairs breeding on the delta, duck their heads beneath the surface to scoop the fish from the water in their great pouched bills, often fishing co-operatively by forming a semi-circle and herding the fish before them.

Other birds dive underwater in pursuit of their prey. As well as a variety of grebes, these include large numbers of Great Cormorants. About 100,000 of these reptilian-looking birds live in the delta, breeding in 60 or so clamorous colonies which they share with a variety of herons. Their large, untidy nests of sticks and twigs lined with the leaves of grasses and water plants, are lodged in the uppermost branches in stands of tall willow or ash trees, which inevitably become whitewashed with the birds' stinking droppings. In the end, the trees are damaged or killed by the acid excrement and the cormorants may have to move to other sites.

The cormorants time their reproductive activities to coincide with the period when the Volga pushes a great mass of floodwater before it into the Caspian. The chicks hatch during the first half of April, and then the whole colony becomes a hive of activity, with skeins of birds constantly coming and going. A cormorant needs between a half and three-quarters of a kilogramme (1 and $1\frac{1}{2}$ lb) of fish every day – an amount equivalent to one sixth of its body weight. When feeding young, it must catch more. To obtain enough food, the cormorants may have to fly up to 50 km (30 miles) into the open Caspian, but usually there are plenty of fish nearer at hand.

Their fishing technique is to swim, dipping their heads frequently beneath the surface to spot the prey, then suddenly leaping forward before submerging. With powerful thrusts of their great webbed feet, they can pursue their quarry for up to a minute before coming up for air. They bring large or awkward prey up to the surface before swallowing it. When their crops are heavy with fish, the adults fly back to the colony in long, weaving lines, the birds behind often taking advantage of the eddies created by the birds in front. On arriving at their nests, the adults are assaulted by their expectant, trembling offspring, which thrust their heads deep inside the parents' bills, reaching into the gullet to seize their next meal.

The cormorants not only sustain themselves. Loafing around the colonies are many quick-witted Hooded Crows. During the early part of the nesting season, they react quickly to any disturbance within the colony and rob any exposed nests of their eggs or very young chicks. Later on, they monitor the parents' feeding visits. As soon as the adults have departed, the crafty crows nip in and tease the youngsters which respond by regurgitating part of the contents of their bulging crops. The morsels that spill into the nest are devoured by the crows in an instant, but the fragments that fall into the amber water below are often engulfed by catfish, which grow fat on the cormorants' scraps.

Fishermen in the Volga delta and Caspian Sea understandably regard these voracious fish eaters as competitors, and have for years culled cormorants. However, research by Russian biologists has revealed that the birds may help to recycle nutrients in the delta to

A Great Cormorant feeds its ravenous, well-grown young in their large,
untidy stick nest. At first, the chicks are given their meals in fluid form,
regurgitated by the adult into its large throat pouch, but later they take more
solid food from within the parent's mouth or gullet.

the benefit of the fish. The cormorants' droppings are rich in nitrogen and phosphorus, and these essential elements are swept downstream to fertilize the shallows where the fish nurseries are located.

The Mighty Sturgeon

There is one group of fishes of great economic importance that is beyond the reach of the cormorants – the sturgeons. The flood triggers the mass migration of sturgeons from the Caspian, up the deeper tributaries of the Volga, the females bringing with them the eggs that will be used to make that most vaunted and expensive of Russian delicacies – caviare. The twenty-five different species of sturgeon, all confined to the northern hemisphere, include the biggest freshwater fish in the world.

Nowadays, sturgeons are quite rare because the unbridled craving for their eggs, river pollution, and the erection of great hydro-electric dams across their migration routes have resulted in the demise of one species after another. However, healthy populations of several species still exist in the Caspian and Volga basins. One of these, the Beluga, can grow to monster size: a specimen probably seventy-five years old was caught in 1926 which weighed no less than a tonne and yielded a king's ransom in caviar – 180 kg (396 lb). Others have been reported to weigh as much as 1.3 tonnes ($1\frac{1}{4}$ tons) and measure 8.5 m (28 ft) in length. The other sturgeon species found in the Caspian and Volga region are the Sterlet, the Sevruga (or Caspian Sturgeon) and the Russian Sturgeon; the Atlantic Sturgeon occurs in the Black Sea only. Fifteen years ago, a hybrid between the Beluga and the Sterlet, called the Bester, was introduced into the Volga: it is now very widespread in the lower Volga.

Sturgeons have a strangely prehistoric look. Indeed, with the related paddlefishes, they are the sole survivors of an ancient group of fishes that lived between 135 and 100 million years ago. Superficially, sturgeons are shaped like sharks and, like them, have low-slung mouths, a tall upper lobe to the tail and a spiral valve in the intestine, and are built around a cartilaginous skeleton. Unlike sharks, however, they are slow swimmers and contain some bone, and are classified with the great group of bony fishes.

Sturgeons differ from the other bony fishes, which are clothed in scales, in sporting bony plates on the head and five rows of spiny studs, or scutes, along the body. With this armour plating and its long snout, a sturgeon exudes a decidedly crocodilian aura. But all the members of this family of fishes are quite harmless inhabitants of deep channels, spending much of their time grubbing in the mud with their shovel-shaped snouts and detecting worms, molluscs and small fishes in the murk, not with their insignificant eyes, but with highly touch-sensitive whisker-like barbels hanging down from their noses. When they detect suitable prey, they suck it up with their powerful lips which can be protruded like a tube.

For many thousands of years, the sturgeons have made their spawning runs at various times of the year, often entering the Volga in the autumn, over-wintering in deep channels beneath the ice, and thrashing upstream during the spring. Hugging the bottom and lashing their bodies against the current, they spawn in the river's upper tributaries where the water is warmer. When the females are ready to extrude their eggs, the males cluster around and shed their sperm, or milt, to fertilize them as soon as they emerge. The older the female sturgeon, the more eggs she manufactures; when she is in her fiftieth year, a female Beluga may produce over three million of them, but she needs two or three years to recuperate. An Atlantic Sturgeon can lay between one million and six million eggs, depending on her size and age.

The eggs, which resemble lead pellets, are sticky, so they adhere to the vegetation or stones on the river bed. While the adults head back towards the Caspian, where they will feed on fish, the eggs begin to develop, and in ten days hatch into tiny, tadpole-like creatures. At first, they continue to be nourished by the reserves held in their yolk-sacs, but when they reach a length of 1 cm ($\frac{1}{2}$ inch) they start eating aquatic insect larvae and crustaceans. By the third week, they begin to look and behave like miniature sturgeons, grubbing along the bottom for their food.

The flow of water gradually carries them downstream and they eventually find themselves in the lower reaches of the river and in the sea. The mortality of these 'fingerlings' is very high indeed, and only one in a hundred will survive their first year. But of the fortunate ones, those that reach five years of age will be about half a metre (20 in) long. Sturgeons mature very slowly and some of the surviving five-year-olds will not venture up the Volga to breed for a further twenty years.

This long life cycle used to be played out not only on the Volga but also on the Don, a river that starts near Moscow and runs into the Sea of Azov, itself a northerly extension of the Black Sea. Nowadays, many of the migrating sturgeon are denied access to their natural spawning beds by hydro-electric dams that block their way, despite the incorporation of fish ladders that allow some of them to get through.

Nevertheless, stocks of Beluga and Sevruga are maintained in the interests of the Volga fishery by one of the largest fish-hatching programmes in the world. The method is to capture gravid females in the Volga's estuary and inject them with hormones to bring their eggs to the point of maturation. A few days later, the fish are stripped of their eggs and these are then stirred with sperm. The resulting fry are kept safely in holding tanks until they are forty days old, when a total of 100 million fingerlings are released into the river and the Caspian Sea. The fruits of this labour will be reaped between eight and seventeen years later when the sexually mature fish emerge from the depths of the Caspian Sea and swim into the nets of the Volga's fishermen.

Fishing for Caspian sturgeon is a lucrative business, employing about 1,000 people

Overleaf: Already displaying the distinctive bony scutes running like saw
blades along their bodies, the shovel-like snout and the sensitive barbels
bewhiskering their mouths, these baby sturgeons were reared
artificially for release into the Caspian Sea. The development in the
1950s of hatcheries for these prized fish has helped to conserve the
sturgeon populations of the Caspian region.

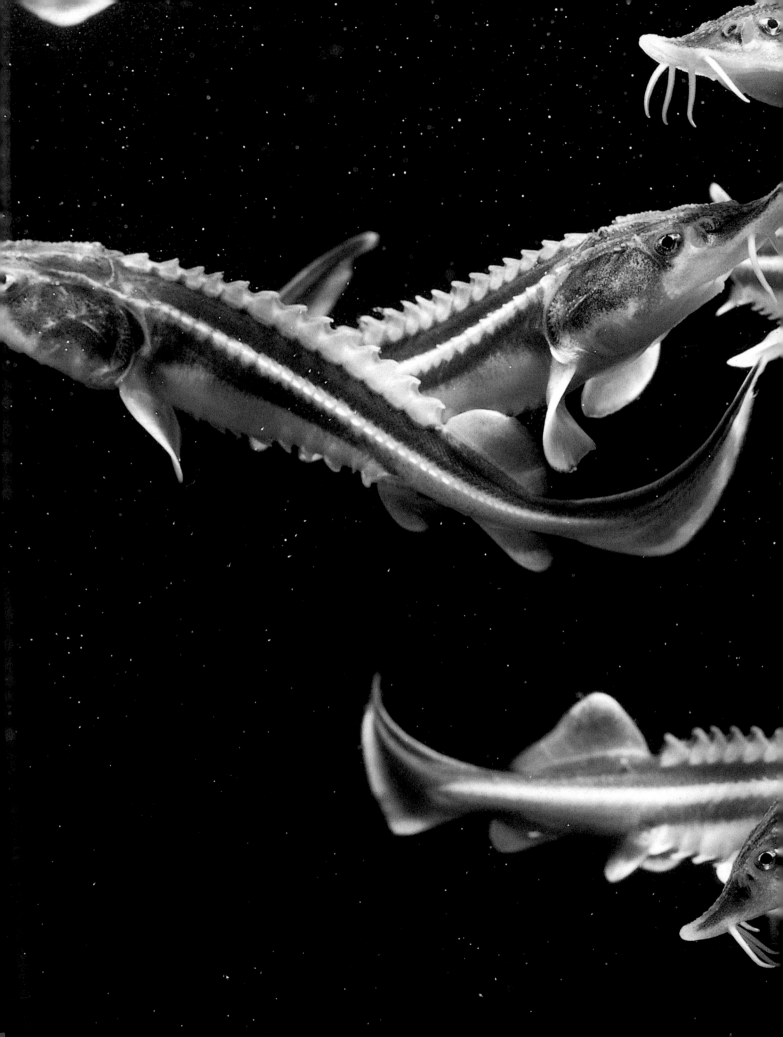

Fishermen land a catch of sturgeon from the Caspian. These great fish have long
been valued for their tender flesh (often smoked), for the isinglass from their
swim-bladders and vertebrae, used as a clarifying and gelling agent, and, above all,
for their eggs, used to make that quintessentially Russian delicacy, caviare.

today. Each spring, teams of fishermen line favoured stretches of the Volga near Astrakhan,
and shoot their nets a dozen times a day across the river. The catches are taken alive in
special holding barges to factory ships where the fish are butchered for their flesh and roes.
The bulky roes are rubbed on scraper boards to separate the eggs from the sinews. These
are then irrigated with a special salt solution until the gleaming eggs – 'the black pearls of
the Caspian' – are ready for canning as caviare.

The rarest caviare, made from the golden eggs of the Sterlet, is especially valued, and
was once reserved for the tables of the Tsar. Even 'ordinary' black caviare is worth almost

its weight in gold in the luxury markets of the world. Each year, the Volga fishery collects about 1,000 tonnes (985 tons) of this prized product, much of which is exported for 'hard' currency.

Islands of Birds

The geography of the delta is always changing as silt brought down in the Volga builds up into banks, which, in their turn, are constantly shifting under the influence of the wind and waves. Some form semi-permanent islands which are settled by a further selection of fish-eaters. One such island is Djemchusny – which is Russian for 'pearl'. This narrow strip of sand lies 85 km (53 miles) beyond the edge of the delta – a day's journey by boat from Astrakhan.

Djemchusny is slowly disappearing beneath the sea. It used to be at least 8 km (5 miles) long, but the rising Caspian has already claimed one third of it. Today, it is 5 km (3 miles) from end to end and only a few hundred metres wide. Despite its impermanence, in spring and summer this sand bar is the site of a huge, noisy, aromatic seabird city, as tens of thousands of pairs of nesting terns and gulls set about the business of breeding.

Foremost among them are the Great Black-headed Gulls. Nearly all of these birds

Among the largest and most powerful of all the world's gulls, a Great Black-headed Gull utters a harsh, gruff croak of alarm at its breeding colony on Djemchusny Island in the northern Caspian Sea.

With her two fluffy chicks nuzzling against her snow-white breast
feathers, a Djemchusny Caspian Tern warns intruders against encroaching
on the small area around her nest in the dense colony.

breed in the former Soviet Union, and 80 per cent of the world population is confined to
the Caspian. With a wing-span of 1.7 m (5½ ft), and a body the size of a small goose, they
are among the biggest and most impressive of all gulls. During the breeding season, their
most characteristic feature is the striking black head, adorned with red-rimmed eyes set in
white surrounds. In the early part of the nesting season, when couples are squabbling over
ownership of their territories, this 'fright' mask reinforces the threats as the birds face one
another with bills poised to strike. The heaviness of these orange-yellow bills, tipped with
black and blood red, indicates that Great Black-headed Gulls can deal with a wide range
of prey. In the Caspian, they are chiefly fish eaters, taking mainly carp, bream, and roach.
But like other large gulls, they are also adept egg thieves and will, without hesitation, pirate
the unguarded nests of their neighbours. They will also eat ground squirrels, voles, other
small rodents and reptiles when the opportunity arises.

There is no shortage of food within commuting distance of Djemchusny and no less
than 25,000 pairs of Great Black-headed Gulls nest on this sandy haven. By the end of

At Djemchusny, Caspian Terns establish their colonies alongside those
of Great Black-headed Gulls (background). Although the gulls may help
in defending the colonies from predators, they also eat tern eggs.

May, the skies are full of the comings and goings of the adults, the crops of the returning
parents bulging with partially digested fish. As soon as a parent lands at its nest, the pattern
of its multi-coloured bill acts as a stimulus for the chicks to peck vigorously at it, which in
turn stimulates the adult to regurgitate a package of fish, softened by digestive juices. The
parent hangs on to this, allowing the chick to peck pieces from it.

For neighbours, these super-gulls have the largest terns in the world. Most terns are
quite small, long winged, elegant birds that justify their popular name of 'sea swallows',
but the Caspian Tern is a thick-set species as big as a Herring Gull, with a hefty, coral-red
beak. Despite its name, it is by no means confined to the Caspian Sea. Indeed, it is an
almost cosmopolitan bird, breeding in places as far removed from each other as New
Zealand, North America, Africa and Spain.

Some 2,000 pairs of Caspian Terns nest on Djemchusny, rearing their offspring on fish
caught by diving from the air into the open waters of the Caspian. They carry their catch
in their beaks back to their ravenous chicks, which gulp them down whole. Caspian Terns

are aggressive birds, and the adults put up a spirited collective defence of their colonies by mobbing and diving at alien intruders, such as a Great Black-headed Gull searching for an unguarded nest.

Havens for Tired Autumn Migrants

As the days begin to shorten and the air starts to chill, vast numbers of waders (North American: shorebirds) and wildfowl (North American: waterfowl), having spent the summer breeding in the north, head westwards into Europe or take a southerly course into Asia and Africa. But like aircraft, migratory birds need refuelling stops, and the Volga delta is one of the most important in the world. It is conveniently placed at the end of the Turgay Depression, a lowland corridor that runs just east of the Urals to the Western Siberian Plain. This is used as a flyway by birds streaming to and from the marshes of northern Siberia and Kazakhstan. In total, over 7 million migrants seek food and rest in the Volga delta during both the spring and autumn passage.

As the summer draws to a close, the shallow bays and lagoons become full of dabbling ducks renewing their worn feathers. Drake Mallard, Northern Pintail, Green-winged Teal and Gadwall no longer sport their dapper courting feathers, but are camouflaged in a dull 'eclipse' plumage similar to that of the females. After a month or two of intensive feeding, the birds grow fresh feathers, and continue their journey to the southern Caspian and Mediterranean regions. They are accompanied by a host of international travellers in transit to faraway places. Long-legged waders, such as Common Greenshank, Spotted Redshank, Ruff, Whimbrel, Eurasian Curlew and Bar-tailed Godwit, freshly arrived from the Arctic, probe the mud frenetically for worms to build up their food reserves before resuming their long journey to the coasts and wetlands of Africa.

Some of the birds that congregate in the Volga delta nested locally. These include flocks of White Spoonbills and Glossy Ibises, which eventually head eastwards towards India and Bangladesh. About 30,000 Greylag Geese, some from Siberia, thrive on a diet tinged with a flavour of the orient. The plant they seek is the Sacred Lotus. In the former

Rising in rosy splendour from among great umbrella-shaped leaves,
the lovely flowers of the Sacred Lotus grace the Volga delta in
summer. When the lotuses are in flower, the region is also full of less
welcome sights – clouds of biting mosquitoes.

USSR, the exotic Sacred Lotus grows only in the far east and on the Volga delta, where it is on the increase, much to the benefit of the birds. It is indigenous to Asia and northern Australia, growing in swampy areas and preferring water no more than 2 m ($6\frac{1}{4}$ ft) deep, with rich, organic mud into which its roots can penetrate.

In summer, the existence of lotus beds is revealed by their characteristic foliage, with large parasol-shaped leaves which flap as they catch each passing breeze. In July and August, the lovely flowers are carried aloft on perfectly straight stems, their whorls of delicate pink petals symbolizing the endless cycle of existence of the Buddhist doctrine – Buddhists call the Sacred Lotus 'the flower of light'. When these beautiful blooms eventually wither, the seed pods are revealed: they are shaped like pepper pots, from which the heavy seeds fall out or are released when the pods rot down. The seeds, together with the roots and rhizomes, are relished by the Greylag Geese. Throughout the autumn and winter, before the surface of the water freezes, the geese settle, often in their thousands, among the lotus beds and, by up-ending, pull the vegetation to the surface, to break it up with their slightly serrated bills.

Wildfowling is a popular sport in Russia and Central Asia, and in September shooting starts in special game reserves in the Volga delta and other wetlands around the great inland seas. In addition to threats such as agricultural reclamation and fish farming experienced by other creatures of the delta, the birds have to face an increasing numbers of wildfowlers. Every autumn the Astrakhan hunters alone kill about 200,000 ducks, geese and coots.

Meanwhile, west of the Ural and Volga river deltas, the salty shallows of the northeast corner of the Caspian Sea are invaded by Greater Flamingos – these individuals are the most northerly representatives of their kind. Strictly protected in the former USSR, between 30,000 and 50,000 of these beautiful, intensely gregarious creatures, all legs and necks, nest on Tengiz, a saline lake in the steppes of northern Kazakhstan. When the flamingos have finished breeding, they follow the Turgay flyway to moult on the edge of the Caspian Sea. Close to the hot desert shore of Kazakhstan, the sea is warm and long lines of delicate pink flamingos, their heads down and bizarre crooked bills straining the ooze, feed on a nourishing diet of planktonic shrimps.

As autumn approaches, great skeins of flamingos make their way towards the southern end of the Caspian, to spend the winter in various places. Two of these sites are especially important. The first is Krasnovodsk, on the south-eastern, Turkmenian, shore of the Caspian Sea. Up to 7,000 flamingos winter in this region of brackish shallows and reedbeds. Many of the remainder head 1,000 km (620 miles) across the Caspian to Kirov Bay, on the south-western, Azerbaijani, shore. This bay embraces the nature reserve at Kyzyl-Agach, which is one of the best wintering sites for wildfowl.

In summer, Kyzyl-Agach supports one of the country's most spectacular heronries and is the only place in the former USSR where Cattle Egrets nest; it also has a healthy breeding population of Purple Gallinules – large, exotic-looking purplish-blue waterbirds with huge red bills and feet that are more typical of tropical Asia, Africa, and Australia. Even flamingos occasionally build their raised mud nests in the shallows. In winter, this part of the Caspian is usually beyond the range of the Arctic's icy breath, and so, as the northerly wetlands freeze over, Kirov Bay and Kyzyl-Agach remain open, acting as havens for nearly half a million wildfowl, including Greylag Geese and swans from the Volga delta.

The Coming of Winter

In October some 20,000 Whooper Swans arrive in the delta from the Arctic and subarctic. The air resonates to the clamour of their trumpeting and the thrashing of their feet and wings on the water as they move from one bay to another. The noisy flocks are not as chaotic as they appear at first sight. Like geese, swans travel in family groups, and the parent Whoopers are never far from the fully grown cygnets which they have led for several

Whooper Swans descend upon the Volga delta in autumn, replenishing themselves with food after the long journey from their breeding grounds on the northern tundra, until the ice forces them further south.

73

thousands of kilometres across Siberia and the Central Asian republics to the welcoming lagoons of the Volga delta. Here they avidly feed on aquatic vegetation until the encroaching ice forces them to retreat southwards. Even so, many will stay as long as possible, crowding into stretches of open water, called polynia, with flocks of diving ducks and Coots. These are often closely watched by White-tailed Eagles which loaf around on the ice, waiting for weak and dying birds to expose themselves. But even a mass of milling birds will not prevent the formation of ice if the temperature is low enough, so ultimately the swans, geese, and ducks will have to seek the open waters of the southern Caspian or even further afield.

In the depths of a hard winter, the once lush, emerald countryside, long since changed to shades of gold and brown, is transformed into a bleak and desolate place. A bitter wind blows from the heart of Siberia, bringing blizzards and leaving the landscape locked in the grip of ice. Little stirs except a few Hooded Crows or a lone White-tailed Eagle surveying the scene from leafless willow trees – looking for signs of death. But unknown to them, Beluga are already stirring in the deep water channels of the frozen Volga, a promise that life will be renewed with the coming of the great flood. The jewel will glint once again in the spring sunshine.

Winter holds the northern Caspian in its grip only once a year, but there are other places in the realms of the Russian bear which are permanently covered with snow and ice – the peaks of the great mountains.

Winter comes to one of the channels of the Volga delta.

CHAPTER THREE

THE CELESTIAL MOUNTAINS

MUCH OF THE spacious hinterland of the Commonwealth of Independent States stretches to the horizon in seemingly boundless, rolling plains, and yet no less than one third of the surface of this enormous region is thrust up into great mountain ranges. Some, such as the Ural, Crimean and Caucasus mountains, are familiar by name. The Urals, which form Europe's eastern boundary with Asia, run in a more or less north-south direction, unlike most of the Central Asian mountains. Although extending for over 2,000 km (1,240 miles), the Urals are relatively low, with their highest peaks in the north at an altitude of only about 2,000 m (6,560 ft). The Caucasus, by contrast, includes Europe's highest peak, Mount Elbrus, 5,642 m (18,510 ft) above sea level. Yet these ranges are insignificant when compared with the great ramparts of rock which run along the southern edge of the Central Asian republics and Siberia, virtually from the Caspian to the Pacific.

These great mountains, which include some of the world's highest, act as a barrier, not only to weather originating in the tropics, but also to the easy passage of animals and plants into the former Soviet Union from the warmer south. Such ranges include the relatively low, earthquake-prone Kopet-Dag, rising to heights of about 2,750 m (9,000 ft) on the frontier with Iran, and the towering peaks of the Pamir-Alai and Tien Shan on the border with China, which include many summits over 5,000 m (16,500 ft).

To the north of the Tien Shan is the Alatau Range, with the highest peaks at about

Among the glittering, perpetually snow-covered peaks of the Tien Shan, or Celestial Mountains, many huge glaciers slowly carve their way over the rock. This is the Inylchek Glacier, at 60 km (40 miles) long the longest of all the Tien Shan glaciers.

4,400 m (14,400 ft). Further east, fringing Mongolia and China, lie the Altai Mountains, with many peaks over 3,000 m (9,840 ft) and the highest, Mt Belukha, reaching 4,506 m (14,783 ft). North-east of the Altai, on the Mongolian border, are the Sayan Mountains, with their tallest peaks at about 3,400 m (11,200 ft). To the east of the Altai and Sayan are the Transbaikalian Mountains, occupying a huge area, and the Stanovoy Mountains. Russia's eastern flank is guarded by the Sikhote-Alin and Kolyma mountains, the former edging into the subtropics and the latter very much in the Arctic domain. Further north are the volcanic mountains of the Kamchatka Peninsula, the Koryak Mountains and the Chukot Mountains in the extreme north-east. Several other impressive mountainous areas are found within Siberia, including the Verkhoyansk Mountains to the north-east of Yakutsk, where the winter climate confers on it the distinction of being the coldest place in the northern hemisphere (see page 19).

Of all these mountains, though, the Tien Shan and Pamir-Alai are the most spectacular, with the tallest peaks and most interesting wildlife communities with origins in both Asia and Europe.

The Tien Shan – The Celestial Mountains

The name 'Tien Shan' is Chinese and means 'celestial mountains'. Although the eastern part of the range is in China, the western half is situated in the former Soviet Union, primarily in Kirghizia, with northern and western spurs extending into Kazakhstan.

These are magnificent mountains, both steep and craggy, with their upper reaches swathed in eternal snow and ice. The highest point of the Tien Shan is on the border with China where Pik Pobeda (Victory Peak) stands at a height of 7,439 m (24,406 ft) above sea level – 1,245 m (4,085 ft) higher than North America's tallest peak, Mt McKinley, and almost 6,096 m (20,000 ft) higher than Ben Nevis, the highest peak in the British Isles. Even more splendid in appearance is its slightly lower neighbour, Khan Tengri, a great pyramid of rock that looms majestically over a bewildering tangle of glaciers and lesser peaks within the massif of the Tien Shan. As evidence of the colossal forces involved in its conception, Khan Tengri is capped by creamy marble, the metamorphosed sediment of an ancient sea-bed, now raised 7,010 m (22,999 ft) above the current level of the oceans.

Due to their altitude and abundant snow, the 'celestial mountains' are well endowed with glaciers. The sides of the mountains are so steep, that, in places, huge edifices of ice cling to them. Some of these frozen cascades of icicles merge with the great ribbons of glacial ice that inch their way down the high valleys, transporting fragments of rock and boulders, and depositing them in huge heaps, or terminal moraines, far from their origins.

The Inylchek Glacier is the longest in the Tien Shan. Grinding along at between 10 and 20 m (33 and 66 ft) a year, it takes the glacier 2,000 years to carry a rock from its origin beneath Pik Pobeda, to its base 60 km (40 miles) away. Because of the current warming of the climate, some glaciers are retreating, leaving isolated pillars of ice at their lower ends, and dumping their cargo to form freeways of rubble.

The Mighty Pamir – The Roof of the Soviet Union

The Pamir include the tallest mountains within the territory of the former Soviet Union. They are located in the south-west of the Pamir-Alai mountain system, close to the frontiers with Afghanistan and China, and most of them fall within the republic of Tadzhikistan. These mountains form a rectangular plateau, with the Trans-Alai Ridge on the northern border, the apex being Lenin Peak at 7,134 m (23,405 ft). To the north-west is the Academy of Sciences Ridge, from which a spur branches westwards. From this ridge rises Pik Kommunisma (Communism Peak), once known as Pik Stalin. At 7,495 m (24,589 ft), this is the loftiest mountain of all.

The Pamir occupies a position within the subtropical latitudes, but its great elevation results in a cold climate. While the western part of the Pamir is precipitous and attracts heavy falls of rain and snow, the landscape of the eastern region is less craggy and very dry. No other area in the realm of the Russian bear receives more sunshine – indeed, this is one of the sunniest places in the world. Here, the sun shines on about 317 days a year, and the annual precipitation is only 25 mm (1 in), producing an alpine, stony desert with sparse, drought- and frost-resistant vegetation. The wildlife here has much in common with that of the Tibetan plateau, with Tibetan Sandgrouse, Tibetan and Himalayan Snowcock, and Bar-headed Geese. Marco Polo Sheep, among the largest wild sheep in the world, also wander these high places.

In the north-west, the snow line stands at 3,600-3,800 m (12-14,000 ft), while in the central and eastern parts, it climbs to 5,200 m (16,000 ft). Despite its arid climate, the Pamir

Overleaf: The gaunt, glacier-honed peaks of the Pamir rise forbiddingly above the broad, flat valleys, creating a rugged, awe-inspiring landscape. Although this harsh mountain region extends into Afghanistan and China, most of the Pamir lies within the territory of the former Soviet Union, mainly in the Central Asian republic of Tadzhikistan. It runs for about 400 km (245 miles) from east to west and 225 km (140 miles) from north to south.

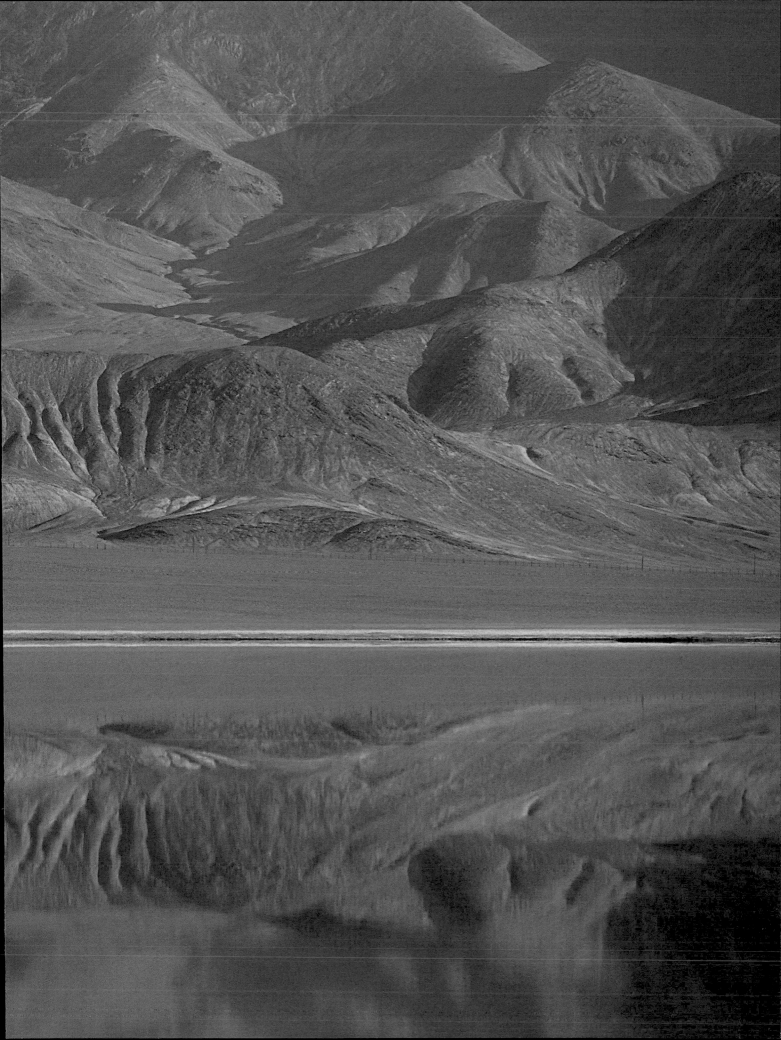

region contains 7,100 glaciers, which cover a total area of 7,500 sq km (2,900 sq miles). The greatest glacier of them all is the Fedchenko, named after a famous Russian botanist. One of the longest glaciers in the world, it is 1,000 m (3,280 ft) deep at its centre, and flows for 77 km (48 miles), at between 10 and 20 m (33 and 66 ft) a year.

The glacial ice cradled in the Central Asian mountains represents a vast store of water – 2,000 cu km (480 cu miles) of it in all. Together with the supply from the melting snowfields, this gives rise to an estimated 10,000-12,000 streams. Some of them form substantial arteries, such as the Panja and Wakhjir, which converge to form the Amu Darya, the most powerful river in Central Asia. Where the icy water funnels through steep-sided valleys, it speeds up and descends in a million chuckling and roaring falls. Where the valleys are wide, with very little gradient, the streams and rivers meander from side to side, repeatedly dividing and coalescing between banks of pebbles like glinting braid. These high river valleys are home to one of the rarest and most striking birds in the Central Asian republics – the Ibisbill.

The Ibisbill

This strange wader (North American: shorebird), boldly patterned in black, grey and white, with a long, downcurved red bill, is found only in river valleys in the Himalayas and some of the high mountains of Central Asia – the Tien Shan and western Pamir-Alai. It starts breeding at the end of April or early May, on stony river beds at altitudes of 1,700-4,400 m (5,575-14,435 ft), sometimes even laying its eggs when the snow is on the ground, when they run the risk of being swept away by flash floods.

In the Central Asian republics, Ibisbills are scarce – there are probably no more than 150 pairs. The couples are strictly territorial, and in locations where there may be two or three pairs, the nests are at least a kilometre (half a mile) apart. Each nest is a simple scrape in the shingle, and the eggs are so well camouflaged that they are barely distinguishable from the pebbles that surround them. Both male and female share the task of incubating the clutch, and their plumage makes them astonishingly difficult to detect when they are sitting tight. The off-duty partner spends its time preening and feeding, using its specialized bill to probe among the water-polished pebbles for the insects, molluscs, crustaceans and small fish which form its prey.

When the chicks hatch, they too are cryptically coloured – long-legged little balls of grey and black fluff. Although they leave their nest scrape soon after hatching, they must be fed by the parents until their beaks grow long enough to be inserted beneath stones.

An Ibisbill picks its way daintily among the boulders and pebbles of a
high-mountain river valley in the Tien Shan Mountains.

Like their parents, they can swim, but do not fledge until they are 50 days old. Ibisbills are
graceful flyers, revealing a striking pattern of black and white on the wings, and use their
mobility to seek lower reaches of the rivers during the autumn, ahead of the deteriorating
weather.

The Cloak of Vegetation

Temperature and humidity vary tremendously in the mountains according to altitude and
aspect. These two factors greatly influence the natural history of these wild places. For
instance, there are scorching, dry plains close to the foothills of the Tien Shan. However,
the air temperature drops by 2°C (3.6°F) for every 305 m (1,000 ft) of altitude. With
increasing height, the climate tends to become wetter as well as cooler, and this is conducive
to the growth of forests.

Many of the lower slopes are covered with Tien Shan Spruce, a narrow conifer that
easily sheds snow in the winter. They often grow with juniper trees, which thrive on stony

slopes where their roots grip the dry soil and prevent erosion. Junipers also replace spruce in the western, drier region of the Tien Shan, extending to the Alai Mountains.

In the moister sheltered valleys of the Pamir, there are groves of walnut and maple at the lower levels. At around 2,800 m (8,000 ft) in the Tien Shan, the trees can no longer grow because of the sharp frosts and the severity of the exposure. Beyond the forest belt, a prostrate form of juniper takes over. With increasing altitude, the juniper scrub gives way to alpine pastures and scree slopes. The plants become squat and cushion-like as protection against the frosts and the withering dry wind. In this respect, they resemble the drought- and cold-resistant kinds that grow in the Arctic.

At high altitudes, sunlight is very intense and contains much ultra-violet radiation, which is potentially injurious to living tissues. Some high-alpine plants therefore synthesize red pigments which act like suntan lotion, thus protecting themselves from the damaging radiation.

Bone Breaker

One of the first birds to show signs of breeding is the Lammergeier. Remarkably, these magnificent birds begin to nest as early as December, siting their nests on precipitous cliffs or crags quite beyond the reach of anything that cannot fly. Each pair returns year after year to the same nest, and refurbishes it before laying a single egg.

This unusual vulture dwells permanently high in the mountains up to 3,500 m (11,000 ft). Here it soars and glides with the elegance of a giant falcon. With slim pointed wings spanning up to 2.8 m (over 9 ft), and a long diamond-shaped tail, the Lammergeier is an impressive bird. When airborne, it is the epitome of grace and power, displaying perfect poise and control as it exploits the upward draughts along the canyons and high ridges, often in the company of Alpine Choughs, Alpine Swifts, Griffon Vultures and Golden Eagles.

The Lammergeier has a pair of fleshy wattles which hang down by its beak, thus accounting for its other name of Bearded Vulture. Unlike that of other vultures, its head and neck are fully feathered because it rarely needs to delve into messy carcases and, alone among vultures, it carries food in its feet. Although the Lammergeier is a scavenger, it does not compete with its larger relatives, the Griffon, Himalayan Griffon and Eurasian Black Vultures. It waits until they have stripped the carcase, because, although it will eat scraps of left-over flesh, it specializes in swallowing and digesting the skin and bones. It swallows small bones – up to 10 cm (4 in) in diameter – whole, but deals with larger ones by dropping them from heights of up to 60 m (200 ft) onto regularly used rocky areas called 'ossuaries' to smash them open and reveal their edible contents. Tortoises, too, are given the same treatment by these remarkable birds.

Lammergeiers may attack sick or wounded animals with powerful beats of their long wings and may even drive prey such as goats and sheep off narrow mountain ledges and, unlike other vultures, probably take small amounts of living prey, such as marmots and snowcocks. But their main diet is bones. Their early nesting may be related to their reliance upon the remains of animals.

By laying their eggs in the middle of winter, Lammergeiers can take advantage of winter casualties scavenged from the melting snows of spring to feed their chicks. The single young does not fledge until the end of July or August. With such a long time needed to complete their breeding cycle, it is not surprising that Lammergeiers are especially sensitive to disturbance.

The Spring Melt

By April, the snow begins to recede, especially on the southern slopes, and the rivers and streams start to shed their ice. It is the unlocking of moisture, as well as the increasing warmth of the sun, that awakens the mountain plants, coaxing the flowers from among the early foliage. Brightly coloured shoots protrude through the ice; among the first bulbs that break the surface are miniature juno irises, followed by several kinds of wild tulips which start to bloom within inches of melting snow.

In the western Tien Shan, of the twenty or more species of tulips, perhaps the most eye-catching is Greig's Tulip. This is the wild parent of many garden hybrids. Masses of its flowers – flamboyant, scarlet and yellow goblets – decorate the hillsides, reaching a density of 60 plants to the square metre (50 to the square yard). They take between six and eight years to mature from seed to flower. Each bloom lasts for ten days, and it is a further two months before the seeds are shed. By midsummer, the ground has dried out and the tulips wither back to their deeply buried bulbs.

With the passage of spring there is a succession of flowers. Particularly noticeable are the spikes of fox-tailed lilies (*Eremurus*), known as desert candles (which are not *bona fide* lilies), Martagon lilies (which are), pale mauve sprays of delphiniums, and blue aconites (monkshoods). There are also the more familiar alpine species such as gentians and edelweiss. Later in the summer, the swaying, purple or mauve drumsticks of various species of wild onions are much in evidence; indeed the name Tsun Lin, given to a subsidiary range

Life renews itself in the Tien Shan as plant shoots emerge from the melting
snows (below left); showy Greig's Tulips adorn an alpine meadow (below right);
fox-tailed lilies sport their flower-spikes, known as desert candles (above left);
and wild onions produce their drumstick-like flowerheads (above right).

Mountain Primula flowers throw up a vivid splash of colour in the Ala Archa Gorge in the Tien Shan Mountains, above the city of Alma Ata, capital of Kazakhstan.

of the Tien Shan, means 'the onion mountains'. High on the dry hillsides, the scrub supports bushy roses, with simple yellow and white flowers.

Across these colourful alpine meadows flits a host of beautiful butterflies – orange and brown fritillaries, gleaming coppers, small blues that glint in the sun like jewels, marbled whites and milky winged apollos sporting red eye-spots evolved to scare birds looking for a meal.

Later in the summer, some of the lighter winged insects will be whisked on the wind and thermals high into the mountains and become stranded on the snowfields and glaciers, where they fall victim to specialized wolf spiders. These remarkable creatures are resistant to cold so that they can retrieve their prey even from the surface of the snow and ice. At these altitudes there are also microscopic springtails which creep around and feed on pollen and other wind-blown detritus.

Spring Birds and Mammals

In the foothills, the nesting season gets underway while the higher levels are still experiencing wintry conditions. Male Red-headed Buntings, saffron yellow with tawny heads, and Persian Robins, with a striking black and white face pattern, blue-grey upperparts and

87

A variety of beautiful songbirds nest in the Tien Shan Mountains.
These include the Blue, or Himalayan, Whistling Thrush (top left),
which lives and breeds by fast-flowing mountain streams; the Persian,
or White-throated, Robin (male, top right), found on hot, dry, stony
slopes with thickets of shrubs at around 1,100 to 2,300 m (3,600 to
7,600 ft); and the Himalayan Rubythroat (male, above), which nests
in juniper forests at about 2,500 to 3,500 m (8,200 to 11,500 ft).

a bright orange-red breast, proclaim their freeholds with sweet songs from the uppermost branches of juniper trees. The stronghold of the Black-crested Tit (also known as the Simla Tit or Rufous-naped Tit) is on the south face of the Himalayas, but in Central Asia, it inhabits the forests of spruce and juniper which clothe the lower slopes, where it usually nests in rock crevices. It looks rather like a dusky chickadee or a Coal Tit with a jaunty crest and black waistcoat.

Also in the forests are white and blue Azure Tits, Yellow-browed Warblers, Red-fronted Serins and several species of rosefinches. Some are high-altitude specialists, such as the Greater Rosefinch; the males resemble hefty sparrows, but are gorgeously coloured – strawberry red with white flecks. Himalayan Rubythroats do not start nesting until June. They fly in from India and settle among the prostrate junipers at around 2,500 metres (over 8,000 ft).

Perhaps the most exotic bird of all to nest in the Tien Shan is the Asian Paradise-Flycatcher. It is a wide-ranging species, breeding from Afghanistan to north-east China and south to Java. In the Commonweath of Independent States, it nests in the lush forests of Ussuriland in the far east, as well as in the dark strips of forest, often of a local species of ash, lining the rivers that course through the foothills of the 'celestial mountains'.

The male Asian Paradise-Flycatcher is stunning. His head and neck are black with a metallic blue sheen and there is a hint of a crest. The eye is encircled by a bare blue ring. The rest of the underparts are white, and the upper plumage is a russet brown. But the most remarkable feature is the tail. The male's central tail feathers are elongated into plumes 50 cm (20 in) long, and cause him considerable difficulty when he tucks himself into the tiny nest of woven moss to incubate the eggs or brood the young. However, they appear to be no impediment when it comes to catching insects, which these lovely birds do with consummate skill in typical flycatcher style, flying out from a perch and snapping them up in mid-air. The drabber female lacks the extravagant tail feathers.

As winter begins to retreat, the larger mammals are able to take advantage of the fresh growth on the lower slopes. As we shall see, Marco Polo Sheep and Siberian Ibex give birth early in the spring. Like their domesticated counterparts, the lambs gambol amongst the first green grass in between their bouts of suckling. Huge, bristly Wild Boars forage on the alpine meadows; although they are forest animals over much of their range, they can be found at nearly 3,000 m (9,800 ft) in the Central Asian mountains. Family groups, including the litters of little striped piglets, plough up the ground with their snouts in search of roots and bulbs. Only a few weeks earlier, the ground would have been locked in ice, but now the animals can gain access to the nutritious food it contains.

Mountain Marmots

Marmots emerge from hibernation as the strengthening sun encourages succulent new shoots of grass to appear. There are five or six species of these large, ground-dwelling squirrels in the Soviet mountains. Spending between eight and nine months of the year somnolent in burrows beyond the reach of frost, they come to the surface only for the brief alpine summer. The Red, or Long-tailed, Marmot of the western Tien Shan and the Pamir is the most colourful. It is a large rodent, about 60 cm ($2\frac{1}{2}$ ft) long, with rich copper-red fur, 45 mm ($1\frac{3}{4}$ in) thick to keep the cold at bay. Its favoured habitat is above the tree line at 3,000 m (9,800 ft), and in the eastern Pamir, it ranges highest – up to 4,700 m (15,400 ft) – where the ground is littered with sharp rocks. Here, the vegetation is thin and, although by day the sun radiates its beneficent heat, the nights are always frosty.

Each family group of marmots commands a territory of about 1 sq km ($\frac{1}{3}$ sq mile). The family consists of an adult pair and their offspring from the previous two years. They spend most of their time in a centrally situated warren which may have been in use for years. There are several entrances leading to a tunnel system about 60 m (200 ft) long, which involves the excavation of a dozen cubic metres of spoil. The burrows connect with both a deep nest and a hibernating chamber 3.3 m (11 ft) underground, and to areas set aside as latrines. In the outlying parts of their territory, the marmots dig a series of fairly simple burrows which act as bolt-holes or as temporary shelters, and are used during the summer when the animals are foraging away from their main base.

Red Marmots wake up in April or May, depending upon the altitude, when there is still snow about, and consume up to 1.5 kg (over 3 lb) of vegetation each day. They have a wide-ranging diet, including some 100 different species of plants. At first, they chew nutritious roots and bulbs, but as the season progresses, they turn to various grasses and herbs, including flowers. The seeds pass through the marmots' digestive systems, and are voided in their droppings, which act as a fertilizer for the young plants. However, marmots are not solely vegetarians; they supplement their diet with insect food – including locusts, caterpillars and ant cocoons – and molluscs.

The marmot's holes are sometimes used as nesting places for other creatures. If there is water nearby, Red-breasted Mergansers and Ruddy Shelduck may take advantage of them. Güldenstädt's Redstarts may frequent the colonies to catch the flies which are

Acting as a sentinel for the rest of the family, a Red Marmot warns the others of impending danger by standing on its hind legs and uttering a piercing whistle. These large ground squirrels excavate complex systems of burrows which they use for hibernating and breeding, as well as resting – and escaping from enemies.

attracted to the marmots' dung. Some of these almost starling-sized birds also breed inside the burrows. They have a rugged constitution, nesting at altitudes of up to 5,000 m (16,400 ft) in the Himalayas, the mountains of Central Asia and in the Caucasus Mountains. They favour glacial moraines and boulder-strewn alpine meadows fed by streams from permanent snowfields. In such places, these gorgeous birds flit from rock to rock, hawking for insects. The male is unmistakable; much of his body is black, but his breast, belly, rump and tail are a deep mahogany-red and his crown gleaming white. When he flies, his black wings reveal conspicuous flashes of white, and the fanned red tail looks as though it is aflame. As with many other birds, his mate is rather more modestly coloured.

Mountain Bears – The Soviet 'Yetis'?

The Tien Shan and Pamir mountains are inhabited by the white-clawed race of the Brown Bear (see pages 30–1). In fact, only animals with really straw-coloured fur possess pale claws; the darker, grey-brown individuals grow normal horn-coloured ones. These Central Asian bears reach a good size, the male's body measuring about 1.5 m (5 ft) long and weighing up to 200 kg (440 lb), although the females are smaller. During May, they emerge from their dens after their long winter's sleep, the females accompanied by their cubs, to feed on fresh grass, juicy wild rhubarb, Cow Parsnip and giant fennel, as well as on the remains of berries and fruit left over from the previous autumn.

As the weather improves and summer reaches the higher ridges, the bears climb to about 3,000 m (10,000 ft) to graze on vegetation and dig out mice, voles, susliks and even the large marmots. Being big and muscular, they can heave up rocks and even turn over boulders in their quest for small mammals, molluscs and large insects. Even carrion is eagerly consumed. Stomping through the elevated snowfields, they often leave surprisingly human-like footprints which may be the source of local Yeti legends. The rear footprints of porcupines, too, can look remarkably like a human's. For this reason, some mountain people will eat neither animal.

Mountain People

During the summer, some of the native people of Kazakhstan and Kirghizia undertake traditional vertical migrations, following the seasonally flowering grasses with their herds of sheep, cattle, goats and horses. Spending only short periods before striking camp, they migrate up the valleys to the high alpine areas, and retreat to lower levels during August, as the weather deteriorates.

These hardy people are of Mongoloid stock, and their oriental features suit them well to the high life. Slanting eyes reduce the intense glare of the snow, and a short, flat nose wards off frostbite. The Kazakhs acquired their name from a Turkic word meaning 'riders of the steppes' and horsemanship has been the secret of their success. They trace their origins back to the Turkic and Mongolian nomads who, under Genghis Khan and his descendants, galloped out of northern China in the thirteenth century, to terrorize and dominate a swathe of land, 3,000 km (1,850 miles) wide, from the Lower Volga in Russia to the borders of Sinkiang Province, China. Nowadays, most of them lead settled lives, but a few still maintain their nomadic existence within the framework of the collective farm system.

The Kazakhs' summer home is the yurt, a domed hut up to 6 m (20 ft) in diameter, supported on a collapsible birch or willow frame, and covered with thick greasy felt. A flap in the roof can be pulled aside to admit light or to allow smoke to escape. It is said that the men can erect a yurt in the time it takes the women to boil water for tea! Although originally conceived as a structure of spartan simplicity, yurts may be elaborately furnished

These Yaks are being herded over mountain grassland in Kazakhstan.
Domestic forms of these hardy, high-altitude cattle are smaller and
more variable in colour than the uniformly plain blackish-brown wild
yaks, which are now rare due to hunting in the past.

with colourful woven rugs, decorative felts, and richly carved beds covered with cushions.
When the fire is glowing, the inside is snug, and guests are offered hot tea from the samovar,
meat, cheese, and a jug of fermented mares' milk or *kumiss* – a thin, smoky yoghurt with
a hint of acidic sharpness.

During the day, the men spend much of the time in the saddle tending and herding
their animals, including herds of horses, which are mostly milking mares. These foal in
April, and the Kazakhs allow the mothers to suckle their offspring for the first month, but
for the next three months their milk is shared between the foal and their human owners.
Five or six times daily, the foal is put to the udder until the milk starts to flow. Then it is
pulled off and tethered in front of the mare to maintain the contact with its mother. A

woman then takes over the teats and milks the mare like a cow. In this way, the mare is encouraged to deliver about 4 litres (1 gal) of milk a day. By August, the foals are weaned and the mares have dried up. They then come into oestrus and become pregnant.

Yaks – High-altitude Cattle

Most of the world's domestic animals have their origins in the lowlands, but there is one that is well adapted to the rigours of life at high altitudes – the Yak. Although wild Yaks roamed the Tuva Range on the border between Russia and north-west Mongolia during the fourteenth century, they are nowadays very scarce creatures, confined to the highest and most inhospitable regions of Tibet and Sichuan, where they reach altitudes of over 6,000 m (20,000 ft) – far higher than any other mammal. The wonder is that these substantial beasts can thrive on the scant vegetation. The bulls may stand over 2 m (6ft 8 in) at the shoulder and weigh about 900 kg (almost a ton). However, their domesticated derivatives are somewhat smaller.

In the mountains of the Central Asian republics and in the Altai, these high-altitude oxen are at the northernmost limit of their range. Here, most are now kept for their meat, not for their milk or wool, or as beasts of burden, as in the Himalayas; out of a herd of 200 Yaks, about 40 may be slaughtered each year. They have a commanding advantage on these elevated pastures; unlike domestic cattle and sheep, Yaks are happiest well above the tree-line and can remain at high altitudes all year round without requiring any supplementary fodder. By contrast, sheep and cattle must be taken down into the sheltered valleys during winter, simulating the kind of vertical migrations that many other wild creatures undertake to escape the grim conditions.

Yaks are rather similar to humped cows, but equipped with short legs and a massive, low-slung head, which in the mature bulls is surmounted by widely spaced horns. Their coat, which is often black, is thick, and a 'kilt' of long hair hangs from their flanks, thighs and tail. This fringe, together with the warm coat, enables them to endure the bitter weather, and insulates them when they rest on the snow. Also, Yaks use their hooves to scrape away the snow cover to expose the vegetation underneath.

High-mountain Lakes

During the last Ice Age, massive landslips dammed some of the mountain river valleys, and formed high-altitude lakes. The largest in the Tien Shan is Lake Issyk-Kul. Occupying a depression at a height of 1,600 m (5,249 ft), it covers more than 6,200 sq km (2,400 sq miles) to a depth of 700 m (2,296 ft). The intense blue of its water and the backdrop of snow-covered peaks give this lake a rare beauty that is perhaps only surpassed in the former Soviet Union by Lake Baikal. In winter, only the shallow edges freeze over and even then acquire only a thin film of ice. Rainbow Trout were introduced into the lake from Armenia, and behave rather like salmon by ascending the streams to spawn during autumn. In the lake, where there is little competition for insect food, this fish now grows into a giant, reaching a record of 15 kg (30lb), although the average is about half of this weight. In Armenia, the trout normally grows to a maximum of 3-4 kg (6-8 lb).

Kara-Kul is the highest lake. Situated in the arid centre of the Pamir Mountains, this stretch of open water lies in a basin at a height of 3,900 m (12,795 ft) above sea level. With a maximum depth of only 236m (774ft), it is comparatively shallow when compared with Issyk-Kul, and freezes over during the winter. During the summer, the wind whips the surface into angry waves, causing it to live up to its name, which means 'black lake'. Being cold and brackish, the waters of the lake are not hugely fertile, but they allow the development of sufficient aquatic invertebrates to support fish and bird life.

High-level Migrants

Islets in Lake Issyk-Kul are the nesting sites of Bar-headed Geese. These birds are high-altitude migrants that are thought to fly across the Himalayas at heights of up to 8,840 m (29,000 ft), where the air is so rarefied that most humans would die without oxygen masks. They are rather dainty, medium-sized grey geese with a white head, adorned with a pair of brownish-black horseshoe-shaped bars across the nape.

Bar-headed Geese are confined to Asia, wintering on the plains of northern India, Assam, and northern Burma. Each spring, the migrating skeins gain sufficient height to cross the Himalayas *en route* to their nesting sites by high-altitude lakes. Most settle on the bitter soda lakes of the Tibetan plateau, but some press on to the southern slopes of the Altai and the region to the south of Lake Baikal. Others head west to the Pamir, on the

Overleaf: Against a backdrop of towering, snow-covered peaks, Lake Kara-Kul in the Pamir Mountains is the highest of the high-mountain lakes of the Central Asian republics. This view, in August, shows a small group of Brown-headed Gulls and their well-grown chicks. Though nesting in larger numbers in Tibet, this is one of the rarest breeding birds in the former Soviet Union, with only 300–400 pairs nesting on Kara-Kul. It migrates south to winter in India, where it is known as the Indian Black-headed Gull.

About 40 pairs of elegant Bar-headed Geese nest on inhospitable soda
islands in the remote soda lake of Ran-Kul, at an altitude of 4,000 m
(13,000 ft) in the eastern Pamir Mountains. Baked in the sun and
blasted by dust storms laden with corrosive salt by day, and freezing
cold at night, this is a tough environment for birds to breed in.

edge of the species' range. They prefer to breed on small islands in the lakes, scraping a hole in the short grass, and often nest in loose colonies. In the republic of Tuva, which borders north-west Mongolia, some are reported to nest in trees.

At these altitudes, it may be July before the eggs hatch. In August, like other wildfowl, the adult geese moult all their feathers simultaneously and are potentially very vulnerable to predators. However, in these high, remote regions, there is little, apart from foxes, to threaten them while they grow their new plumage.

Bar-headed Geese also thread their way through the high valleys to reach Lake Ran-Kul, which is situated 80 km (50 miles) to the south-east of Lake Kara-Kul, only a stone's throw from the Chinese border in Tadzhikistan. This lake is even shallower than Kara-

Kul, being barely a metre or two (3-6½ ft) deep, and so warms up quite quickly during the summer, and gives rise to a good hatch of midges and caddis-flies – ideal food for the goslings. The geese nest on dusty islets of gleaming white caustic soda, the largest of which is only about 365 m (400 yd) across. The isolated islands give them a good measure of protection from marauding foxes, but not from Ravens, which sally forth from the surrounding hills to raid unguarded nests and eat the addled eggs.

Caspian, Common, and Gull-billed Terns nest on these high lakes, as well as various hooded gulls, including the Great Black-headed Gull described in Chapter 2 (see pages 67-9). Two other hooded gulls resemble the familiar Black-headed Gull, a common breeder in northern Europe. The rare Brown-headed Gull is rather larger than the Black-headed, and can be distinguished at close quarters by its pale eyes and slightly different wingtip markings. It nests in noisy colonies like its lowland cousin and, like it, loses the chocolate brown face mask at the end of the breeding season.

The Mysterious Relict Gull

The Relict Gull is another 'hooded' species, but in contrast to its relatives it is one of the rarest and most enigmatic gulls in the world. It is reminiscent of a small Great Black-headed Gull, with blood-red beak and legs, and white circles around its eyes. For many years, it was not recognized as a distinct species but was thought to be a hybrid, perhaps between the Mediterranean and Great Black-headed Gulls.

The whereabouts of the Relict Gull's breeding sites also remained an utter mystery, until 1963, when a colony was found on Lake Barun-Torei, in Trans-Baikalia, on a remote part of the Mongolian border. Then, in 1969, a further site was discovered on Lake Alakol in Kazakhstan close to the Chinese border. For a long time, these were thought to be the only breeding sites of this very special gull, but then, in 1984, a single nest was found on Lake Balkhash among a colony of Caspian Terns. Much more significant, in 1987, a Chinese ornithologist found one of the largest breeding colonies near Ordos in Inner Mongolia – the only known breeding location for the species in China.

In the former Soviet Union there may be no more than 2,000 breeding pairs of Relict Gulls, all nesting at Lake Barun-Torei and Lake Alakol. The birds breed in dense colonies, with their nests only half a metre (1½ ft) apart and often close to those of Caspian Terns. To avoid mammalian predators, they are located on islands a long way from the shore. The eggs are unusually coloured for a gull's, having a chalky-white ground colour rather than green or brown, and decorated with dark blotches.

99

Sadly, these rare birds give conservationists much cause for concern because the number of nesting pairs tends to fluctuate every year. For example, on Lake Alakol, there may be a thriving colony of as many as 1,200 pairs one year, but the following year only 30 or so pairs arrive to nest. Storms and cold weather may conspire to hold the population in check either by flooding the nests or by reducing the amount of insects on which the gulls and their chicks depend.

Snowcocks

Few birds occur on the high snowfields, but snowcocks habitually frequent these upper realms. Although their camouflaged brown, grey, black and white plumage makes them difficult to see among the rocks and snow, their ethereal whistles are readily heard. Indeed, these long-drawn-out calls which echo around the crags are evocative of these high altitudes. They are uttered by surprisingly big birds. Built rather like partridges but as big as guineafowl, snowcocks strut around the snow line.

Male snowcocks measure up to 56 cm (22 in) long and weigh up to about 3 kg (6½ lb), but the hens are a great deal smaller and reach only about 1.8 kg (4 lb). Two species are found in the Tien Shan and Pamir mountains. The most widespread is the Himalayan Snowcock, while a rarer species, the Tibetan Snowcock, occurs in the Pamir. These birds are swift runners and often gather in flocks to feed on the edge of the snow line, taking buds, seeds and berries, as well as bulbs, which they excavate with their strong, broad bills. Being plump and tasty, they are fair game for Golden Eagles and Grey Wolves.

The End of Summer

As in the far north, summer is a brief season in the mountains and soon comes to an end. The onset of inclement weather begins high up and gradually extends into the valleys, bringing sleet and snow and very cold nights.

By the end of July, the vegetation starts to dry out, and the marmots prepare for hibernation. About a month before they finally disappear underground, they turf out their old bedding and allow it to dry in the sun. They also put on about 2 kg (4 lb) of fat to see them through the winter. By mid-September, the marmots have settled down on their refreshed bedding and started their deep winter sleep.

Meanwhile, the Güldenstädt's Redstarts of the Pamir descend to the foothills and plains along the Zeravshan valley as far west as Samarkand. Siberian Buckthorns, which form almost impenetrable thickets along the streams and river beds, are now covered with

Among the most exciting birds of the high mountains are the rare
Relict Gulls (above), seen here at one of their few breeding colonies,
on small islands in Lake Alakol, in southern Kazakhstan, near the
Chinese border. Others are the snowcocks, of which all five species
are found in the mountains of the former USSR: this pair of Himalayan
Snowcocks (below) are in a river valley in the Pamir Mountains.

bright orange berries, and the redstarts join many other migrants to feast on this autumn fare.

The Brown Bears also leave the high, alpine meadows and retire to the forests and thickets, where they feast on hawthorn berries, oil-rich walnuts and wild apples in preparation for their long winter lie-in.

Early snow drives the hardy snowcocks lower down the slopes, although they still spend the winter above the tree line. In November, there is an outburst of courtship. A male chases his intended mate in a crouching position, with his tail cocked, fluffing out his neck and tail feathers, his head lowered. Every now and then, he sprints to the top of a rock, throws back his head and utters loud, wild whistling calls. However, the pairs will not nest until the following spring.

The Thrifty Pikas

Of those mountain residents that need to make forward plans for the winter, the pikas are perhaps the most remarkable. Several species occur in the former Soviet Union, but the Large-eared and Red Pikas are those most commonly met with in the mountains of Central Asia. They are cute little creatures, a little larger than guinea pigs but with longish ears and

A thrifty Altai Pika busies itself with gathering supplies of plant food which it will dry and store as a diminutive haystack in spaces under and between the rocks. In winter, it will survive on these hidden food stores – if other animals have not found them first.

whiskers to match. They live in colonies in alpine meadows, mostly among scattered rocks under which they place their nests.

In places where pikas are common, their communities are spaced about 100 m (330 ft) apart, usually on south-facing slopes. This is no accident, because these industrious relatives of rabbits and hares need the warmth of the sun to dry their winter food stores. Since pikas do not hibernate, they need to lay up sufficient stores of plant food to see them through the winter. They do this by literally making hay while the sun shines.

Pikas zealously defend their mountain plots against encroaching neighbours because the vegetation is their key to survival. Throughout the summer, they busily harvest grass and leafy twigs, and stack them on stones, to enable the sun's heat to convert them into hay. The miniature haystacks are regularly turned so that as much moisture as possible is driven out of the cut vegetation. When it is sufficiently desiccated, the material is ferried away and stored out of the reach of rain and snow under slabs of rock or in crevices for use during the most rigorous period of the year.

A single family of pikas may make up to a dozen stacks on 1 hectare ($2\frac{1}{2}$ acres) of mountainside, with a total weight of 10 kg (22 lb). When the snow lays thickly on the ground, the pikas manage to live well on their preserved fodder. However, there is always the danger that other herbivores will profit from their resourcefulness. In areas where the ranges of pikas and musk deer (see pages 239-41) overlap, the deer sometimes stumble upon one of the stores, and, using their hooves to dig away the snow, reveal the mass of nourishing, sun-dried foliage.

Goats and Sheep

Wild goats and sheep are the mountaineers of the mammal world, but even they move down from the bleakest areas during the winter and so avoid the worst of the weather. However, their most dramatic activity – the rut – occurs in November and December. Since the ewes give birth in spring, they must mate at the end of the previous year, due to their short gestation period. The most vigorous males with the largest horns copulate most.

Rams challenge one another by rearing on their hind legs and striking their heads together with a clash of horns. Were it not for their reinforced skulls, the force of the butting would shatter their heads. The highest-ranking rams gather harems of 20-30 females and mate with them as they come into heat.

Wild sheep and goats owe their success to their robust digestive systems which enable them to thrive on hard and abrasive vegetation that flourishes at high altitudes close to snow fields and glaciers. The grasses and herbs are often covered in grit, and so, to counteract the wear on their teeth, sheep have evolved batteries of long molars which grow continuously.

Six species of goats are distributed across Western Europe through the Mediterranean to India, extending as far north as Siberia. The Siberian Ibex is one of the most widespread in the mountains of the former Soviet Union. It is a large animal, standing up to a metre ($3\frac{1}{4}$ ft) at the shoulder, with the mature rams sporting spectacular, scimitar-shaped horns up to 1.5 m (5 ft) long. Those of the females are much more modest, growing to barely one third of this length.

Ibex are agile climbers and confident jumpers, at home on steep slopes beyond the reach of wolves. Their surefootedness is enhanced by the nature of their hooves. As in all ungulates, the horn of the hoof is constantly being renewed, but ibex hooves are fairly soft and adhere strongly to the surface of slippery rocks. The Siberian Ibex is a particularly versatile goat which can occur at fairly low altitudes near to the forest zone as well as occasionally venturing as high as 5,000 m (16,000 ft). In the realm of the Russian bear, there are approximately 500,000 head of ibex.

The Markhor – Greatest of the Goats

The largest and most magnificent of all the goats, the Markhor, is by comparison with the Siberian Ibex a very scarce species. Although there are some in Afghanistan and Pakistan, only 400 occur in the former Soviet Union, and these are all confined to the mountainous areas of Tadzhikistan, such as the Dashti Dzum Nature Reserve in the foothills of the Pamir. The mature rams are handsome creatures, standing about 1.1 m (over $3\frac{1}{4}$ ft) at the shoulder, and vary in colour from reddish-brown to grey; the older ones have a heavy beard hanging from the neck and chest, and this is especially long during the winter, when a skirt of long hair sweeps down from the flanks.

However, it is the horns that are the male Markhor's crowning glory. Each is a great twist of bone and keratin, shaped like a corkscrew and projecting over 1.5 m (5 ft) above the head, thus accounting for the Russian name of *vintorogy kozyol* – 'the spiral-horned goat'. In Tadzhik Markhors, the horn generally executes three full turns. Of Persian origin, the word 'markhor' means 'snake-eater'.

For much of the year, Markhors live in small groups of five to seven individuals, although they will congregate during the winter months. They favour slopes and canyons with a certain amount of scrub – often of juniper or pistachio – and usually range no higher

An old male Markhor shows off his impressive corkscrew-shaped horns – this
is the rarest of the five species of wild goats found in the former USSR.

than 2,600 m (8,500 ft). The mating season begins in mid-November and carries on through
December. During May, the kids are born, often as twins, and within a day or so, they are
on their feet and following their mothers.

Marco Polo Sheep

Few animals remain to endure winter in the grimly inhospitable upper reaches of the
mountains, but among those that do are Marco Polo Sheep – the giant sheep of the Pamir.
They eke out an existence in wide valleys at 2,500-4,600 m (8,200-15,000 ft). As the
snowfall is relatively light, they are able to scrape a living where the strong winds have
blown away the snow from the poor vegetation. By virtue of their evolutionary history,
wild sheep do well at these high altitudes because they are pioneers, fitted to exploit the
meagre resources left by retreating glaciers.

Over the past one million years, the ancestors of wild sheep spread from their original
home in Central Asia into the mountainous areas of Europe, North Africa, Asia, and North
America, to become some of the most widespread of the cloven-hoofed mammals. The
fragmentation into so many discrete populations across three continents has resulted in a
bewildering variety of races. Today, there are some 36-40 races of wild sheep, belonging
to six separate species: Bighorn and Thinhorn Sheep from the USA and Canada, the
Siberian Snow Sheep, and the Urial, Mouflon, and Argali from Eurasia. The Marco Polo

105

CHAPTER FOUR

THE GREAT CENTRAL ASIAN DESERTS AND STEPPES

DESPITE THE FACT that much of the former Soviet Union is cold and snow-covered for a large part of the year, such is the size of this huge country that it is also possible to experience the hot blast of the desert there. The sun-scorched arid lands stretch for 1,000 km (620 miles) in a vast crescent across Central Asia and Kazakhstan, extending from the foothills of the Tien Shan and Pamir-Alai Mountains to 48°N – the same latitude as Vienna – where a kinder climate prevails. To the west, their spread is blocked by the salt encrusted shores of the Caspian Sea, while to the east, they merge into the cold, barren wastes of the Gobi Desert.

Some areas of the Central Asian deserts are virtually lifeless, having been scoured by wind, etched into gullies by rare rainfalls, and baked by the blazing sun into a surface as stark as any lunar landscape. These and other desert and semi-desert regions cover a total area of 2 million sq km (772,260 sq miles), almost equivalent to the combined areas of the United Kingdom, France, Spain and Germany, or more than those of California, Arizona and Texas.

Together, by far the largest of the arid areas are two great sandy expanses in Central Asia. The Karakum, named from Turkic words meaning 'Black Sands', is located between the Caspian Sea and the Amu Darya River. The sand was originally deposited in ancient times by the river as it overflowed its banks and changed course over the plains of Turkmenistan. At Repetek, just south of Chardzhou on the border between Turkmenistan

A herd of Kulan, or Asiatic Wild Asses, raises the dust as it thunders across the dry savannah semi-desert at the Badkhyz nature reserve, in southernmost Turkmenistan, near the border with Iran and Afghanistan. This reserve was established in 1941 to protect these beautiful mammals.

(18,400 ft). They range from the southern Himalayas northwards through Pakistan and into Central Asia and southern Siberia. In the former Soviet Union, as in the rest of their range, these big cats exist at very low densities, and there may be only about 2,000 of them scattered throughout the high ridges and boulder-strewn slopes of the Pamir, the western Tien Shan, and the eastern Sayan Mountains. Although fully protected by law, they suffer from poaching, and, much more seriously, from conflict with the owners of domestic sheep and goats, as well as from the destruction of their habitat by the overgrazing that often results as the mountain slopes are increasingly colonized by livestock.

Like all cats, Snow Leopards are wonderfully agile; they easily take ravines up to 8 m (26 ft) wide in their stride and can leap over barriers 3 m (nearly 10 ft) high. Being surefooted, they can balance on narrow ledges, and have no fear of heights in the pursuit of their victims. These may include smaller mammals, such as hares and marmots, as well as larger ones such as Siberian Ibex, wild sheep, and Wild Boars.

Snow Leopards are so elusive, and their home terrain is so difficult to negotiate that few worthwhile observations have been made on their behaviour in the wild. However, captive individuals have a placid nature and appear to make friends among themselves. They spend a great deal of time rubbing heads, lying in contact with each other and mutually licking each other's coats. Furthermore, Snow Leopards which are acquainted will greet each other with a brief purring, made by softly blowing air through the nostrils.

This long-term social bonding may be of survival value to these lovely animals in their wild mountain domain where prey is sparse. By associating in pairs, they may maximize their chances of making regular kills. Also, the females come into heat for only a very limited time each year (they are receptive every five days a month between December and March) so it may be of advantage if each individual has a member of the opposite sex close by. Once the kittens are born, both parents may be needed to provide enough food to keep the offspring alive.

During the winter, Snow Leopards may follow their prey down to the tree line where it is more sheltered. Unlike the other great predator found in the mountains, the Brown Bear, these cats must keep hunting throughout the coldest months of the year.

Some of the snow that settles in the Pamir and Tien Shan mountains eventually melts and finds its way into the great rivers of Central Asia, which run across the hottest and driest region in the former Soviet Union – the only realm not tramped by bears.

Sheep is a race of the Argali. Like all Asiatic sheep, Marco Polo Sheep have long, slender legs, a diffuse rump patch and a narrow tail, and the rams possess deeply ringed horns.

Sheep are intensely gregarious creatures, although not particularly placid ones; despite proverbs alluding to their gentleness, they have pugnacious dispositions. Sheep societies are based upon the lasting bonds between the ewes and their grown-up daughters. The sexes segregate into their own groups, the bachelors consorting together while the females and their lambs form tight flocks. When moving from one pasture to another, the rams line up behind the highest-ranking individual with the most impressive horns, and the females follow the oldest ewe and her offspring.

The thickset rams of Marco Polo Sheep grow curled horns of spectacular proportions (although those of the Siberian Argali are even bigger). A ram may carry horns up to 1.9 m ($6\frac{1}{4}$ ft) long and 50 cm (20 in) round at the base; such a set of monstrous horns tips the scales at 22.5 kg ($49\frac{1}{2}$ lb), and weigh more than the rest of the skeleton. The head and skull alone account for 13 per cent of the animal's total weight.

Heavyweight horns are basically status symbols. A ram's rank is determined by the size of his horns. As they become more impressive with age, young rams have to defer to their elders which possess bigger headgear. They show off their horns in special strutting displays so that rivals can assess each other's strength by their profile. If the dispute escalates, the horns double up as weapons. Whereas many horned animals engage in contests of strength based upon hooking or wrestling with locked horns or antlers, sheep deal out seemingly skull-shattering blows, often standing on their hindlegs as a preliminary to clashing with their opponents. Accordingly, these living battering rams have evolved hefty horns and greatly reinforced skulls to assist and protect them in their sexual jousting.

The Elusive Snow Cat

In the high, desolate mountains of Central Asia lives one of the world's most enigmatic creatures – the Snow Leopard. Sometimes referred to as the phantom cat, this low-slung, long-tailed predator has been observed only fleetingly in the wild.

Snow Leopards are completely committed to mountain life and although they have been seen as low as 700 m (2,300 ft), most of them dwell at altitudes of between 3,000 and 4,500 m (10,000 and 15,000 ft) above sea level, with the odd individual reaching 5,500 m

Preceding pages: Its long bushy tail dragging in the
deep snow, this elusive Snow Leopard is superbly adapted to
life in the highest mountains of Central Asia.

An old male Markhor shows off his impressive corkscrew-shaped horns – this
is the rarest of the five species of wild goats found in the former USSR.

than 2,600 m (8,500 ft). The mating season begins in mid-November and carries on through
December. During May, the kids are born, often as twins, and within a day or so, they are
on their feet and following their mothers.

Marco Polo Sheep

Few animals remain to endure winter in the grimly inhospitable upper reaches of the
mountains, but among those that do are Marco Polo Sheep – the giant sheep of the Pamir.
They eke out an existence in wide valleys at 2,500-4,600 m (8,200-15,000 ft). As the
snowfall is relatively light, they are able to scrape a living where the strong winds have
blown away the snow from the poor vegetation. By virtue of their evolutionary history,
wild sheep do well at these high altitudes because they are pioneers, fitted to exploit the
meagre resources left by retreating glaciers.

Over the past one million years, the ancestors of wild sheep spread from their original
home in Central Asia into the mountainous areas of Europe, North Africa, Asia, and North
America, to become some of the most widespread of the cloven-hoofed mammals. The
fragmentation into so many discrete populations across three continents has resulted in a
bewildering variety of races. Today, there are some 36-40 races of wild sheep, belonging
to six separate species: Bighorn and Thinhorn Sheep from the USA and Canada, the
Siberian Snow Sheep, and the Urial, Mouflon, and Argali from Eurasia. The Marco Polo

snow fields and glaciers. The grasses and herbs are often covered in grit, and so, to counteract the wear on their teeth, sheep have evolved batteries of long molars which grow continuously.

Six species of goats are distributed across Western Europe through the Mediterranean to India, extending as far north as Siberia. The Siberian Ibex is one of the most widespread in the mountains of the former Soviet Union. It is a large animal, standing up to a metre ($3\frac{1}{4}$ ft) at the shoulder, with the mature rams sporting spectacular, scimitar-shaped horns up to 1.5 m (5 ft) long. Those of the females are much more modest, growing to barely one third of this length.

Ibex are agile climbers and confident jumpers, at home on steep slopes beyond the reach of wolves. Their surefootedness is enhanced by the nature of their hooves. As in all ungulates, the horn of the hoof is constantly being renewed, but ibex hooves are fairly soft and adhere strongly to the surface of slippery rocks. The Siberian Ibex is a particularly versatile goat which can occur at fairly low altitudes near to the forest zone as well as occasionally venturing as high as 5,000 m (16,000 ft). In the realm of the Russian bear, there are approximately 500,000 head of ibex.

The Markhor – Greatest of the Goats

The largest and most magnificent of all the goats, the Markhor, is by comparison with the Siberian Ibex a very scarce species. Although there are some in Afghanistan and Pakistan, only 400 occur in the former Soviet Union, and these are all confined to the mountainous areas of Tadzhikistan, such as the Dashti Dzum Nature Reserve in the foothills of the Pamir. The mature rams are handsome creatures, standing about 1.1 m (over $3\frac{1}{4}$ ft) at the shoulder, and vary in colour from reddish-brown to grey; the older ones have a heavy beard hanging from the neck and chest, and this is especially long during the winter, when a skirt of long hair sweeps down from the flanks.

However, it is the horns that are the male Markhor's crowning glory. Each is a great twist of bone and keratin, shaped like a corkscrew and projecting over 1.5 m (5 ft) above the head, thus accounting for the Russian name of *vintorogy kozyol* – 'the spiral-horned goat'. In Tadzhik Markhors, the horn generally executes three full turns. Of Persian origin, the word 'markhor' means 'snake-eater'.

For much of the year, Markhors live in small groups of five to seven individuals, although they will congregate during the winter months. They favour slopes and canyons with a certain amount of scrub – often of juniper or pistachio – and usually range no higher whiskers to match. They live in colonies in alpine meadows, mostly among scattered rocks under which they place their nests.

In places where pikas are common, their communities are spaced about 100 m (330 ft) apart, usually on south-facing slopes. This is no accident, because these industrious relatives of rabbits and hares need the warmth of the sun to dry their winter food stores. Since pikas do not hibernate, they need to lay up sufficient stores of plant food to see them through the winter. They do this by literally making hay while the sun shines.

Pikas zealously defend their mountain plots against encroaching neighbours because the vegetation is their key to survival. Throughout the summer, they busily harvest grass and leafy twigs, and stack them on stones, to enable the sun's heat to convert them into hay. The miniature haystacks are regularly turned so that as much moisture as possible is driven out of the cut vegetation. When it is sufficiently desiccated, the material is ferried away and stored out of the reach of rain and snow under slabs of rock or in crevices for use during the most rigorous period of the year.

A single family of pikas may make up to a dozen stacks on 1 hectare ($2\frac{1}{2}$ acres) of mountainside, with a total weight of 10 kg (22 lb). When the snow lays thickly on the ground, the pikas manage to live well on their preserved fodder. However, there is always the danger that other herbivores will profit from their resourcefulness. In areas where the ranges of pikas and musk deer (see pages 239-41) overlap, the deer sometimes stumble upon one of the stores, and, using their hooves to dig away the snow, reveal the mass of nourishing, sun-dried foliage.

Goats and Sheep

Wild goats and sheep are the mountaineers of the mammal world, but even they move down from the bleakest areas during the winter and so avoid the worst of the weather. However, their most dramatic activity – the rut – occurs in November and December. Since the ewes give birth in spring, they must mate at the end of the previous year, due to their short gestation period. The most vigorous males with the largest horns copulate most.

Rams challenge one another by rearing on their hind legs and striking their heads together with a clash of horns. Were it not for their reinforced skulls, the force of the butting would shatter their heads. The highest-ranking rams gather harems of 20-30 females and mate with them as they come into heat.

Wild sheep and goats owe their success to their robust digestive systems which enable them to thrive on hard and abrasive vegetation that flourishes at high altitudes close to

Resembling a scene from a science-fiction planet, this dramatic view
across the rift edge at Badkhyz shows a salt flat gleaming white in the
summer sun, and the strange, conical, flat-topped remains of ancient
volcanoes, called *kazans*, rising above it.

and Uzbekistan, the loose sand is blown into high, crescent-shaped dunes called *barkhans*.
These shift a few metres every year, according to the direction of the wind, and form a
region of rolling ridges of sand reminiscent of Arabia or the Sahara.

Beyond the Karakum lies the Kyzylkum – or 'Red Sands' – which stretches across
Uzbekistan into Kazakhstan where the Syr Darya River forms its eastern boundary.
Together, these two areas constitute the fourth largest desert in the world, with a combined
area of 640,000 sq km (247,000 sq miles).

Different Types of Desert

The sandy wastes of the Karakum and Kyzylkum are not the only kind of Central Asian
deserts. They eventually give way to areas of rubble, rocks and clay, each with its own
characteristics. A thin belt of clay desert runs along the foothills of the Kopet-Dag, Tien

One of the harshest environments in Central Asia is that of the salt
deserts, although these occupy a relatively small area of the desert region.
In some places, the seasonal salt lakes are completely
devoid of life.

Shan and Pamir mountains. With time, the friable soil has become dissected by a network
of ridges and deep gullies reminiscent of the 'badlands' of the western USA.

The largest clay desert is Betpakdala, lying between the Syr Darya River and Lake
Balkhash, a large lake with the outline of a beached sturgeon. By contrast, a stony desert
extends across the Ustyurt Plateau between the Caspian and Aral seas. As the name suggests,
the ground is littered with fragments of shattered rock.

The extreme aridity of the air, combined with natural salts, is responsible for a further
kind of desert called *solonchaki*. These areas have developed on the terraces of the rivers
that carve their way across the desert regions. Moisture seeping from them into the
surrounding soil is sucked to the surface by capillary action, bringing minerals into the top
layers. In the intensely dry atmosphere, the water evaporates, leaving soil bitter with salts
in which only a few kinds of salt-tolerant (halophytic) plants will grow.

The location of the deserts is determined by their remoteness from sources of moisture. By the time they reach Central Asia, the Atlantic weather fronts, borne on the westerly winds, have long since lost their capacity to generate much rain. Also, humid air flowing from the tropics is blocked by the forbidding peaks of the Tien Shan and Pamir Mountains, condensing the moisture from the clouds. This falls as snow, which eventually feeds the numerous rivers that run, like thin veins on a marble slab, across the lowland deserts. Some, such as the Tedjen, Zeravshan, and Murgab, simply vanish into the porous sand. Many thousands of years ago, these were probably tributaries of the great Amu and Syr Darya rivers which still flow into the Aral Sea. Unfortunately, their sweet water is insufficient to freshen and fertilize the arid countryside through which they flow.

The dynamics of global atmospheric circulation also contribute towards the formation of deserts in these latitudes, by bathing this area in dry air. The phenomenon starts at the equator where humid air is heated and rises in powerful convection currents high into the atmosphere. As it ascends, it cools, and the water vapour condenses, producing billowing clouds and torrential rain which nurtures the equatorial jungles. The air, now deprived of its moisture, flows away from the equatorial regions and slowly descends in the middle latitudes, where it produces dry landscapes. The Sahara and Gobi deserts and the arid lands of Central Asia come under its withering influence.

The humidity of desert air is so low that the skies tend to be cloudless. As a consequence, the ground receives the full force of the sun; at night, without the insulating blanket of cloud, the heat rapidly radiates into space, causing the temperature to plunge. The winters are almost universally cold throughout the former Soviet Union, and it is during this time that the arid lands receive most of their meagre ration of moisture, sometimes as snow, which must satisfy the desert plants' and animals' needs for the rest of the year.

By definition, deserts have a rainfall of less than 250 mm (10 in) a year, and this might fall within a very limited wet season, the rest of the year being completely dry. The climatic details are known for Repetek, because this nature reserve has been a centre for studying the Karakum Desert since 1928. The records reveal the harshness of the desert's conditions.

At Repetek, the average rainfall is 114 mm ($4\frac{1}{2}$ in) a year, but this figure conceals the fickle nature of the precipitation. Severe drought prevails in some years when a mere 6 mm

The great dune systems of the Central Asian
sand deserts create a scene reminiscent of the Sahara.
Tough desert grasses help to stabilize
the shifting dunes.

($\frac{1}{4}$ in) of rain is recorded; this barely wets the surface of the sand. At other times, 200 mm ($7\frac{3}{4}$ in) is recorded in a single year, and this causes the desert to bloom luxuriantly.

The temperature also fluctuates widely with the seasons; in winter, the average temperature hovers just above freezing point, while in July – the hottest month – it soars to 29°C (84°F). However, even these statistics belie the extremes of climate that are experienced in the Karakum. In January 1969, the temperature sunk to a Siberian level of -31°C (-23.8°F) and in July 1983, Repetek became like an oven, with the mercury in the official thermometer registering 50.1°C (122.18°F). Such dry heat causes a moisture deficit of major proportions in the desert, even in years when the winter rain has been plentiful, because the equivalent of 1000 mm (39 in) of water can be evaporated from the soil.

The Russian word for desert is *pustinia*, which, like its English counterpart, means an empty place. However, the arid lands of the Central Asian republics are far from uninhabited. In Repetek alone, 1,000 species of insects and of arachnids (spiders and their kin) have been recorded, along with 23 species of reptiles, 196 of birds, and 29 of mammals. The reserve also contains an impressive 211 species of plants. These animals and plants have come to terms with the inhospitable conditions by evolving methods of economizing on water and keeping cool.

Escaping the Heat

Most animals survive in the deserts by simply opting out of the difficulties. For instance, many avoid the debilitating daytime heat by adopting a nocturnal life-style. Others become active around dawn; when it gets too hot for comfort, they retire into the shade or disappear into burrows where it is cooler.

Horsfield's Tortoises cram their living into the three kindest months of the desert year. These reptiles are up to 18 cm (7 in) long, and are distinguished from other tortoises by having four rather than five toes on their front legs. They appear during the spring when the land is covered with fresh, succulent vegetation. Clawing their way to the surface from their subterranean chambers, they feed and breed with gusto.

By the end of May or the beginning of June, the female tortoises have mated and each one is busy burying about a dozen eggs in the sand. Afterwards, the adults lay up stores of body fat, in preparation for the long period they will spend underground. By midsummer, the scorching sun and withered vegetation stimulates them to tunnel up to 2 m ($6\frac{1}{2}$ ft) into the ground, where they retire for the next nine months in a state of torpidity – this process is called aestivation, and is the hot climate equivalent of hibernation. Meanwhile, the

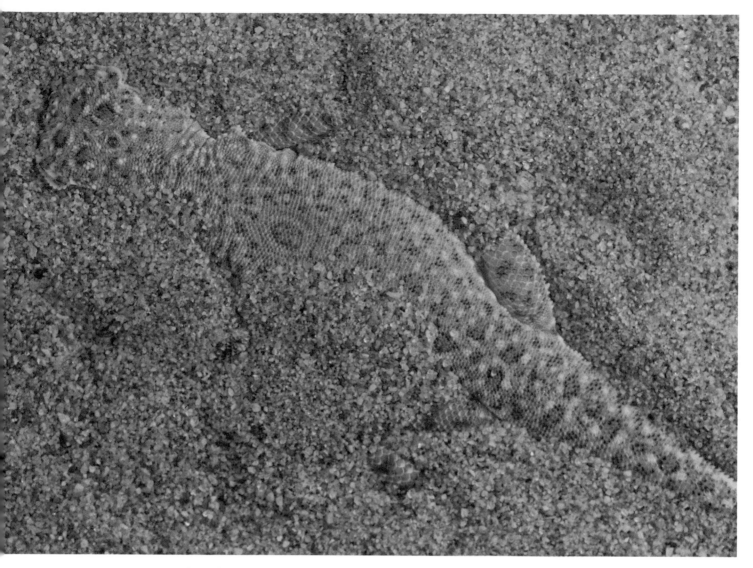

Pushing the sand out from beneath it with rapid sideways movements of its
well camouflaged body, a Toad-headed Agama lizard buries itself almost instantly
beneath the sand to escape from danger. The head is the last part to disappear
and the first to re-emerge, as the little reptile checks that the coast is clear.

tortoises' eggs develop in the solar-heated soil and hatch between August and October.
However, the tiny young may make no attempt to surface until spring.

A Wealth of Lizards

The Central Asian Agama is a common lizard of the deserts which occurs where there are
bushes and grows to about 30 cm (1 ft) long. Just after dawn, these agamas can be seen on
the very tops of the shrubs catching the early morning sun. Neighbouring males express
their dominance towards each other by nodding and showing off their blue throats. When
it becomes too hot for them, they scurry off into the shade.

One remarkable lizard of the Central Asian deserts is the 25 cm (10 in) long Eared
Toad-headed Agama because it has startling territorial defence and threat displays. The

males spend much of the day patrolling their territories, holding their tails high, coiling and uncoiling them like watch springs. They are difficult to surprise because they often station themselves on the top of sand dunes. Even if one is taken unawares, it can bury itself in the loose sand in an instant like so many lizards. But if a toadhead has the misfortune to be cornered, then it shows its annoyance by gaping and unfolding dramatic red flanges at the corners of its mouth.

Rival males of the smaller Sand Toad-headed Agama signal a warning to one another to keep away by waving the black and white banded tips of their tails. These conspicuous little warning banners may also be the lizard's downfall, though, because many of them are caught by White-winged Woodpeckers and Bukhara Tits and fed to their nestlings.

A young Desert Monitor lizard explores its surroundings. Eventually, it will
grow to over 1.5 m (5 ft) long. This voracious predator eats a wide range of
prey, from rodents, tortoises and other lizards to poisonous snakes.

By far the most impressive of all the Central Asian lizards is the Desert Monitor. Weighing up to 2.5 kg (5½ lb), this reptile is the biggest and most muscular lizard in Central Asia. From the end of its nose to the tip of its heavy tail, a fully grown Desert Monitor measures 1.6 m (5¼ ft), has a bite like a crocodile, and can deliver a blow from its tail that will leave the skin badly bruised. Some of these giant lizards enlarge the burrows of gerbils to act as bases, from which they sally forth for up to 0.5 km ($\frac{1}{3}$ mile) to hunt, their forked tongues continuously testing the air for interesting scents.

At first sight, a prowling Desert Monitor looks prehistoric and clumsy, but it can sprint fast enough to intercept a fast-moving rodent, seizing it in its powerful jaws which remain clenched for several minutes, then devouring the dead or dying victim in one gulp. Almost anything that can be accommodated within its terrifying mouth is consumed with great speed. Desert Monitors pillage the nests of birds, eat tortoises, and do battle with snakes. Even the spines of hedgehogs are no defence against these voracious creatures.

There are many other lizards in the Karakum, including the Reticulate Racerunner, another small species that skitters across the sand on fringed toes which spread the animal's weight and prevent it from sinking beneath the sand, in a similar way to snow shoes. These little lizards also engage in 'sand dancing'. The surface of the sand can reach 70°C (158°F), so they rhythmically raise alternate legs to prevent their toes from becoming burnt. Other lizards rest on their heels with their toes in the air to keep them cool.

Desert Birds

Birds have body temperatures that are feverish by our standards – typically around 41°C (105°F) – and so they probably suffer less from heat stress than other desert animals. Like reptiles, they produce little urine, do not sweat and have impermeable skins. Their covering of feathers is the finest form of insulation, both for conserving body heat and for keeping heat out. Many of the true desert birds seem able to survive without drinking. One such species is the Desert Sparrow.

The Desert Sparrow is basically a cream-coloured bird, the female almost entirely so, and the male adorned with a grey crown and mantle and a bold black bib and eye-patch, as well as some black and white in the wings. The birds endure their desiccated surroundings all year round by feeding upon seeds. The kernels provide enough moisture for the sparrows' needs.

Desert Sparrows have a very fragmented distribution, and occur across the deserts of North Africa, Iran and Turkmenistan, where they prefer a scattering of trees in which to build their large nests. Each nest is a miniature haystack about the size of a football, built 1.5-4 m (5-13 ft) above the ground, often in a Sand Acacia tree. These nests provide a modicum of air-conditioning to protect the nestlings against the extremes of temperature. During the day, the ball of material helps to insulate the interior from the heat, and at night, the interior is kept several degrees warmer than the air outside. Furthermore, many nests are sited among the lower layers of an old, large nest of another bird, such as a crow or bird of prey, thereby gaining additional protection from the sun's heat.

Many birds need to quench their thirst every day, and their ability to fly enables them to commute great distances to and from water. The three species of sandgrouse of Soviet deserts, for instance, follow a strict daily routine relating to their need for water. Related to pigeons, and maybe also to waders (North American: shorebirds), sandgrouse fly up to 60 km (37 miles), usually in large flocks, to drinking places where they wade into pools to slake their thirst. When they have chicks in the nest, the adult males carry water back to their families in their specially modified breast feathers which absorb water like a sponge. First, they rub their bellies in the sand to remove the waterproofing preen oil coating their feathers, then they wade into the water until their bellies are covered and rock their bodies up and down to work as much water as possible into their breast feathers. When a male returns to the nest, he stands erect so the water runs down a central groove in his belly feathers, and the chicks drink it.

Plants of the Desert

Plants face a fundamental problem in that they cannot exist without evaporating water from their leaves; the hotter it is, the more moisture passes from their foliage into the atmosphere. The solution adopted by many desert flowers is to compress the whole of their life cycle into a few weeks of spring, when the soil has been moistened by winter snow or rain, and before the sun becomes too fierce. They then die, and survive only as resilient seeds that remain viable for years if necessary, until revived by moisture and warmth. Such plants are called 'ephemerals'.

But plants have other strategies, too, for coping with the desert conditions. When it becomes hot, many shrubs simply shut down and lose their leaves to save moisture, while others die back to their perennial roots, bulbs, or rhizomes.

If the winter rains are sufficient, the strengthening sunshine brings about a miraculous renewal of life in a pageant of vivid colours. In the sandy regions of the Karakum, the moisture is first intercepted by miniature sedges, the roots of which form a thick felt to absorb the water as it trickles downwards through the ground. These and the grasses flower in a flurry of feathery heads. Wild rhubarb, with thick ruby stems and leaves like dark green plates, also grows well in the damp depressions between the dune ridges. It spreads its leaves overnight so that they are firmly pressed onto the ground to prevent the wind from drying them out. Even so, they last only about a week while the fleshy flower spike

Poppies create a blaze of colour against a background
of Pistachio trees at Badkhyz nature reserve.

is carried aloft. Their useful work finished, the flowers and leaves shrivel and blow away, but the root lives for about ten years.

By April, the desert turns red with swards of scarlet peacock poppies and blazing tulips. The poppies are short-lived annuals, but the tulips die back and survive the summer's heat by means of their fleshy bulbs, which store sufficient water and nutrients to support the following year's growth. These wild tulips are the ancestors of the familiar garden tulips which were taken to Europe in the sixteenth century by a Flemish diplomat. The Turkmen people called them *tulbant*, referring to their turbanlike flowers – and the name became corrupted as 'tulip'.

After the dramatic red flowers of the poppies and tulips, there is a succession of dominant flower colours, from pale blue malcomias, yellow senecios (ragworts) and dazzling white marguerites with sulphurous centres to pale purple irises. With the arrival of summer, all these herbaceous plants either set seed and die, or wither back to their corms and bulbs.

'Jungles' in the Desert

Some of the larger plants, such as the Black and White Saxauls, have a different method of survival. Black Saxauls are trees highly adapted for life in the desert. At Repetek, they grow in thick groves that are difficult to penetrate because of the tangle of fallen branches. They look rather like gnarled willows, with a drooping canopy of wispy, green stems that bear no leaves. The trees can make food by photosynthesis, using the chlorophyll in their green stems, yet are also able to conserve moisture because they do not have the large surface area of leaves. Their roots probe very deeply for water, even reaching the saline water table, because they can tolerate salt.

In these arid areas, the Black Saxaul is much valued for its timber; although sufficiently heavy to sink in water and hard enough to blunt a saw, it is used for fuelling the fires of

The leafless branches of a saxaul tree hang limply in the searing heat
of the midday sun at the Repetek Biosphere Nature Reserve in the
south-east Karakum sand desert.

desert nomads. The saxauls bloom at the end of March, but during the hotter months the active growth of branches slows almost to a standstill. This is a further measure for minimizing the need for water. In September, when the weather cools, the tiny fruits fall like grains of desert dust and are dispersed on the wind.

The Black Saxaul 'jungles' provide shade and humidity for a whole community of animals and plants. About 100 species of plants find a home in the gaps between the trees. In March, these glades take on a festive appearance, with a profusion of flowering grasses and carpets of ephemeral poppies, studded with creamy chamomiles and delphiniums in various shades of pink. The saxaul roots nurture giant broomrapes or *cistanches*. These parasites are ghostly pale, lacking chlorophyll to make their own food. Instead, they tap moisture and nutrients from their host's roots 3 m (10 ft) below the surface, and thrust their 15 cm (6 in) wide flowering spikes, like giant hyacinths, through the sand to a height of nearly a metre ($3\frac{1}{4}$ ft). The florets are an exquisite blend of violet, gold and cream.

During this bountiful period, before the summer heat sets in, the saxaul thickets hum with life. Pollinating bees abound, and the fresh seeds are sought by a host of insects. Long-

Giant broomrapes thrust their flower spikes aloft like sentries through
the baking sand of the desert at Repetek. These plants live by
parasitizing other desert plants for their food and water.

legged desert ants (*Phaeton*) patter across the hot sand, abdomens held high, carrying their bounty back to subterranean galleries. Some fall prey to ferocious beetles. One, which rejoices in the scientific name *Anthia mannerheimi*, is a formidable black giant, 5 cm (2 in) long, decorated with six white spots and equipped with scimitar-shaped jaws. This carnivore seizes ants, pierces their bodies, and, after sucking them dry, spits out the empty 'husks'.

Many kinds of rodents also inhabit these areas where there is relief from the heat. Ground squirrels called susliks are very much in evidence. These fall prey to snakes and birds of prey, such as Long-legged Buzzards, which swoop without warning from the sky. These predators obtain all the moisture they need from the blood and flesh of their victims.

A variety of birds actually live within the saxaul forests. Over 200 species have been recorded at Repetek, but many of them are migrants, such as Eurasian Cuckoos, Bluethroats and redstarts, which briefly gorge themselves on succulent insects before continuing on their long journey north. The majority of those that stay depend upon the plants for food. One of the most striking is the Black-billed Desert Finch, an attractive dove-grey bird with lovely pink and black wings. Its powerful, stout bill is an adaptation for crushing and eating seeds. Each pair builds a cupped nest deep in the shade of a saxaul tree, and the arrival of the nestlings coincides with an abundance of nourishing flower seeds. The adults are kept busy supplying their ever-hungry chicks with a sloppy, wet mixture of crushed kernels regurgitated from their crops.

Pander's Ground Jay is one of the few birds of Repetek that lives there all year, and is also unique to the saxaul forests of the Karakum and other sandy deserts of the former USSR. It is an unusual thrush-sized member of the crow family that spends most of its time on the ground, preferring to run from danger at high speed on its long legs, rather than taking flight. Pander's Ground Jay is an elegant bird, with a pale grey crown and back, pinkish-buff underparts, black in front of the eye, a large black patch on the breast and bold black and white wings. It thrives on insects and seeds, digging them out of the sand with its sharp, slightly downcurved bill, and prepares for the leaner times of the year by laying up stores of food near the roots of desert shrubs or in the trunks of trees.

Growing in the saline soil along some of the desert river valleys, such as those of the Syr Darya and Amu Darya, can be found another type of 'jungle', a remarkable habitat known by its Russian name of *tugay*. It consists of impenetrable forests of trees, shrubs, prickly salt-resistant plants and creepers. Special animals of the *tugay* include a race of the Red Deer called the *Khangul*, or Bukhara Deer, various races of the Common Pheasant such as the Syr Darya Pheasant, and – formerly – the Caspian race of the Tiger.

The Underground Option

One strategy adopted by a variety of animals to cope with the harsh desert conditions is to spend most of the time underground, where conditions are cooler and more humid than on the surface. Even a mere 0.5 m ($1\frac{1}{2}$ ft) below the surface, the temperature is an equable 20-25°C (68-77°F), with a relative humidity of 75 per cent.

Rodents are accomplished burrowers, and foremost among them is the Great Gerbil, a very common mammal throughout the arid zones of the Central Asian republics. Although they are more closely related to the hamsters, gerbils are built rather like elegant rats, though they are more endearing because of their furry rather than scaly tails. With a head and body length of about 15-20 cm (6-8 in) and a 13-16 cm (5-6¼ in) long tail, the Great Gerbil is about three times the size of the Mongolian species which is so popular as a pet in Europe and the USA. It has a sandy coloration that camouflages it superbly against the desert background.

Gerbils have various interesting ways of coping with their hot, dry desert habitat. Generally, they extract enough liquid from their vegetable food and have dispensed with the need to drink, although they sip dew if the chance arises. Almost all trace of water is

A Great Gerbil pauses to check for danger as it travels
across the desert in search of plant food.

absorbed from the food in their intestines to minimize moisture loss in their droppings, and they possess such efficient kidneys that they excrete only a drop or two of concentrated urine each day. Most gerbils are nocturnal, but the Great Gerbil is active by day, foraging intermittently in the baking heat and then retiring to the cooler conditions underground.

Great Gerbils dig out huge warrens up to 50 m (160 ft) across, consisting of a number of tunnels each measuring 4½-6 cm (3-4 in) in diameter. Such prodigious excavations are often the work of just one couple and their offspring. A network of horizontal tunnels is excavated on three levels, linking a series of chambers, each the size and shape of a rugby ball. These chambers have different functions. Some are for storing food that will see the occupants through winter, while others serve as toilets. The central nest chamber is sited at a depth of at least 1.5 m (5 ft) below the surface.

Female Great Gerbils are tremendously fertile. If conditions are suitable, there are two peaks of breeding during the year – one in spring (February to May) and another during August, which coincides with the time when seeds are plentiful. A female produces about four litters a year, each containing up to a dozen pups. Those born early in the year attain sexual maturity within a few weeks of being weaned, and reproduce later on in the year. The gerbil population therefore has the capacity to multiply enormously as the summer progresses.

In places where the gerbil population is densest, there may be as many as 7,000 burrows per hectare (2,800 burrows per acre). The effect upon the soil and vegetation is profound. With so many rodents excavating their tunnels, the ground is regularly mixed and churned to the benefit of some of the desert plants. Where saline subsoil is brought to the surface, salt-tolerant plants become established. In other places, the desert diggers eject salt-free spoil to cover salty topsoil, encouraging a different kind of vegetation to take root.

The gerbil's catacombs provide a refuge for a host of other creatures. Over seventy species of animals have been recorded squatting in the shade of the tunnels. Many beetles and lizards retire underground when the heat of the day becomes too much for them. The Isabelline Wheatear habitually looks to these rodents to provide a cool and secure site for raising its own family. This is a creamy-buff bird with a white rump and a bold black and white tail which it flashes to startling effect when hunting for insects on the open plains. The male also employs this dazzling signal during courtship to draw his mate's attention to potential nesting holes.

If the female wheatear accepts one of the burrows recommended by the male, the couple builds an untidy nest of grass and feathers up to 3 m (10 ft) down the hole. Within the sanctuary of the burrow, the eggs are incubated and the nestlings reared. They emerge from the gerbil's tunnel at least ten days before they can fly, and until then are fed on the surface. This might be a way of reducing the risks for the young of being discovered by many of the predators that lurk in the warrens.

The Saw-scaled Viper is one of these. Like the American Sidewinder, it is one of the few snakes that moves by 'side-winding' across loose sand, making a series of little jumps, with the body momentarily touching the ground only at the front and rear ends. This curious method of locomotion enables the snake to move across dry, soft, shifting sand and keeps most of its body off the dangerously hot surface. The Saw-scaled Viper also has a noisy alarm

display. When threatened, it warns off its own predators by writhing its coils against each other so that the side scales produce a dramatic swishing sound rather like that of sizzling fat. Its warning should be heeded, because it is one of the world's most venomous snakes.

The adult vipers prefer to eat newborn gerbils, whereas the young content themselves with insects. Racer snakes (*Coluber* species) and venomous Central Asian Cobras squeeze into the gerbils' tunnels when the temperature on the surface becomes too high for comfort. The latter species is the most impressive of Soviet snakes, with scales like burnished bronze. When disturbed, the cobra hisses, lunges, and erects a characteristically flattened hood. This acts like a fright mask and may prevent the snake being trodden upon and injured. Only if the display fails to intimidate its adversary, does the cobra risk breaking its fangs on a defensive strike. These snakes prefer to reserve their highly lethal venom for paralysing prey, such as amphibians, other reptiles, small birds and rodents. About 350,000 Central Asian Cobras live in the foothills and deserts of Central Asia. The rodent runs are also used as lairs by real-life dragons – the Desert Monitors (see pages 118–19).

The Night Shift

Many desert dwellers avoid heat stress by emerging only at night. After sunset, when the blue sky is transformed into a velvety black panoply in which the stars twinkle with a piercing clarity, the desert can be a surprisingly busy place. From all quarters, one can hear mysterious rustles, the hooting of owls, the sounds of stridulating insects, and perhaps the howling of wolves to set the spine tingling. A night-time stroll may reveal some of the creatures responsible for this nocturnal chorus.

Small mammals, lizards and spiders often freeze under the glare of a powerful lamp. The eight beady eyes of the small Sand Tarantula shine in the light. This spider builds itself a vertical lair, reinforced with silk so that it will not cave in; if approached, it quickly dives inside. At night, it is not difficult to find scorpions as they scurry about their business. It is not wise to touch them, however, as their stings are sufficiently poisonous to be very painful.

By day, the scorpions live inside rodent burrows, under rocks, or in cracks in the soil. They feed on beetles, cockroaches and spiders, first locating their prey by the tiniest vibrations they make, which they detect with a pair of sensitive abdominal combs that rest on the soil. Given away by the merest tremor of footsteps, the prey is rapidly seized by the scorpion's long pincers, injected with venom from the sting in the tip of its tail, and finally chewed to pieces.

Scorpions have a curious property. When they are illuminated with ultra-violet light, they glow green. No-one knows the significance of this fluorescence; perhaps it is merely a by-product of the chemistry of their outer covering.

Seen in close-up, solifugids – or sun spiders – are horrific-looking creatures, their heads armed with enormous pincers. They are related to spiders but do not spin silk. They are fast-moving, gluttonous little animals, catching not only small animals which skitter over the sand but also insects buried beneath the surface; the solifugid locates them and rapidly unearths them with its front legs.

The beam of the lamp picks out two sparkling points of light on the slopes of a dune. These are reflected by the bulbous eyes of a jerboa which give it virtually all-round vision. In an instant, this 'mouse-on-stilts' leaps into the darkness and is gone, elegantly demonstrating the use of its greatly lengthened hindlegs.

A diminutive jerboa pauses before leaping off across the sand.

There are sixteen species of jumping jerboas in the Central Asian republics, and all are built like miniature kangaroos, with lanky legs and long tails which help them maintain balance when they are hurtling along at nearly 36 km/hr (22 mph). At night they need to travel far and wide – perhaps as much as 7 km (4$\frac{1}{4}$ miles) – searching for tubers and insects, before returning by morning to the relatively cool sanctuary of their burrows.

The demands of living in the desert are reflected in the design of the jerboas' bodies. Most have enlarged ears, and those that inhabit sandy places possess hairy pads on their hind feet, enabling them to obtain better traction on the loose sand. If inhaled, loose sand could choke a small mammal, so some jerboas have evolved protective tufts of hair to seal

their ears, and one species is equipped with a loose flap of skin which can be lowered over the nostrils to prevent sand from being inhaled, especially when the animals are excavating their tunnels.

Jerboas are self-sufficient in water, manufacturing it from fats and carbohydrates in their food. As befits any desert creature, they are very thrifty with water, excreting very little urine, and conserving even the moisture in their exhaled breath, which condenses in their enlarged nasal chambers. Should the desert become too hot for them during the summer, these remarkable rodents can become torpid, aestivating deep inside their burrows.

At night, jerboas must be on their guard for snakes. They are not only fast movers on their two hind legs, but also are extremely agile, suddenly changing direction in an attempt to shake off a predator.

One of the most interesting desert snakes is the Sand Boa, which lurks beneath the

Life and death in the desert: a Sand Boa swallows a lizard.

surface. Although it grows to only 80 cm (2½ ft) long, this snake tackles quite large quarry. Both its behaviour and design are keys to its success: the Sand Boa is modified to take advantage of the loose sand. Instead of being positioned on the side of its head, its eyes are located on top, so that when the snake is lying in ambush just beneath the surface, it can still see.

Like its larger cousins, the Sand Boa kills by constriction. Should an unsuspecting rodent or lizard come within striking distance, the boa seizes the unfortunate creature, quickly wraps its body around it and squeezes the life out of it. The snake does not always simply lie in ambush, but sometimes slithers through the sand to stalk its quarry.

129

There are creatures abroad at night in the Central Asian deserts that are more usually associated with Africa – porcupines, Honey Badgers, Caracal Lynxes and the elusive Striped Hyena. The latter species is a master scavenger which ranges from East Africa through Arabia and the Central Asian republics to India. It is typically hyena-shaped with sloping shoulders and low hindquarters, but attractively marked with yellow and black stripes.

Unlike Spotted Hyenas which sometimes hunt in menacing packs on the East African savannahs, Striped Hyenas are less sinister creatures. They tend to live in pairs and require vast territories which they mark with a strong-smelling paste secreted by their anal glands. At dusk, they set out to scavenge, making short work of carcases, bones and all, with their formidable teeth and powerful jaw muscles. But to survive in the arid areas of Central Asia, they also need to be opportunistic, and eat a whole range of other edible items, such as birds' eggs, insects and vegetable matter. Their presence is a reminder that this part of the world is populated by an animal community of mixed origins; these species have their roots in Africa, while others are clearly of Eurasian ancestry.

The Long-eared Hedgehog lives in desert regions from Morocco to Mongolia, and is

The Long-eared Hedgehog, a desert specialist, is smaller and much more active than the familiar European Hedgehog.

Left: One of the most surprising of the animal inhabitants of the Central Asian deserts is the Striped Hyena.

widespread in Central Asia. Lighter in build and faster moving than its European relative, this hedgehog has very large ears which presumably help it to hear well, and also act as radiators for cooling the blood — a common feature of many desert mammals that face the danger of overheating. The Long-eared Hedgehog is a rapacious hunter and will eat a whole range of insects and reptiles. It is quite fearless of snakes, including poisonous ones, such as young Saw-scaled Vipers, which have a venomous bite and are very aggressive. Even their defiant and noisy display is ineffective against a hungry hedgehog.

There are several species of nocturnal lizards in the Central Asian deserts. As night falls, geckos wake up and stalk insects by the light of the moon. These lizards possess great goggling eyes that help them see well in dim light. But, unlike other lizards, they have no

This little nocturnal gecko, which rejoices in the scientific name
Teratoscincus scincus, avoids the searing heat of the day in the Central
Asian deserts by retiring to its burrow and plugging the
entrance with moist sand.

eyelids to wipe their eyes clean. They solve the problem by using their long, moist tongues to lick the corneal surfaces of their eyes clear of grit. By day, they live in burrows, blocking the entrances with moistened sand.

Small lizards are fair game for the Piebald Shrew, among the fiercest of all mammals for its size. Confined to the Karakum, this pretty ash-grey and white creature would sit comfortably in the palm of one's hand, but it is a ball of fury. Like all shrews, it lives at a tremendous pace, and needs a great deal of food each day to sustain it. Quivering with energy, it darts hither and thither, exploring every likely crevice and piece of vegetation which might conceal a locust or small reptile. Should the puny predator encounter one, even if the victim is as large as itself, the shrew launches into battle, delivering a deadly succession of bites until the prey succumbs or is dismembered.

Not all the desert birds roost during the hours of darkness. The ghostly shapes of nightjars wheel and glide with great agility from dusk onwards, hunting large juicy moths and other sizeable insects. These are long-winged, long-tailed rather hawklike birds with a mottled and barred owl-like plumage that camouflages them superbly during the day, when they rest on the ground. They have large eyes for spotting their aerial prey in the dim light, and their tiny bills are fringed with stiff bristles to funnel the insects into their outsized gapes.

Owls are also designed for the night, and are very much part of the nocturnal desert scene. Little Owls rest underground by day, sometimes squatting in gerbil holes. They start to hunt at dusk, their huge, sensitive eyes and acute sense of hearing enabling them to penetrate the darkness. The forward facing eyes with overlapping fields of view give them stereoscopic vision, which is useful for judging distances, and the asymmetrical ears, each set in its own parabolic dish, enable the owls to locate the precise whereabouts of their prey from the faintest of sounds.

Little Owls home in chiefly upon crickets and beetles, either tearing them to pieces or swallowing them whole. The indigestible chitinous plates of the insects' outer skeletons are regurgitated later as tightly bound pellets.

One of the largest owls in the world lives and hunts in the Central Asian deserts. The Northern Eagle Owl is aptly named as it is the nocturnal counterpart of a diurnal eagle. It is a magnificent, extremely powerful bird. With wings of the burlier females spanning nearly 2 m ($6\frac{1}{2}$ ft), Northern Eagle Owls have been known to fly with prey as heavy as a Red Fox gripped firmly in their talons, though they feed mainly on gerbils and hares.

As the reddening horizon in the east heralds the start of another scorching day, the

animals of the night-shift disappear into their day-time retreats. Only the soft desert soil betrays the intense activity of the waning night with a myriad of criss-crossing tracks – miniature tank trails left by six-legged beetles, the characteristic sideways curves of a viper produced as its body coils thrust against the sand, the excavations of a porcupine unearthing tulip bulbs, and a patch of disturbed soil where the gerbil met its demise. There is a story behind all of the signs in the sand, but these will soon be eradicated by the desert wind.

The Successful Camels

Many large herbivorous mammals have taken to the deserts. The camel is by far the largest of the desert brigade, and perhaps the most outstandingly successful of them all. There are about 12 million camels in the world, and over a quarter of a million of them plod the arid lands of what was Soviet Central Asia. Both of the two species of camels occur there; the two-humped Bactrians live in the northern deserts of Kazakhstan whereas the single-humped Dromedaries roam the Karakum and Kyzylkum deserts. There are even Drom-

Above: A group of shaggy Dromedary Camels stops to feed in the
Karakum Desert.
Left: Orange eyes blazing, a huge Eagle Owl glares defiance after
being disturbed from its daytime slumber in a rock crevice.

edaries wandering through the saxaul forests in Repetek, where they look remarkably at home browsing on the wispy, dry foliage.

Camels are herded in large numbers by partly nomadic people in the arid lands of Turkmenistan. As in Arabia, the camel is a useful beast of burden, and can carry as much as 400 kg (880 lb) on its back, travelling steadily at 10 km/hr (6 mph) for eight hours, day after day. But most of the feral camels are grazed, turning the poor vegetation into valuable commodities. The females yield up to 400 litres (88 gals) of milk a year, used to make *koumiss* (a fermented milk drink), cheese and butter, and their down and fur is made into felt and fine fabrics. The camel's fat and flesh are eaten, and its skin tanned to make leather.

Feral camels in the semi-desert and desert regions still give the impression of living much as their wild ancestors did in ancient times. As with most other hoofed mammals, the central core of the camel community is made up of the females and their young.

The large males become the focus of attention only during spring, when they become preoccupied with sex. At this time, they froth at the mouth and become very pugnacious, biting and striking out at each other, occasionally with lethal consequences, until the dominant individuals have established their priority in the mating league. Drooling with scented saliva, which gives them sex-appeal, the passionate bulls react to the solicitations of the females, who offer themselves for mating in a sitting position. A pregnancy of thirteen months ensues, and the resulting calf will be suckled for about a year on 5 litres (1 gal) of milk a day.

The origin of these domesticated creatures is something of a mystery. It seems that feral Bactrians appeared in eastern Turkestan approximately 2,000 years ago, whereas the smaller and more lightly built dromedary occurred in Arabia at about the same time. About 800 genuinely wild Bactrians still survive in Mongolia, but there are no traces of the ancestors of the Dromedary. Presumably, its wild progenitors lived somewhere in the Middle East. However, there is one theory that the Dromedary is a purely domesticated beast derived from the Bactrian. One intriguing piece of evidence supporting this idea comes from the Dromedary's foetuses, which display two miniature humps before they coalesce into one, perhaps recapitulating the recent evolution of the race.

The Hoofed Herds

Other kinds of hoofed mammals thrive in Badkhyz, a magnificent wilderness in the most southerly tip of Turkmenistan, close to the border with Afghanistan and Iran. This is the realm of Asian Wild Asses and Goitred Gazelles.

Framed by the walls of a cave – the daytime retreat of an Eagle Owl –
the great Yer-Oilan-Duz Depression of Badkhyz stretches into the
distance, with salt lakes and flat-topped *kazans*.

Badkhyz is a beautiful place and very different from the scorching sand dunes in the heart of the Karakum. Like most of Turkmenistan, it suffers from a scanty supply of water. An average of 250 mm (10 in) of rain falls each year, mostly during the winter. However, the presence of impervious rocks concentrates the water and causes a number of springs to gush from the ground, at least until May. These keep the nearby Murgab River flowing, which acts as a lifeline to many creatures during the long, baking hot summers.

Much of Badkhyz consists of a rolling plateau, partly covered with Pistachio trees and dissected by ravines. Its southern limit is marked by a spectacular escarpment, 500 m (1,600 ft) high, which runs for 20 km (12 miles) and overlooks the great depression of Yer-Oilan-Duz. In the depths of this rift valley lies a series of saline lakes which are normally rendered into gleaming salt flats by the furnacelike heat of summer. From them, loom a picturesque group of cone-shaped hills – or *kazans* – which are the relicts of volcanic activity. Although the scene is one of lunar dryness, the ground is littered with fossilized oysters, testifying to the fact that the area was once covered by a shallow sea - the Tethys (see page 32). The pink sandstone cliffs and terraces of Yer-Oilan-Duz eventually run into the Kyzyl-Dzhar, a dramatic 'red' canyon that winds for 18 km (11 miles) into the tableland like a giant gash, up to 450 m (1,500 ft) deep, in the surface of the planet.

The canyons and cliffs generate powerful updraughts which make Badkhyz a paradise for birds of prey. About thirty species ride the swirling currents of air, including several species of vultures, Golden Eagles, and snake-eating Short-toed Eagles. There are also many Long-legged Buzzards in Badkhyz which take advantage of the bonanza of gerbils on the plains. In summer, the scree slopes are settled by pairs of rock thrushes and prettily marked Finsch's Wheatears – prey for Peregrine Falcons. In places, the grassland is dotted

Dwarfing the poppies that grow around it, the trunk-like stem of a
giant fennel blazes with yellow umbels of flowers
only once every nine years or so.

with stands of the tall spikes of ferulas – or wild fennel plants. In spring, each plant raises a tapering stem 10 cm (4 in) across at its base, and up to nearly 2 m (6½ ft) high. Although it seems to die back during the summer, the ferulas continue to sprout for a further nine or so years, when they burst into glorious yellow flowers, then die, entrusting their winged seeds to the wind.

Large areas of Badkhyz resemble the East African savannahs. However, instead of flat-topped acacias breaking up the monotony of the landscape, in this area, there are Pistachio trees. The illusion of Africa is given further credence by the herds of Asiatic Wild Asses instead of zebra, and groups of Goitred Gazelles in place of Thompson's Gazelles. And in the skies above, vultures wheel in the vortexes of rising air. Even a few Leopards of the Iranian race survive in the rocky ravines of Badkhyz, although these great cats are now very rare in this part of the world. Until quite recently, Cheetahs used to streak across these Central Asian savannahs in hot pursuit of the Goitred Gazelles, but unfortunately no wild individuals have been seen on former Soviet territory since 1960.

The dainty Goitred Gazelles, known locally as Djeran, that grace the arid landscape of

A buck Djeran, or Goitred Gazelle, with an impressive
set of horns, pauses to sniff the air as he travels through
a saxaul grove.

the Central Asian republics, have virtually dispensed with the need to drink. The lithesome bucks are distinguished by a pair of lyre-shaped horns and also possess an enlarged larynx or 'goitre' which gives them their Western name. These little antelopes are able to survive in very inhospitable countryside, eating as many as a thousand different species of plants, many of which are so loaded with toxins that sheep die from eating them.

Also, if driven to drink, Djeran can tolerate bitter brine, equivalent to 50 per cent sea water. With such a tough constitution, it is not surprising that this species is distributed across the deserts of Arabia, Central Asia, West Pakistan and western China. In the dry lands of the Central Asian republics, there are about 30,000 of them, and several special nurseries have been established for breeding from captive animals.

By contrast, the Asiatic Wild Asses, whose local race is known as the Kulan, must have a daily drink, although, like camels, they can tolerate the loss of one third of their body weight through water loss. Herds of these pretty fawn-and-white asses with short, black manes and black stripes down the centre of their backs once inhabited huge areas of the dry steppes which ran almost continuously from the eastern slopes of the Urals to the Gobi Desert, and southwards into Arabia and northern India. Unfortunately, their need to drink was their downfall because people gradually took over their vital watering places. Everywhere, they were considered fair game; their meat was wholesome and their hides produced the finest morocco leather.

As great areas of the dry steppes vanished before the relentless onslaught of irrigated agriculture, the range of the wild asses began to shrink and fragment. Nowadays, Kulan are reduced to a few, widely scattered relict populations, one of which is located in Badkhyz. In 1941, it was made into a nature reserve specifically as a haven for these rare mammals. In those days, there were only 150 on the reserve, but under protection, the number of Kulan has increased to a satisfying 3,000 or more, and progress is being made in the former Soviet Union to populate other regions from which they have vanished.

The Precious Pistachio

The Pistachio tree is crucial to the natural economy of Badkhyz. It is a hardy Central Asian plant with a distinctive silhouette; each Pistachio has a short, stout trunk, on which sits a dense, rounded crown of dark green leaves. The secret of this nut-bearing tree's success in the arid lands lies beneath the ground. After breaking out of the seed, the Pistachio concentrates all of its resources into sending roots deep into the soil to establish a connection with moisture.

By the end of its second growing season, the young Pistachio tree is still only 15 cm (6 in) high but its roots reach down 2.5 m (8 ft) below the surface. They also continue to grow sideways so that they are able to soak up water percolating through the soil over an area way beyond the diametre of the canopy. By the time the Pistachio has reached its full stature of 10 m (33 ft) – which may take between three and four centuries – its roots may run sideways for about 30 m (100 ft). It is the competition between their root systems that prevents the Pistachio trees from growing too close to each other. With such a leisurely

The Pistachio savannah stretches for many kilometres across the rolling
hills of Badkhyz, providing food and shelter for people and animals alike.
Pistachios grow best on high, hilly terrain, and conditions at Badkhyz,
which rises to an altitude of over 1,000 m (3,500 ft), are ideal.

rate of growth, the Pistachio makes very heavy and solid wood, with a fine dark brown grain that is ideal for furniture. When burnt, it yields a smokeless charcoal.

The groves of Pistachio trees have been called Badkhyz's most precious botanical treasure because so many animals benefit from their presence. During the summer, several species of birds nest within the welcoming shade of the branches. Holes in the trunks may be taken over by the Bukhara, or Turkestan, Tit – a rather grey version of the familiar Great Tit of Eurasia, but now recognized as a distinct species. Colonies of Spanish Sparrows build their untidy domed nests of dry grass in the outer branches, and Bay-backed Shrikes nest nowhere else, hunting for insects and small lizards that scurry across the intervening ground. The largest constructions that the Pistachios have to bear are the nests of Eurasian Black Vultures. A few pairs place their huge platforms of sticks on top of trees situated on the sides of hills from which these jumbo birds can conveniently launch themselves. But it is the Pistachio nuts that provide a huge bonanza during the autumn for animals and people alike.

Pistachios are dioecious – that is the male and female flowers are confined to separate plants. The female trees do not bear fruit until they are between 15 and 20 years old. When they are fully mature, each can yield up to 100 kg (220 lb) of nuts in their shells a year (equivalent to 45 kg/100 lb of shelled nuts). In fact, the normal yield is much lower; a tree is more likely to produce about 2 kg (4½ lb) of shelled pistachios a year. But each nut is concentrated nourishment; by weight, 57 per cent of the flesh is high energy fat, 22 per cent body-building protein, and the rest is moisture and carbohydrate.

In Badkhyz, no less than 400 sq km (154 sq miles) of desert has been planted with Pistachios, and every 3–5 years there is a bumper crop. In autumn, the Pistachios become the focus of intense activity. Kulan and the wild sheep called Arkhar move between the trees to feast on the nuts. Gazelles with their long necks and the ability to stand on their hind legs, nibble them off the lower branches. Those nuts that drop onto the ground are eagerly collected by Great Gerbils which take them back to their burrows to eat and store.

At night, White-tailed Porcupines feast on the fallen harvest and even Corsac Foxes and Striped Hyenas take advantage of this sudden glut of food. Birds, too, feed on the

A small group of the wild sheep called Arkhar turn to check for danger in
the Yer-Oilan-Duz Depression. These splendid creatures, with their great
curling horns, have been hunted almost to extinction in other parts of
Central Asia, but here at Badkhyz they thrive under protection.

Pistachio nuts; Rock Buntings, Crested Larks and Chukar Partridges creep around under the trees to peck at them, while Eastern Rock Nuthatches fly off with the nuts and wedge them in cracks in rocks, which serve as anvils as they hammer the shells to obtain their tasty contents. They eat only a proportion of the rich kernels, stowing away the rest of the nuts in nooks and crannies on the cliffs, saving them for the bleak winter months.

A great deal of the crop is collected by Turkmenian people. The nuts are picked from the trees, shells and all, and then spread out on the ground to roast in the sun. The heat splits the outer casings, which are then separated from the valuable kernels in a winnowing machine. A hectare ($2\frac{3}{4}$ acres) of good trees produces 88 kg (194 lb) of cleaned seeds; 2,000 tonnes (1,960 tons) are exported from Badkhyz each year.

In addition to its crop of nuts, the Pistachio also produces galls on its foliage which are induced by the attacks of aphids. After the aphid *Slavum lentiscoides* has pierced a leaf, a nut-shaped growth appears; the bite of a different aphid, *Forda hirsuta*, results in the formation of 3 cm ($1\frac{1}{4}$ in) long, hollow gall which the Turkmenians call a *buzgunch*. *Buzgunch* were once harvested for their contents. Whereas a healthy Pistachio leaf is only 9 per cent tannin, the galls contain 44 per cent, and when rendered down, yield a source of medicinal and industrial tannin. They also contain a light green aromatic resin, and dark red, black and blue pigments that were once used for dying leather and fabrics, worn to stunning effect by Turkic women.

The Coming of Winter

As autumn dissolves into winter, the sun takes a lower course across the sky, shedding less warmth upon the brown and dusty landscape. The winds now begin to blow from the north, bringing a Siberian chill to Turkmenistan and the likelihood of frosts at night. The Pistachios have lost their nuts and foliage, and the ferulas stand in dead, bleached ranks like everlasting flowers. Most of the birds have migrated south to escape the winter except for the vultures, which will continue to thrive on the misfortune of others. Underground, the reptiles, hedgehogs, and jerboas are in deep torpor, induced by the cold. Great Gerbils survive the winter by huddling for warmth in groups of one or two dozen individuals, reaping the benefit of nuts and dried vegetation stored in their subterranean 'barns'.

Of the larger mammals, only the Djeran are spurred into feverish rutting activity at this time of year. At the end of November and the beginning of December, the bucks become boisterous, staking out territories of about 3 hectares ($7\frac{1}{2}$ acres) which they mark with scent from glands located between their horns, on their hooves and in front of their eyes. Even their droppings are pressed into service as territorial markers, left in little piles or rutting 'closets' every 20 m (65 ft).

All the while, the mature bucks bleat and canter around, constantly fending off the challenges of younger males. The young bucks trespass continually and cheekily leave their own scent by urinating and defecating on the older buck's closets before making a quick exit. Should the challenge be more serious, the interloper and owner stiffly strut around one another, each sizing up the opposition, before clashing horns. These encounters may last only a minute or two if the contestants are of unequal strength. But if the rivals are more evenly matched, then the fights can be exhausting and result in injury or even the death of one of the animals.

The buck's objective is to attract females. Parties of does tiptoe through the scrub, assessing the merit of the various bucks by the size of their territories and the quality of the foliage they encompass. The better the feeding, the longer they linger.

A dominant male Djeran in his prime should be able to maintain between eight and eleven does on his patch, although the average is nearer half this number. As the females and their virgin daughters barely seven months old become receptive, he will mate with them, thus passing on his genes to the next generation. This is crucial for the bucks, because many will not have another chance to breed. Establishing and defending an adequate mating ground for nine hours each day takes a great deal out of them. With little time to feed properly, they steadily lose weight from 41 kg (90 lb) to 28 kg (62 lb). When their passion has cooled, the bucks will not be in the best of condition to face the worst weather ahead, and many will die, becoming food for the scavenging foxes, hyenas, and ever watchful vultures.

Djeran give birth in early May to coincide with the good grazing. The nursery is often a bed of brilliant spring flowers. The younger females bear just one fawn, but the more mature does give birth to twins. Although the fawns can stagger onto their spindly legs just after they are born, their mothers tend to leave them hidden among cover for the first two weeks while they go off to forage on the lush vegetation, returning regularly to suckle them. After two weeks, the fawns are strong enough to bound along beside their mothers.

Death of a Desert

Unfortunately, not all of the arid lands of the old USSR are as halcyon as Badkhyz or Repetek in spring. They include some of the worst cases of ecological despoliation in the world. In the late 1940s, a plan was devised to deploy the waters of the Amu Darya,

A group of Uzbek women harvest cotton on land won from the desert by irrigation schemes on a grand scale. The economic advantages gained have been more than offset by the huge environmental problems caused by diverting Central Asian rivers to provide water for this thirsty crop.

Murgab and Tedjen Rivers, diverting some of them along a newly excavated canal to the north of the Kopet-Dag Mountains, past Ashkhabad, to link up with the Caspian Sea. The objective was to irrigate vast areas of Uzbekistan and Turkmenistan. Work on the 1,000 km (620 mile) long Karakum Canal was started in 1954, but was halted before it reached the Caspian – though not before vast areas of the arid landscape had been irrigated at a huge environmental cost.

Bringing water to the dry regions enabled immense areas of Uzbekistan to become dependent upon just one crop – cotton. In the early 1980s, nearly 7.5 million tonnes (7.4 million tons) of the fluffy seed heads were harvested each year, mostly from Uzbekistan. Cotton is a particularly thirsty plant, and as the demand for this 'white gold' increased, so the two great Central Asian rivers were reduced to mere trickles and the Aral Sea began to shrink and die (see pages 35–7).

There were also problems with the soil itself. When the sweet river water was applied to the parched land, it evaporated, drawing salts into the surface layers. This increased salinization was not the only difficulty. The inherently poor desert soil could be coaxed into productivity only by the application of huge quantities of inorganic fertilizers. Spiralling production targets during the Brezhnev era were achieved only by the use of ever more chemicals, which, in the end, soured the very soil that was desperately needed for agriculture. The problem was exacerbated by the need to defoliate the cotton plants so that the fluffy heads could be more easily harvested. This was – and still is – effected by the liberal application of herbicides. These further poison the soil and the ground water, which finally finds its way into the domestic water supply.

It is difficult to see a solution to the results of this ruinous policy. At last, the scheme for diverting some of the northern rivers to replenish the Aral Sea has been officially cancelled; perhaps the Amu Darya River should be allowed to retain more of its own water, although this will be at the expense of agricultural productivity. With so many intractable problems to deal with, it seems likely that the ecological difficulties in this part of the world will remain, and may even increase, for years to come.

The Rolling Steppes

The steppe zone stretches for some 5,600 km (3,200 miles), almost without interruption, from Romania's eastern border to Manchuria, in northern China.

The steppes boast a unique combination of drought-resistant plants, although the species vary from one part to another, with tougher kinds occurring in the east where the severe winters linger for longer and the springs are cold and dry. The turf is composed of a number of fescue, oat and rye grasses and sedges. However, it is the feather grasses that are most characteristic of great areas of steppe. During the summer, their long, feathery, silvery-green flower heads catch the wind which blows relentlessly across these lonely, flat landscapes. The billions of swaying plumes are an unforgettable sight as the early morning sun illuminates them with shafts of golden light.

The steppe grasses conceal a richness that is revealed only by a close examination of the vegetation. In fact, it is possible to count over 80 plant species growing in a single square metre of northern steppe, perhaps the highest tally for anywhere in the former Soviet Union. Many of these perennials burst into flower during the spring and summer, adding yet more beauty and colour to the otherwise green countryside. The flora includes flowers that we, in the west, normally grow in our gardens, such as perfumed hyacinths, scarlet tulips, crocuses, valerians, irises, and wild onions.

Their feathery flowerheads rippling gracefully like waves in a sea of vegetation, the aptly named feather grasses dominate large areas of the southern steppes. Despite their apparent monotony, the steppes contain a wealth of plant and animal species.

After this blaze of dazzling blooms, the scorching sun shrivels and bleaches the vegetation, as hot winds drive the temperature on the steppes to 40°C (104°F) in the shade. At times, sudden thunderstorms can deluge the ground with 80 mm (3 in) of rain or pelt it with huge, glistening hailstones.

Although about one sixth of the former Soviet territory falls within the steppe region, there is precious little of the original steppe left, because of the nature of the soil that lies beneath it. This is the famous *chernozem*, or black earth, which is among the most fertile of all the world's soils. The productivity of the black earth zone, running from the Ukraine eastwards across the middle Volga and into northern Kazakhstan, underpinned Soviet agriculture. Virtually the whole of the European steppes have fallen to the plough and the unique drought-resistant herbs and feather grasses have given way to corn, wheat and sugar beet. A few fragments have been preserved on special reserves, of which Askaniya-Nova in

147

the southern Ukraine is best known. Greater areas of the drier Central Asian grasslands have escaped being converted into farmland, and it is across them that one of the most spectacular of all mammal migrations takes place – that of the Saiga.

The Strange Saiga

The Saiga is to the Central Asian steppes what the Wildebeeste and Pronghorn Antelope are to the African savannahs and American prairies respectively. It is an unusual creature and both it and its sole close relative – the Tibetan Antelope, or Chiru – are unique to the Central Asian high plateau and steppe regions. Male Saiga stand about 75 cm (30 in) high, with females slightly smaller. The amber-coloured, somewhat lyre-shaped horns are grown only by the rams.

The Saiga's most distinctive feature is its grotesquely inflated nose. Although it gives its owner a comical appearance, this great bulbous nose has been shaped by natural selection to enable Saigas to cope with life on the windy, dusty steppes. Inside each nostril is a sac, lined by mucous membranes, which undoubtedly warms and moistens the air before it is inhaled into the lungs. This natural 'air conditioning' mechanism may be important to Saiga during the winter when the air is both very dry and bitterly cold. It has also been suggested that the nasal chambers act as filters, removing the fine grit that is both carried on the wind and continually kicked into the Saiga's face by the hooves of its ever moving companions, especially when they are panicked. They then put their heads down and gallop at 50 km/hr (30 mph), raising clouds of stifling dust.

Although the Mongolian race of the Saiga is now very rare and endangered, there are two major concentrations of 'Russian' Saiga. About 100,000 live in Kalmykia, on the west bank of the Volga, just north of the Caspian Sea. However, the majority, totalling about one million animals, wander the steppes of Kazakhstan.

In winter, the Saiga move south and grow thick, woolly white coats to combat the worst effects of the Central Asian winter. But the severity of the climate does nothing to dampen the Saiga's ardour, because the rut occurs in December, when there may be a

Preceding pages: A herd of Saiga pounds across the great steppes of
Kazakhstan in an almost ceaseless wandering in search of good grazing.
The rescue of this remarkable antelope from the brink of extinction is
one of the most outstanding success stories of conservation in the world.

sprinkling of snow on the ground and the vegetation glistens white with hoar frost. At this time the mature rams are frenetically active, marking their territories with oily secretions from their pre-orbital glands, seeing off rivals, and rounding up as many females as possible into their harems for mating. The unsuccessful and immature males are banished into bachelor groups. Their turn at mating may come the following year.

For the successful territory holders, this is a crucial period, because their chances of surviving the season are not high. While the ewes are able to maintain their vigour by browsing on wormwood leaves – their favourite food – the dominant rams have breeding on their minds. Accordingly, they fail to feed, and by the time they have finished mating, most of them are exhausted. Out of every every six rams, no less than five succumb to the cold and wolves.

After mating, the Saiga turn north, migrating at between walking pace and 15 km/hr (9 mph). Their journey may take them as much as 1,500 km (930 miles) away from their breeding areas. On the way, small groups combine to form herds 100,000 strong, crossing roads, railways and even large rivers in their quest for fresh pastures.

A Time of Vulnerability

During May, the heavily pregnant female Saigas pause to drop their calves. Those that are breeding for the first time each produce a single calf, but the older ewes tend to give birth to twins. For the first few days, the calves stay where they are born, crouching should danger threaten, but stagger onto their long, spindly legs to greet and suckle from their mothers when they return from grazing.

Although the mothers are fearless in lashing out with their hooves when defending their offspring, the calves are nevertheless highly vulnerable at this stage – 20 per cent of them will die within a month – and many are killed by Grey Wolves and Steppe Eagles.

The Saiga calves are soon strong enough to stay close to their mother's heels, and the great herds continue their long trek northwards. As the summer draws on, the animals gradually disperse as they wander off in all directions, searching for nourishing vegetation. By August, the quality of the grazing has deteriorated, and the Saiga head south towards their wintering quarters, once again coalescing into large herds.

The winter takes its toll, and by the following May, less than 40 per cent of the calves will be alive. However, the most astonishing fact is that 85 per cent of the surviving female calves will be ready to mate in December, barely eight months after they were born, and after having migrated 2,000 km (1,240 miles) or more! This means that Saiga have a great capacity for restoring their numbers after periods of decline – a capacity that has stood them in good stead during their recent history.

Back from the Brink

Saiga were not always as numerous as they are today. Severe over-hunting and a series of catastrophic droughts reduced the population to a mere 1,000 or so by 1930. The depredations of a parasitic fly were also partly to blame for the population crash, although with such low numbers of its host, the fly itself died out. For the Saiga, extinction became a real prospect.

Fortunately, the value of the great herds was recognized, and a successful conservation programme was implemented in the nick of time. Under rigorous protection, the numbers increased until a critical point was passed, when the build-up of Saiga became a population explosion. In 1951, there were 900,000 in Kazakhstan and 100,000 in Kalmykia. Today, the Saiga herds are in a healthy state, and can once again withstand sensible exploitation. Each year, 110,000 are killed on the Kazakh steppes, yielding wholesome meat and useful hides.

Steppe Birds

As spring casts its rejuvenating magic over the steppes, the Saiga are joined by many migratory birds which commence their own nesting activities. In areas of saline soil, Black Larks establish their territories, the cocks resplendent in their glossy jet black plumage, while their mates are predictably well camouflaged in shades of brown and grey. Here, there are no trees from which the territory holders can broadcast their songs, so many steppe songsters, such as Tawny Pipits and Black and Short-toed Larks, proclaim their freeholds far and wide by singing during display flights. Other birds have evolved far more dramatic displays that can be seen over a great distance across this open landscape.

The most amazing of all is that of the Houbara Bustard, whose courtship rivals that of any bird of paradise. Bustards are medium-sized to large birds that are distant relatives of the cranes. Houbaras range from the Canary Isles and North Africa eastwards as far as Mongolia, occurring in the driest areas of steppe and semi-desert, with little vegetation. The western populations make only modest seasonal movements, but the Houbaras of Central Asia make long migrations to winter in Pakistan, north-west India and the Middle East. There, many fall prey to hunters, particularly wealthy Arabs and their falcons, and the species is regarded as endangered.

When the surviving males return to the Soviet steppes and semi-deserts, they summon a mate by turning themselves into a prancing confection of feathers. Although an alert male blends into the background, an enraptured bird in full display catches the eye from a great distance. He begins by erecting his white head feathers like a powder puff. He then inflates and partially withdraws his neck into a mass of long white breast plumes which are framed by black quills. While these confusing plumage adjustments are taking place, the drama is enhanced. The male breaks into a high-stepping strut which shuffles the feathers and gives his performance more impact. Not surprisingly, he often blunders into the vegetation because he simply cannot see through his veil of fluffy feathers. No-one can fail to be impressed by this virtuoso act, least of all the females of the species!

But far from the home of the Houbara Bustards in the hot arid lands of Central Asia is a region that calls for quite different survival techniques – the cold wilderness of the far north of Russia – the realm of the great white bear.

A male Houbara Bustard puts on a spectacular performance to attract
a mate, fanning out his plumage and mincing along with exaggerated
steps in circles, zigzags or straight lines. After mating, he leaves the
female to incubate the eggs and look after the young alone.

THE ARCTIC FRONTIER

AT THE END of March, an enchanting scene is enacted on remote, bleak Wrangel Island in the north-east of Arctic Russia. The interminable polar night has long since retreated before the returning sun, and the daylight reveals an ethereal landscape of dazzling white hills and dells. Everything seems to be sprinkled with diamond dust as shafts of sunlight scatter off myriads of ice crystals. The deep blue vault of the sky contributes towards the illusion of pristine perfection. But this lovely scene belies the harshness of the environment. Even at midday, the temperature reaches only −30°C (−22°F) and a vigorous wind blowing from the north is sufficient to drive the Arctic chill deep into the very marrow of one's bones. Despite these grim conditions, life stirs beneath the blanket of snow.

The first sign appears half-way up a slope where a black object pokes through the snow. It roots around, pauses, and then emerges to reveal itself as the wet, dark nose of a female Polar Bear beginning to rouse herself in her den from her long winter lie-in. At first, she exposes only her head and blinks in the blinding glare. She is stiff and sleepy after five months of confinement within her cramped shelter beneath the snow, and it is some time before she summons enough strength to haul her shaggy bulk out into the open. Straddling the entrance to the den, she tests the air for familiar scents, and scans her surroundings thoroughly. Suddenly, from between her pillar-like legs, a diminutive, bleating cub emerges to take its first view of the outside world. The fleecy little creature is much more interested in maintaining contact with its warm, comforting mother, and scarcely gives the awesome Arctic scenery a second glance before nuzzling onto one of her nipples. At three months,

Dwarfed by its mother, a Polar Bear cub emerges in March from its nursery
under the snow to gaze in awe at the stark white landscape of Wrangel Island.

the cub can barely reach it while the she-bear is standing, so after a few minutes, they both disappear back into the relative snugness of the den and will not surface for another day.

Without doubt, the Polar Bear is one of the most impressive creatures in the world. A fully grown male may weigh ten times as much as a man, and ranks as the largest of four-legged carnivores. Despite the name, no Polar Bears live anywhere near the North Pole; in fact, they are rare at latitudes above 82°N.

Polar Bears are not unique to the Arctic regions of Russia – they are found right around the northern polar regions. Between 20,000 and 40,000 of these great white bears live at these high latitudes, approximately 25 per cent of them in the Russian Arctic. On Wrangel alone, up to 250 females make their dens each year, and a further 50 settle for the winter on Gerald Island, conferring on it the distinction of hosting the highest density of denning Polar Bears in the world.

The cubs are born between the end of December and the end of January. Almost three out of four female Polar Bears produce twins, with most of the rest giving birth to single cubs. Only 5 per cent have triplets. Like those of all bears, the new-born babies are blind, with a sparse covering of fur, and minuscule compared with their parents. Those of the Polar Bear are only the size of a rat, making them the smallest in relation to their mother of any placental mammal – if women produced such tiny babies, we would emerge merely thumb-sized from our mothers' wombs!

The mother Polar Bear does not hibernate during her nursing period, but maintains a normal body temperature and can wake up quickly if she is disturbed. Her prey – seals and young walruses – are far away on the frozen sea, so she must sustain herself and her diminutive offspring on her internal resources of fat, proteins and minerals. Polar Bear milk is the consistency of thick cream and is second only to that of seals in the amount of fat that it contains. The mother bear continues to lactate for nearly six months, during which time the cubs grow at a phenomenal rate.

When the little creatures first set foot outside their snow nursery, they will already be the size of small dogs. Most mothers continue to use their dens for a week or two while the cubs become stronger and more confident. Then, after a few brief excursions, the female bear leads her family across the snow-covered land towards the frozen sea. Here they are in mortal danger from the powerful males, which are up to three times the weight of their mates and have no compunction about killing and devouring infant bears. The cubs' safety therefore depends upon the skill and cunning of their mothers, who will avoid mating with the males for at least another year.

Out on the sea ice, the bears spend a distinctly relaxed summer; they pass more than 80 per cent of their time simply lying around on the pack ice. Here, the youngsters enjoy their first taste of seal or walrus, and develop their prodigious appetites. Dieticians are amazed at the capacity of Polar Bears to consume huge quantities of meat, rich in saturated fats and low in fibre – the kind that gives humans severe cardio-vascular and kidney problems. However, by some quirk of body chemistry, these great carnivores are protected from any dire consequences of their diet.

A Treasured Island

Wrangel Island lies in the Chukchi Sea at the extreme north-eastern corner of Russia, 140 km (87 miles) off the Siberian mainland. About 150 km (93 miles) long, and up to 125 km (78 miles) wide, this mountainous island straddles the 180 degree meridian, and were it not for the fact that the international date line deviates to the east, to pass between Alaska and Russia, it would be possible for a visitor to move freely backwards and forwards between consecutive days!

Wrangel Island is named in honour of the Russian explorer Ferdinand Petrovich Wrangel (1796-1870), who graduated from the Imperial Lycée near St Petersburg with Alexander Sergeyevich Pushkin. While Pushkin turned to writing lyrical poetry and became the founder of modern Russian literature, Wrangel travelled to the Arctic and mapped the Siberian coast. In Kolyma in 1824, he inferred the presence of the island from descriptions of the flight lines of seabirds given to him by native people. However, the island was not properly charted until 1867, when an American whaler sailed close by, and it was subsequently named after Wrangel.

Today, Wrangel is inhabited by a small settlement of Chukchi and Inuit people, introduced together with herds of Reindeer, in 1926; the much smaller Gerald Island, 60 km (40 miles) to the north-east, is uninhabited. These two islands constitute one of Russia's most treasured refuges for wildlife; since 1976, the area has been designated an

Overleaf: Wreathed in cloud and mist, the forbidding ramparts of the
mountains on Wrangel Island loom up out of the sea. This Arctic
island, off the remote north-east coast of Siberia, contains a 7,956 sq km
(3,072 sq mile) nature reserve, the home of up to 250 breeding Polar
Bears, great gatherings of Walruses, herds of Musk Oxen
and colonies of Snow Geese.

Stretching right across Russia, the tundra forms a great carpet of low-growing
vegetation, broken up by innumerable lakes, ponds and rivers.

International Biosphere Reserve, and special measures have been taken to preserve the
integrity of the unique community of Arctic wildlife that lives there.

Defining the Russian Arctic

There is no universally accepted definition of what constitutes the Arctic. A cold, extreme
climate is the essence of the place, and so most geographers consider it as the region in
which the average highest summer temperature does not exceed 10°C (50°F). The 10°C
(50°F) July isotherm which meanders around the high latitudes of the planet closely
corresponds to the northern limit of tree growth, and so marks the fairly abrupt boundary
between the coniferous forests of the *taiga* and the bleak *tundra* zone which unquestionably
falls within the Arctic domain.

Of the $7\frac{1}{2}$ million sq km (2.9 million sq miles) of Arctic land, only a little over one-
quarter – 2 million sq km (770,000 sq miles) – is in Russia. Nevertheless, the Russian
Arctic embraces a great sweep of land and sea. The narrow band of tundra which borders
the Arctic Ocean stretches for 5,000 km (3,500 miles) from Finland to Uelen on the
Chukotka Peninsula, only a short distance from Alaska. *Tundra* is a Lappish word for this

Occupying the same latitudes as northern Greenland, the Taimyr Peninsula is
a harsh place, even in summer – this photograph was taken in June!

treeless plain, dominated by mosses, tussocks of sedges, rushes, grasses, dwarf shrubs and heaths. The landscape is pockmarked with countless lakes and ponds, often contained within polygonal ridges caused by the rhythmic heaving of the ground as it alternately freezes and thaws with the passage of the seasons. Across the vast, lonely expanses of the tundra, many rivers wriggle wildly, like giant silvery serpents, on their tortuous journey towards the sea.

Not all of the Russian Arctic consists of flat tundra. The great fold of the Urals continues northwards and emerges from the icy sea as Novaya Zemlya (New Land), a pair of islands that were used for testing nuclear weapons. To the east, another crease in the Earth's crust produces the Byrranga Mountains of the Taimyr Peninsula, the world's most northerly continental peninsula, and Severnaya Zemlya (North Land), a group of ice-covered islands.

Russian territory reaches to within 700 km (435 miles) of the North Pole: Rudolf Island, the northernmost of a cluster of about 800 islands just east of Spitsbergen, collectively known as Franz Josef Land, lies at latitude 82°N. These islands are heavily glaciated, with the ice in places calving straight into the sea; there are also steep cliffs rearing up in great ramparts against the erosive force of the Arctic Ocean. Here, the Arctic is at its bleakest;

even in summer, one can find only about 40 species of higher plants in this polar desert. Nevertheless, the cold sea is bountiful, with a wealth of marine life, enabling every habitable quarter of land to be occupied by noisy breeding colonies of seabirds.

Arctic Terns, the greatest of all animal migrants, which make a round trip of up to 36,000 km (22,400 miles) annually between their Arctic breeding grounds and their wintering sites in Antarctica, breed on the beaches. Brünnich's Guillemots (North American: Thick-billed Murres), Northern Fulmars, Glaucous Gulls and Black-legged Kittiwakes

A handsome White-billed Diver at its nest in the tundra displays the
great upturned pale dagger of a bill that gives the species its name.
Nothernmost of the five diver species, it occurs right across Arctic
Siberia and North America, where it is called the Yellow-billed Loon.

line up in close-knit bird bazaars on the cliff ledges; and clouds of Little Auks (North American: Dovekies) settle to nest on the mountainous slopes of scree and boulders. The coastal tundra is the realm of nesting Brent Geese (North American: Brants), divers (North American: loons), Purple Sandpipers and prettily patterned Sabine's Gulls. Neat little black-and-white Snow Buntings flit around on the screes close to the sea, and pure white Ivory Gulls establish small colonies near glaciers.

Further east, the New Siberian Islands, at latitude 75°N, rise to a maximum elevation of just over 500 m (1,600 ft), but have no glaciers and are very sparsely vegetated. The mountains on Wrangel Island range up to 1,096 m (3,596 ft) above sea level and, during the long Arctic night, the weather is so inhospitable that the animals that brave out the winter in such forbidding places exist on the very edge of survival.

The Arctic is less well endowed with species than many other parts of the world. For example, Texas alone can boast a flora of over 5,000 species of plants, while the whole of the Arctic can muster only 1,000. About 200 plant species, such as the Arctic Buttercup, are circumpolar in their distribution. This also holds true for animals. For instance, Arctic Foxes, Polar Bears and Snowy Owls are found in both the North American and Russian parts of the Arctic. And yet, as we shall see, the Russian Arctic has some very interesting specialities.

The Tundra's Past: Beringia

Much of the Siberian tundra has had a different history from that of North America. At the height of the last Ice Age, 18,500 years ago, most of Canada was smothered with ice. By contrast, north-eastern Siberia and a narrow area of land called Beringia, which once formed a bridge connecting Asia with the Seward Peninsula of Alaska, remained relatively unglaciated and acted as a refuge for many cold-loving species of plants and animals.

Today, the Russian tundra is a mere remnant of a great treeless steppe that once ran from the edge of the Caspian Sea to Alaska. It had a maximum area about 18,500 years ago, when the reduced sea level caused the northern Siberian shoreline to extend beyond the New Siberian Islands. At the same time, the Beringian land bridge broadened into a corridor 1,000 km (620 miles) wide, making Alaska an extension of Asia.

In places, the vista must have resembled a Serengeti of the north, with a rich mixture of carnivorous and hoofed mammals, including mammoths, the most magnificent of all the creatures that lived there. The isthmus between the two continents allowed the unrestricted migration into the New World of these shaggy elephants, together with bison, Saiga, Reindeer (North American: Caribou), wild horses and Musk Oxen. Man also extended his sphere of influence by following his prey across the Beringian bridge. However, movement further east was blocked by the Brook's Range and walls of ice which ran from the Aleutian archipelago across Canada to Greenland. But this situation was to change.

About 13,500 years ago, the climate warmed, the glaciers retreated, and sea levels rose so that the Bering and Chukchi seas once more reclaimed the corridor between Siberia and Alaska. The rising Arctic Ocean melted the permafrost beneath the northern 'mammoth steppes' and much of it vanished beneath the sea. With the onset of snowier winters and sudden spring thaws, the grasses which dominated these Ice-Age steppes gave way to sedges and mosses that were not to the liking of horses, bison, and mammoth, so these animals disappeared from the Arctic landscapes.

Some creatures which live in the Siberian Arctic are part of the Beringian heritage. For example, charcoal-and-white Emperor Geese nest on both sides of the Bering Straits. Sandhill Cranes, Pectoral Sandpipers and Long-billed Dowitchers are birds whose main populations breed in northern North America but which have established themselves on the Siberian tundra. There are also species unique to the Russian side, such as Siberian White Cranes, Sharp-tailed Sandpipers and the lovely Ross's Gulls, which breed solely on the coastal plain that was formerly part of Beringia.

The best remnant of this ancient landscape is the section of tundra that rolls east from the Lena River to the Kolyma River. This coastal lowland (Primorska Nizmennost) is overlain by a plateau of fine, wind-blown soil called loess which, in places, has been carved out by twisting rivers, exposing crumbling cliffs. Upon the ancient soil that formed these cliffs once grew the grasses and herbs which the mammoths relished. Today, the friable loess often yields the sub-fossilized bones of these mighty mammals.

Woolly mammoths were undoubtedly hunted by our Stone-Age ancestors, but the chief cause of their final demise about 11,000 years ago was probably the deterioration of their pastures. A vast tonnage of their mighty tusks has been preserved in both Alaska and Siberia; it is estimated that 550,000 tonnes (539,000 tons) are still buried along the 1,000 km (620 miles) of coastal tundra between the Yana and Kolyma rivers. Some deep-frozen mammoths have even been recovered from the permafrost in a remarkably good state of preservation. From these remains, it has been possible to build up an accurate picture of what the living animals looked like.

An adult bull of the Siberian race stood 3 m (10 ft) high and possessed a characteristically domed head and humped shoulder. But his most striking asset was a pair of immense twisted tusks, often turned inwards at the tips and carried like snow ploughs. The coat was divided into two layers, an inner one of short fur overlain by a layer of long coarse hairs. Although these tundra elephants, with their huge bulk, must have been well able to withstand the cold, they possibly migrated southwards during the winter into the sheltered forest zone, like Reindeer. Not so with another Ice-Age relict that still survives today.

The Hardy Musk Oxen

Musk Oxen brave the grim winter weather on the tundra and polar deserts – indeed, they are the only ruminants to do so. These sturdy, shaggy relatives of sheep and goats thrived in Siberia between 10,000 and 12,000 years ago, but climatic changes and hunting by Stone-Age people conspired to eliminate them from the Russian Arctic. In recent times,

A trio of hardy Musk Oxen send the snow flying in a rare bout of activity.
The Musk Ox is the most specialized of all the Arctic mammals.

most wild Musk Oxen have been confined to the Canadian Arctic and Greenland. However, in 1975, a small herd was reintroduced to Wrangel Island from North America. Today, there are about 100, and another herd has been established on the Taimyr Peninsula.

Musk Oxen manage to exist in these harsh northern environments by virtue of their thick, insulating fur coats which give the impression of being draped over their bodies. When the wind howls across the tundra, these act like very warm skirts. Also, Musk Oxen move relatively little as part of their survival strategy – their slothfulness helps them save energy. During the winter months, they continue to graze, exposing the deep-frozen fodder by hoofing away the snow.

The calves are born at the end of April when Wrangel Island and the rest of the Russian Arctic are still firmly in the grip of winter weather. At the onset of labour, the cow lies down in the snow, possibly surrounded by other members of the herd. This offers her added protection from the elements. Eventually, her small, helpless offspring emerges from beneath her 'skirt', soaked in steaming placental fluid. How it fails to become chilled to death is nothing short of a miracle. Despite the cold, it takes a little time to gather its strength before staggering to its feet and taking its first drink of milk. On Wrangel, there are no wolves, and so the adult Musk Oxen rarely need to form a defensive ring around their calves to protect them, as they do in the rest of their range, where wolves are their main predators.

The Brief Arctic Spring

Spring is so brief in the Arctic that winter virtually gives way to summer on the tundra over the course of a few days. The precise date depends upon how quickly the snow clears and allows the vegetation to start growing. The blanket of snow, which may be up to 50 cm (17 in) deep, tends to cover the flat landscape for between 200 and 280 days a year. If the weather is relatively warm and the snow thinly spread, or blown away by strong winds, then the tundra bursts into life at the end of May. However, in cold years, the events which mark the beginning of the Arctic breeding season may be delayed for a further three weeks, thereby jeopardizing the chances of many species raising young.

During May, the sun no longer sets but circles the sky in a great ellipse, climbing a little higher day by day and casting a benevolent warmth over the tundra. The Arctic appears to 'breathe' in tune with the movement of the sun in the sky. Each day, fog and low cloud, generated by the mixing of cold and warm air, dissipate under the influence of the morning sun. But then, as the sun gradually sinks and swings low across the western horizon, the power of its slanting rays is insufficient to keep the mists at bay. Towards 'midnight', shallow ponds and puddles may glaze over with ice, and the fog banks roll back from the north. It is then easy to believe that these far northern lands are among the most overcast on Earth. However, little by little, the tundra warms up.

The chief heralds of spring are the birds. Some 200 million of them head for the Russian tundra from all over the world, eager to start nesting and raise their broods before the first frosts and flurries of winter snow arrive in early August.

The most important places for waders (North American: shorebirds) and wildfowl (North American: waterfowl) are the great river deltas and their associated swamps and lakes. The mouth of the Pechora River and the Yamal Peninsula teem with wild swans, ducks and geese, especially during the moulting period. Another major refuge for wetland birds is the Khatanga Estuary that forms the eastern boundary of the Taimyr Peninsula. Most important, just east of the Urals is the largest breeding ground for wildfowl (North American: waterfowl) in the whole of Eurasia. Here the mighty river Ob and its tributaries, the Irtysh and Ishim, form a vast, swampy basin beneath which are huge frozen deposits of gas and oil that rival those of Saudi Arabia. On the surface, the riches are ornithological. Like all Siberian rivers, these three bring warmth from the south, and this contributes towards the productivity of the region. By the end of summer, there are an estimated 5 million ducks in the area, 90 per cent of them Long-tailed Duck (North American: Oldsquaw), Northern Pintail, Eurasian Wigeon and Green-winged Teal.

The Advent of Summer

Summer on Wrangel Island is heralded by the cackling calls of Snow Geese, 60,000 of which make the annual journey from their wintering grounds in the western USA, chiefly in the Sacramento Valley, California, and Puget Sound, Washington. The Wrangel population is an isolated outpost, most Snow Geese breeding across Arctic North America. In the past, numbers breeding on Wrangel were much greater – as many as 400,000.

Elsewhere on the mainland of north-east Siberia, Sandhill Cranes have also flown across the Bering Sea from North America, where their main breeding populations live. Pacific Golden Plover, resplendent in their yellow-spangled breeding plumage with black 'waistcoats', wing their way across the Pacific Ocean from Hawaii to establish territories on the Siberian tundra. Sharp-tailed Sandpipers outfly all these, spending their winters in India and Australia. Other waders, wildfowl and songbirds stream in from different points of the compass – from Asia, Africa, and Europe.

Many of the arriving migrants carry payloads of fat equivalent to 15-30 per cent or more of their total body weight. These energy-rich food stores enable the birds to survive for some time without having to feed should the tundra be covered by snow and ice, and, in some species, may even provide the materials for egg formation and the energy for incubation. However, the females of other species must find a local source of protein-rich food before they can lay their eggs.

As the tundra awakens, the air rings to the sound of birds proclaiming ownership of their territories. In the tundra around the Kolyma delta, Willow Warblers form the background chorus, pouring forth their descending scales of silvery notes from the highest sprigs of dwarf willow. Little Buntings likewise sing from the best perches available. However, the disadvantage that bird songsters face here is the absence of trees from which to broadcast their messages of love and defiance, so many species have evolved ways of 'perching' in the sky to make their songs carry. Bluethroats, Red-throated Pipits, and Arctic Redpolls (North American: Hoary Redpoll) deliver their spirited songs on the wing. So do Lapland Buntings (North American: Lapland Longspurs) and Snow Buntings

Countless waders of many species breed in the Russian Arctic. They
include the Pacific Golden Plover (top left), the Spotted Redshank
(top right) and the Ruff, the males of which indulge in dramatic
courtship displays (above); remarkably, no two male Ruffs have
exactly the same pattern of colours.

which, like Arctic Redpolls, are truly birds of the high Arctic. Cock Snow Buntings perform a courtship flight in which they display their dazzling black-and-white wings by fluttering them in front of their prospective mates.

Waders also join the medley of true songsters, some producing instrumental sounds to draw attention to themselves. Snipe use their stiff outer tail feathers to generate a bleating sound which supplements their monotonous vocal calls. Pin-tailed Snipe circle and swoop

This dapper male Snow Bunting is about to deliver a beakful of insect
food to its chicks in a nest concealed among rocks.

high above the tundra in an impressive display of aerobatics, generating a deep roar from their quivering tail feathers when they dive. Elsewhere, Spotted Redshanks in their smart dusky breeding plumage yodel, Pectoral Sandpipers that wintered far away in South America float on wings held high above their backs, uttering deep booms like miniature foghorns, extravagantly plumaged male Ruffs gather at traditional display sites, or 'leks', to engage in elaborate tournaments evolved to impress the watching females, and tiny Temminck's Stints hover over the river banks, giving trilling calls that sound like the tinkling of tiny bells.

Arctic Vegetation

By early June, the carpet of vegetation is rejuvenated with fresh, new growth. It is a dense weave of prostrate plants, about 35 cm (14 in) thick, soft underfoot and presenting an intricate mosaic of textures and colours. The spongy mosses form a velvety patchwork of reds, browns and greens. There are also bizarre growths of lichens, some resembling coiled, off-white pasta, and others like amoeboid scabs of yellow and deep orange. Set among this sumptuous carpet are tussocks of grasses, and sedges, and hummocks of herbaceous plants, dwarf willows and birches.

On calm, fine days, the hum of insects and the fragrance of honey pervade the air. And, yet, beneath the mat of plants and lichens, the ground is held in the grip of ice, as it has been for thousands of years. Even during the summer thaw, the ice releases only the top 15-30 cm (6-12 in) of soil from its clutches. Indeed, were it not for this layer of frozen ground, known as permafrost, the Arctic landscape would resemble a desert rather than a swamp, because meltwater and the meagre summer rain would quickly drain away. Instead, the permafrost keeps all the water on the surface. It is, therefore, little wonder that the tundra is a more favourable place for waders and wildfowl than for birds that prefer to keep their legs dry.

Here, as everywhere else, the productivity of plants is crucial to the whole ecosystem. Although there is round-the-clock daylight during the summer, the growing season is brief, so the majority of Arctic plants are perennials, with seeds that may need a second season to mature.

The physical conditions faced by Arctic plants are very taxing – except close to the ground. Here, the air may be quite calm and very warm, even if a cold, brisk wind is blowing a metre or two above the surface. Ground-hugging plants are therefore at an advantage in the tundra, because they escape the withering effect of the unremitting polar winds, and take advantage of the beneficial microclimate which speeds up the development of flowers and seeds.

Many plants, such as willows, saxifrages and Thrift, retain their old, shrivelled foliage from the previous year as a protective layer against the biting wind and the abrasion caused by the snow. Louseworts and many other Arctic plants are muffled against the climate by a thick felt of hairs on their stems, leaves and flowers. Such hirsute species are able to retain an insulating layer of air next to their surface and trap some of the sun's radiation. Cotton grass wraps its developing seed heads in tufts of white fluff which serve as miniature greenhouses; the temperature inside the floss may be 20°C (36°F) warmer than the air outside. The dense basal rosettes of saxifrages have the same effect of retaining pockets of warm air. Being dark, they absorb so much heat from the sun that there may be a 15°C (27°F) difference between the temperature inside the cushion and that of the air outside. The first miniature leaves of Dwarf Birch to unfurl are cup-shaped and act as parabolic reflectors, focusing the heat of the sun onto the axillary buds.

Some flowers, too, act as miniature solar collectors. The bowl of petals focuses the heat

Arctic flowers are superbly adapted to their harsh environment:
louseworts (top left) and Arctic Forget-me-Nots (above right) have
a dense felt of hairs on their stems, leaves and flowers that trap heat;
many plants, including Purple Saxifrages (top right), grow as low
cushions that escape the worst effects of wind abrasion; and the Arctic
Poppy (above left) has flowers that track the sun.

of the sun onto the central anthers, stigma and ovaries. This creates a 'hot spot' that attracts pollinating insects and also enhances the development of the seeds. Some, such as the attractive yellow flowers of mountain avens (*Dryas* species) are mobile and track around so that they constantly face the sun for maximum effect.

Coloured blooms are advertisements attempting to lure pollinating insects in exchange for a little nectar. Research undertaken on the Taimyr Nature Reserve revealed the importance of insects as pollinating agents in the Russian tundra. In the Taimyr reserve, there are about 236 species of flowering plants, including 60 wind-pollinated grasses and sedges. Of the rest, no less than 137 species need insects to effect the transfer of pollen. Between 140 and 150 different species of insects visit the flowers and are therefore capable of performing the task of pollination, including half a dozen species of hoverflies, a damselfly, three species of moths and a sawfly. However, by far the most effective are three large, furry species of bumblebees.

Bumblebees are very much in evidence in the Arctic. They are among the few kinds of insect that can keep warm and therefore remain active in cold conditions. They achieve this by vigorously 'shivering' their massive wing muscles; their covering of coarse 'fur' traps the heat that this exercise generates and prevents it from being dissipated.

The ability to generate heat also helps the bumblebees to reproduce quickly. The queens mate at the end of the summer and overwinter underground within the security of rodent burrows. They surface in spring to feed on nectar and pollen, producing a first generation of workers, before laying the eggs which will eventually hatch into a second generation of sexual drones and queens. The rapid development of the brood is ensured by the maintenance of a cosy nest with a temperature of about 30°C (86°F). But the queens of one species of bumblebee, *Bombus hyperboreus*, are less industrious. They have a longer winter lie-in, and usurp the queens of another species, *Bombus polaris*, taking over their task force of workers and redirecting them to nurture their own broods of drones and queens.

Flower-shopping insects can be very selective and will tend to visit only those plants that yield plentiful supplies of nectar. This was confirmed by another Soviet research project. It revealed that only 6 per cent of louseworts, 24 per cent of Adams' Oxytrope and 34 per cent of Middendorf's Larkspur were visited by bees; the figure for Middendorf's Oxytrope, by contrast, was 96 per cent. Not surprisingly, the latter species produces abundant nectar to 'pay' the pollinating insects for their services.

The Arctic Willow epitomizes the tundra. The harsh, windy conditions have dictated its bonsai-like form, with stem and branches that creep horizontally over the ground. They are often covered by a sward of moss, through which the willow's twigs and leaves emerge into the sunshine. But even the willows need the wind for dispersal. During the early part of summer, these prostrate plants thrust their catkins into the air, so that they stand up like furry candles above the surface of the tundra.

The low, creeping growth of the stem and leaves of Arctic Willow,
seen here with a fine crop of erect catkins, is determined by its genes,
whereas the stunted habit of some other Arctic shrubs is due to
environmental effects, such as abrasion caused by wind and snow.

These and the catkins of other bushy species that border the rivers and lakes are welcomed by Willow Grouse (North American: Willow Ptarmigan). Like those of lemmings, populations of these gamebirds build up and crash according to regular cycles. When a population is at a peak, there may be twenty pairs to every square kilometre (eight pairs to every square mile) of tundra. The cocks in their handsome white and russet breeding plumage claim their territorial rights by fighting and performing display flights, uttering loud, provocative 'go-back..go-back...go-back' calls. The objective of each male is to secure a rich patch of willow close to a water course that will provide food for him and his mate. She is remarkably well camouflaged to match the tundra carpet on which she lays her clutch of up to a dozen eggs, barely covering them with her breast until the striped chicks emerge.

The seeds hidden within the fluffy heads of cotton grass are an important source of protein for lemmings, which themselves form a vital link in the natural economy of the tundra. When these rodents are abundant, they devour virtually all the seeds, to the detriment of female Bean Geese, which need to build up their own protein reserves before laying their eggs. In addition to the busy little lemmings, other, much larger, tundra mammals rely on the brief summer flush of vegetation for survival.

Reindeer

Chief among these is the Reindeer, known in North America as the Caribou. Currently, some 80 per cent of the world population of Reindeer live in Russia – a total of 2.2 million feral animals and 900,000 wild ones.

During the Arctic summer, both wild and feral Reindeer migrate north from the taiga onto the open tundra to calve and to graze on the fresh growth of vegetation. Reindeer farming has always been a profitable occupation for the indigenous peoples who live in high latitudes because these animals are able to convert the unpromising tundra turf into meat, milk, skins and horns – all useful commodities in the sparse Arctic landscape. The tribal peoples that occupy the far north of the Russian Arctic are no exception – indeed, the reforms initiated by *perestroika* have reinstated the nomadic existence of herders after a period where settlement was the order of the day.

There is evidence that Reindeer cults existed 1,500 years ago, although people such as the Nentsy of the Yamal Peninsula and the Chukchi of north-eastern Siberia can trace back their involvement with Reindeer husbandry only as far as the eleventh century. Reindeer are their obsession; the Chukchi, for instance, have at least twenty terms to describe their animals, depending upon their sex, the shape of their horns and their body size. Even the feral Reindeer possess the same nomadic lifestyle of their forebears, and the people themselves follow suit.

In spring and early summer, the Reindeer herders drive their herds for hundreds of kilometres along traditional routes towards the northern Siberian shoreline with their tundra sledges and *yarangas* – circular tents of Reindeer skins. The sea breezes that blow across the summer pastures keep the merciless mosquitoes partially at bay. On the way, the female Reindeer give birth to their calves, and some of the animals will be deprived of their new antlers. These are sawn off while still covered in a layer of 'velvet' and the products sent to the lucrative aphrodisiac markets in China and South-east Asia.

Unlike the other members of the deer family, to which they are only distantly related, Reindeer sport antlers on both sexes, although the bulls grow much heftier ones than the cows. During the autumn rut, the bulls engage one another in trials of strength, chasing each other, intermeshing the tines of their antlers and pushing with all their might.

This herd of reindeer, seen here in the Kolyma region of eastern
Siberia, is on a long northward migration across the tundra.

Occasionally, a pair of wild Reindeer bulls become permanently locked in combat and are
destined to die together of starvation. Under normal circumstances, the bulls shed their
antlers in December after the rut, but the cows retain theirs until April. As antlers are a
sign of dominance, the females suddenly find themselves deferred to by the naked-headed
bulls, and so they are able to gain better access to food at the coldest time of the year when
they are pregnant.

Reindeer are fussy feeders. Although they will graze on fresh willow foliage and small
mushrooms – on which they occasionally become inebriated – they prefer lichens, especially
species of *Cladonia*, popularly known as 'reindeer moss'. In winter, they dig up the fronds
with their sharp hooves. At first sight, the lichens appear dry and unappetizing, but they
are full of fungal threads, rich in a kind of starch, vitamin B-12 and protein. However,
reindeer moss grows at a rate of only 5 mm ($\frac{1}{5}$ in) a year, so a passing herd nibbles away
many years' worth of productivity in a matter of seconds, and it then takes another ten
years for the vegetation to regenerate. If for no other reason, then, Reindeer must keep
moving. Of necessity, the stocking rate is low: in some areas, 60 hectares (150 acres) of
tundra are needed to support just one of these useful animals.

Unfortunately, lichens concentrate heavy metals and strontium-90, a dangerously radioactive element that has been spread over parts of the Russian Arctic by nuclear tests carried out on Novaya Zemlya. The Chukchi people claim that their health has been affected, and that they suffer a high incidence of throat cancer as a result of eating contaminated Reindeer meat, but this is not proven.

Rare Breeding Birds of the Arctic

The Russian Arctic is home to some birds that breed nowhere else: all of them are rare. Perhaps the most elusive is the Spoon-billed Sandpiper, which nests on the Chukotka Peninsula in the far east of the Siberian Arctic. As its name suggests, this little wader possesses an extraordinary spoon-shaped beak, which it uses for sifting through semi-liquid mud when searching for worms and small crustaceans. There are so few of these birds that only a handful of nests have ever been discovered on the tundra. The exact location of their major wintering areas was also a mystery until 1989, when 257 were counted among the huge conglomeration of waders on islands off the south coast of Bangladesh. By good fortune, two of them wore coloured tags which positively identified them as Chukotka birds, ringed the previous season.

The Siberian White Crane is another Russian speciality. It is an impressive species, standing about 1.4 m (just over $4\frac{1}{2}$ ft) high, and mostly white, with black wing-tips and a bare red face. These extremely wary birds once nested across a wide expanse of the Siberian tundra, but hunting, disturbance and loss of suitable habitat, especially on their migration routes, have steadily eroded the population to only about 2,000 individuals.

Today, Siberian White Cranes nest in two widely separated areas of tundra: one is in Yakutia, between the Yana and Alazeya rivers, and the other is over 3,000 km (1,860 miles) to the west, along the lower reaches of the River Ob. After breeding, these beautiful birds fly south, uttering loud, wild bugling calls as they go. The two populations have different destinations. The Yakutian birds wing their way across Siberia and Mongolia and overwinter on Lake Poyang in China, while most of those that nest along the Ob head for Bharatpur, a wetland sanctuary in India; small numbers of the Ob breeding population winter in Iran. Unfortunately, such long journeys put these conspicuous birds at risk and a concerted effort is being made to stem the losses in a conservation project involving both Russian and North American scientists under the auspices of the International Crane Foundation. Captive breeding is one technique that is being used to help increase the numbers of these elegant birds.

For almost ninety years, the location of the breeding grounds of Ross's Gull was one

A pair of rare Siberian Cranes take to the air at the approach
of danger, uttering loud alarm calls to warn their single chick on
the tundra below to conceal itself.

of the great ornithological mysteries of the Arctic. This dainty 32 cm ($12\frac{1}{2}$ in) long bird is arguably the prettiest member of the gull family; during the nesting season, its body and tail plumage is flushed with an exquisite shade of pink, accounting for the Russian name of *Rosovaya Chaika* (Rosy Gull).

A legend is told by Siberian people to explain the origin of this coloration. The birds are supposed to be the spirits of two attractive young girls who died in their quest for even greater beauty. An old spinster, envious of their good looks, advised them to bathe at the height of winter, whereupon their complexions would become red and healthy in response to the ice-cold water. Alas, they paid a high price for their vanity because they became numb and eventually drowned, but their souls return year after year in the form of lovely pink birds.

The real explanation is more prosaic, but remarkable nonetheless. The pigment comes from the gull's marine diet of planktonic shrimps and is exuded with the oil from its preen gland. This is spread onto the feathers to condition and waterproof them when the birds preen them with their bills. The colour is most noticeable during the spring, and is all but imperceptible by the end of the breeding season.

Its ethereal pink hue has always given Ross's Gull a magical aura. Also, the details of its life were shrouded in mystery until comparatively recently. The bird's discovery dates from the heroic period of polar exploration during the nineteenth century. The first specimen was collected by the Scottish Royal Navy officer Sir James Clark Ross (1800-62). He undertook several courageous expeditions to find the elusive North-West Passage, during which he located the North Magnetic Pole. On his third trip to the Arctic, in 1823, Ross shot a small gull new to science with red legs and plumage tinted with 'the most delicate rose colour on its breast'. It was subsequently christened Ross's Gull in his honour, and although his name is not now remembered in its scientific name, *Rhodostethia rosea*, an abandoned scientific name was *Larus rossii*.

The whereabouts of the gulls' nesting grounds remained unknown until 1905, when Sergei Alexandrovich Buturlin, a Russian High Court Judge, who later became a distinguished ornithologist, found three colonies on the tundra near the Kolyma River.

We now know that, apart from a few very small colonies discovered recently in the Canadian Arctic, Greenland and Spitsbergen, the entire world population of 50,000 or so Ross's Gulls nests in the north-eastern quarter of the Siberian tundra. The colonies are situated in the swampy plains of the Kolyma-Indigirka Depression, and along the lower Yana River. Furthermore, breeding is by no means regular; in some years, when conditions are not favourable, the gulls fail to grace the most commonly used nesting sites.

The appearance of the birds in these remote regions of the tundra coincides with the spring melt. Surprisingly, they do not arrive from the direction of the Arctic Ocean, but fly in from the south-east, across the frozen tundra. It seems that by April, the bulk of the

The exquisite pale rose-pink body and tail of this Ross's Gull contrast with the clear blue sky of the tundra in summer. Almost all of the world's 25,000 pairs of this dainty little gull breed in north-eastern Siberia.

population is situated off Kamchatka and in the Sea of Okhotsk, and so the journey to the Siberian river deltas involves an overland journey.

When the gulls reach their destinations at the end of May, the pools alongside which they nest are usually frozen. At first, they are more at home with the feel of ice under their feet and settle, often in pairs, on the frozen pools. During this period, they feed on dead invertebrates and suffocated fish, such as sticklebacks, which have become released from the thawing ice. The gulls bring these to the surface of the pools by paddling vigorously with their vermilion feet.

The bonds between pairs are cemented by regular courtship feeding, the females begging their mates enthusiastically for gifts of partially digested food. The males oblige by regurgitating their offerings onto the ice, whereupon the females devour them in an instant. This extra nourishment helps the females lay their eggs as soon as the vegetation by the edges of the pools or on islands is clear of snow and melt water. This happens very quickly. Overnight, the birds move to their nests on small islands or peninsulas projecting into shallow tundra lakes.

Ross's Gulls do not form large and raucous colonies like many of their relatives. Theirs vary in size from a minimum of two or three nests to a maximum of fifty. However, an average sized colony consists of about thirteen pairs spread over several hectares. The eggs are khaki-coloured with dark brown blotches, and are superbly camouflaged – as well they might be, because the colonies are constantly patrolled by hungry Glaucous and Herring Gulls. When the Ross's Gulls rise into the air in defence of their nests, they are usually assisted by neighbouring Arctic Terns, which are more ferocious in pressing home attacks on intruders. Despite this, raiding gulls, as well as Pomarine, Arctic and Long-tailed Skuas (North American: Pomarine, Parasitic and Long-tailed Jaegers) occasionally devastate a colony, stealing nearly a third of its eggs.

To the west of the range occupied by Ross's Gulls nests another rare endemic Russian bird, the Red-breasted Goose, which has evolved an intriguing relationship with the Peregrine Falcon and other predatory birds. Red-breasted Geese are among the most beautiful of all waterfowl, strikingly patterned in glossy black and white, with glowing terracotta breasts and ear patches. Although there are about 28,000 of them, only about 5,000 pairs attempt to nest each year in a relatively restricted area of the Russian Arctic.

By world standards, these geese are rare and becoming rarer. In the days of the Pharaohs, they used to be familiar winter visitors to Egypt – at least, if the accurate representations of them in ancient tombs can be believed. In more recent times, flocks of Red-breasted

An anxious parent Red-breasted Goose shepherds her brood of six
newly hatched fluffy goslings on the Taimyr Peninsula in July.

Geese used to winter in the southern Caspian region and the mouth of the Syr Darya where it entered the Aral Sea. Today, their main winter quarters are restricted to the Danube delta, mostly in Romania, with some birds in northern Bulgaria, and a few wintering irregularly in Greece, Turkey and Iran.

In spring, these small geese fly some 4,000 km (2,500 miles) from their wintering grounds across the steppes and taiga by way of river valleys, until they reach the tundra. The Taimyr Peninsula is one of their breeding strongholds. The objective of many of them is to settle on cliffs and bluffs carved out by meandering rivers. Such places are the preferred nesting sites of predatory Peregrine Falcons. Pairs of these falcons are spaced about 8 km (5 miles) apart in the southern tundra zone. Although the geese might be expected to avoid such committed bird killers, in fact they are attracted to precisely those spots where the falcons are nesting.

By mid-June, each Peregrine's eyrie may have a cluster of up to a dozen Red-breasted Geese sitting on eggs within 30 m (100 ft) of it. Many are situated on the south sides of the slopes so that the birds benefit from the warmth of the sun. Also, such elevated sites

This pair of Snow Geese at their nest on Wrangel Island have rust-
coloured stains on their heads from iron oxide in the Arctic soil.

Right: A hungry Arctic Fox prepares to eat a Snow Goose's egg it
has stolen from a breeding colony on Wrangel Island.

catch the breezes, which give the incubating geese some respite from the clouds of
mosquitoes that swarm over the tundra in summer.

However, no-one knows for sure what advantages the geese gain by nesting so close to
the Peregrines. The adult geese have nothing to fear from the falcons, which target smaller
prey, taking perhaps 5 per cent of the song birds and small waders which abound on the
tundra during the summer. However, the goslings may be at risk from some of the other
predatory birds, such as Rough-legged Buzzards (North American: rough-legged Hawks)
and Herring Gulls. Surprisingly, the geese also nest in association with these birds, despite
the fact that they are not averse to grabbing a gosling or two.

Perhaps the Peregrine Falcons protect the geese from Arctic Foxes. These wily little carnivores are a real menace to incubating birds, especially when their main prey, lemmings, are in short supply, as happens periodically when the lemming cycle is at its nadir. If an inquisitive fox approaches too close for comfort, the cackling of the geese might alert the falcons to the danger, and encourage them to attack the intruder and drive it away. This certainly happens with Herring Gulls, which put up a very spirited defence of their nests. So in this case, the benefits of protection from foxes may outweigh the risk of losing a few goslings to the gulls.

On Wrangel Island, Snow Geese and Arctic Foxes coexist. The birds nest communally on the tundra where their white plumage makes them easy for predators to locate. Furthermore, the colonies are generally situated in areas where there are plenty of lemmings so the foxes gravitate naturally to the goose nesting grounds to hunt their favourite prey.

In years when there is a glut of lemmings, the foxes ignore the geese, but when the rodents are in short supply, they turn to feeding on goose eggs and goslings. During the early part of the breeding season, these plucky little mammals bound in among the nesting birds, infuriating the ganders guarding their mates. Drawing themselves up to over 1 m (3 ft) high, the geese are formidable opponents, using their wings to batter an attacker. A healthy adult goose is too strong and pugnacious to fall victim to an Arctic Fox, but the eggs, when left unguarded in the commotion, are quickly seized by the agile, fast-moving predator and either crushed and consumed, or buried to provide a store of food to help it survive the leaner times ahead.

Later in the summer, when the goslings appear, the parents must remain very vigilant and give predators no quarter. Even so, Arctic Foxes account for about 15 per cent of the eggs and goslings during the years when there is a shortfall of lemmings. This is not a catastrophic toll; Snow Geese live for up to twenty-five years and have plenty of opportunity to nest again.

The Tiny Hordes

The arrival of the young birds coincides with the richest time on the tundra. As the summer wears on, the sward, warmed to tropical temperatures by the sun, seethes with life, much of it so small that only a microscope will reveal its full extent. A hidden workforce of bacteria helps to break down the vegetable matter and make it available to larger species, such as nematode worms. There may be between 1 and 5 million of them squirming away in every square metre, together with up to a quarter of a million springtails. The latter provide food for spiders, many of which stalk their prey between the hummocks of vegetation.

Although there are only a few thousand species of insects in the entire Arctic region, some of them occur in astronomical numbers. Towards the end of June, when there is a mass emergence of midges and mosquitoes, humans and animals alike can be driven demented by their attentions. They rise like grey smoke from the water and vegetation, covering exposed flesh and entering the mouth and nostrils to suffocating effect. However, it is perhaps the non-biting chironomid midges that are the most numerous of the Arctic flies. There may be between 6,000 and 27,000 midge larvae per sq metre (5,000 and 22,500 per sq yard). Together with those of craneflies, these larvae form an important part of the diet of birds. They have life-cycles perhaps six years long. As adults, chironomids may never feed but live only to breed.

Temperature is critical for insects. On the tundra, those that fly tend to keep close to the ground where it is warmer. Butterflies, several species of which grace the Russian Arctic, bask in the sun with open wings. Many tend to be darker and so better able to absorb heat than their relatives which live in more southerly climes. These terrestrial insects are eagerly devoured by a host of warblers, pipits, and other songbirds. Wheatears, for example, have a taste for bumblebees, while Bluethroats are adept at catching craneflies and damselflies. All these birds stuff great balls of insects into the imploring gapes of their ever-hungry chicks. By contrast, Willow Grouse (North American: Willow Ptarmigan) chicks, all stripes, can walk and follow their parents an hour or two after they have hatched. They are self-supporting and eagerly peck at mosquitoes and aphids as they scramble through the vegetation on their little legs.

The pools and lakes warm up more slowly than the turf of the tundra, and so the aquatic inhabitants reach their peak populations rather later, in July. At this time, the water contains a frenzied mass of crustaceans and larvae of all kinds, especially those of midges and mosquitoes. The two common species of Arctic mosquitoes, *Aedes impiger* and *A. nigripes*, spend their larval lives in water. It is this abundant and easily caught supply of food that makes it worthwhile for so many waders and wildfowl to fly so far north to nest. Phalaropes are particularly skilful at intercepting prey beyond their reach. These dainty little waders agitate the water by pirouetting on the surface, and this brings small shrimps and larvae to within range of their bills. Marine ducks, such as Greater Scaup, Long-tailed Duck (North American: Oldsquaw) and the three species of eider move from the sea to fresh water to rear their families on this glut; at any moment, a young eider may have

The drake King Eider has a spectacular breeding plumage.
This species is one of the most northerly of all ducks, and one
of the most abundant, too.

2,000 midge larvae in its crop. In July, the sun never sets and so young protein-hungry birds have double the amount of feeding time of their more southerly nesting relatives.

The young Ross's Gulls hatch during late June and early July, when the population of mosquito larvae is at its peak. For the first few days, the dappled brown chicks eat large amounts of these larvae, as well as midges, craneflies and sticklebacks, brought to them by their parents. Then, in striking contrast to other gull chicks, which remain dependent on their parents for food for up to eight weeks, they feed themselves, mostly on small snails called *Siberinauta*. Although they are well camouflaged when skulking around the edges of the lakes, nearly 40 per cent of the chicks may be taken by predators, including powerful grey-brown or ghostly white Gyr Falcons, which occasionally hunt around the gulls' nesting colonies. The few gull chicks that survive are ready to fledge when they are 16–17 days old. They bear no resemblance to their parents, having predominantly dark plumage and a bold black-and-white pattern on the wings.

Arctic Fish

The rivers and lakes of the Russian Arctic are very productive in fish life. There is plenty of food in the form of insect larvae and small crustaceans and many of the water systems are deep enough not to freeze solid during winter. Many of the Arctic river fish migrate from the deeper, saline estuaries during the summer when the thaw sets in and the rivers once more start to flow freely. These fish and the countless billions of fry they produce are important to the natural economy of the Arctic, and are exploited by both the animals and the people of these high latitudes.

Several species of whitefish inhabit Siberian rivers. The majority are migratory and therefore escape becoming frozen in during the winter. Their chief feeding grounds are in the lower, brackish parts of the rivers, where some specialize in feeding on plankton and others thrive on bottom-dwelling organisms. The *Tugun*, which lives in some of the lakes between the Ob and Yana rivers, reaches a length of only 20 cm (8 in) and a weight of barely 1 kg ($2\frac{1}{4}$ lb). In the Kolyma River, the *Tschirr* grows into a relative giant, reaching a weight of 16 kg (35 lb).

Most Siberian fish grow slowly and may not reach sexual maturity until they are over ten years old. As spawning time approaches, they ascend the rivers during the latter half of the summer, and deposit huge numbers of eggs over stony areas in October and November, often under the ice. Although the adults are exhausted by their efforts, most survive to breed again. The small eggs develop into fry by the following spring and are swept downstream.

Many fish fry are swept into the lakes by meltwater and grow enormously year by year while they await a big melt to flush them back into the rivers. Like whitefish, Arctic Char are closely related to salmon and trout, and are just as tasty. They are essentially coldwater fish, and have penetrated further than any other species of coldwater fish into the Arctic domain. They have been recorded as far north as 82°N in the New Siberian Islands and in Novaya Zemlaya. Some Arctic Char attain a weight of 10 kg (22 lb) when they are twelve years old, but others remain quite small throughout their entire lives.

Like salmon, Arctic Char are normally migratory, but many have become cut off in lakes so that isolated populations develop their own characteristics. Those that are free to do so migrate in September and October and spawn during the winter, often under the ice, on gravel bottoms in lakes or near the upper courses of rivers. While breeding, the males are gorgeously coloured, with brilliant red fins and bellies. It is fish like these that are caught by the various species of divers (North American: loons) that nest on the Russian tundra lakes.

Smaller fish are taken by Ross's Gulls. Many of the tundra streams and ponds are inhabited by Twelve-spined Sticklebacks. They move in from the estuaries during the summer thaw and, if the meltwater level is high enough, swim into the tundra pools. Their presence in large shoals close to Ross's Gull colonies generates feeding frenzies among the birds, which mill around and rapidly dip into the water to seize the fish in their bills. Those survivors that cannot escape into the rivers before winter sets in become entombed in the ice. When the ice thaws during the following spring, their preserved bodies are a source of nourishment for the gulls as they return to the tundra.

Predatory Northern Pike lurk in the Arctic rivers. They spawn in the spring and are caught in large numbers by people camping on the tundra, who split them open and make an extremely salty, golden 'caviare' from the roes. It is alleged that some Russian Arctic lakes harbour populations of Northern Pike that sustain themselves by cannibalism. Apparently, the smallest individuals thrive on aquatic insect larvae and, in the absence of smaller species of fish, the larger pike prey upon the smaller ones.

Pallas's Arctic Grayling is another common fish species of the eastern Siberian rivers. It is more colourful than the European Grayling, with a larger dorsal fin, and feeds voraciously on insects and small fish.

Perhaps the most remarkable of all these Arctic fish is the Blackfish. It grows to 20 cm (8 in) in length, and lives in small lakes, meltwater channels and bogs that are rarely free of ice in the Chukotka Peninsula and Alaska. As its name suggests, it is very dark in colour, but the fins are edged in red or orange during the spawning season. Blackfish are active for only a short period, feeding on fly larvae. As winter approaches, they bury themselves in the silt, and can apparently tolerate a certain amount of freezing. However, many die if they are frozen for too long.

Rodent Cycles

Although Ross's Gull chicks and other young birds may provide a major source of food for some tundra carnivores, it is lemmings and voles that form the staple diet of many of the predators. Arctic Foxes, Snowy and Short-eared Owls, Rough-legged Buzzards (North American: Rough-legged Hawks) and Pomarine and Long-tailed Skuas (North American: Pomarine and Long-tailed Jaegers) all profit from large populations of these rodents.

However, both voles and, to a greater extent, lemmings experience great population swings on a three or four year cycle, and the creatures that depend upon them follow suit. The build-up is due to the lemmings achieving sexual maturity early in life, and to a long breeding season that may extend into the winter.

During peak years, when there may be between 200 and 400 lemmings to every hectare (80-160 to every acre), Rough-legged Buzzards may nest only 0.8-2 km ($\frac{1}{2}$-$1\frac{1}{4}$ miles) apart and lay clutches of as many as seven eggs. Over the course of the summer season, a couple of these buzzards may succeed in killing 1,000 rodents, thus accounting for 10 per cent of the lemmings or voles in their own hunting territories during a plentiful year. Likewise, Snowy Owls are numerous when lemmings are at a peak, and may be able to raise families of eleven owlets.

However, after a year or two of feasting, the inevitable famine follows. The lemmings exhaust their supply of high-quality food and the little creatures fail to breed because of

A female Snowy Owl prepares to feed one of her chicks with a lemming. This
magnificent owl feeds almost entirely on lemmings in the breeding season.

malnutrition and stress induced by overcrowding. Many try to move to better areas but drown while attempting to cross lakes or rivers, and are snapped up by eiders, pikes and salmon – one salmon was found to contain the bodies of ten lemmings. Even Reindeer eat the odd lemming. Fly maggots consume many lemming carcases on the tundra and the vegetation is nourished by the minerals that leach from the putrefying remains. There is even a bright green moss that grows on lemming bones.

Those predators that survive the lean times during a 'crash' in the rodent population may fail to breed for a year or so. This is the period when Arctic Foxes try to survive on birds and carrion but the supplies are usually insufficient, and many of the adults and their cubs starve to death.

Coping with Winter

By August, the prospect of winter looms in the Russian Arctic. The sun is already dipping below the horizon, and flurries of snow begin to powder the landscape. It is time for the polar creatures to prepare for the worst times ahead. Some simply escape from the harsh conditions. Most of the birds head south with their offspring, from the Red-breasted Geese flying south-westwards to Romania to the Snow Geese bound south-eastwards for California. By contrast, Ross's Gulls and their newly fledged juveniles appear to meet the threat of the impending polar winter head-on by flying northwards into the Arctic Ocean. Many will then fly east past Wrangel Island, and then move with the leading edge of the

pack ice as it spreads into the Chukchi and Bering seas. They thrive in the bitterly cold conditions, plucking shrimps and small fish from the icy waters with their bills.

Many Arctic insects, such as mosquitoes, overwinter as eggs, while midges survive in their immature stages by seeking refuge in the unfrozen, deeper parts of lakes. Others, including the caterpillars of some butterflies and moths, cope by allowing themselves to become frozen solid in suspended animation. They must prepare their bodies for enduring the sub-zero temperatures. This often involves excreting water so that their body fluids or blood become very concentrated and resist freezing. As the summer draws to a close, some synthesize chemicals that act as a natural antifreeze. There is even an amphibian in the tundra, the Siberian Salamander, that appears to freeze, surviving temperatures down to $-35°C$ ($-31°F$).

The warm-blooded mammals have evolved different methods of coping with the

The pristine white plumage of the Ivory Gull (left) echoes the ice and snow of its High Arctic habitat; the most northerly breeding of all the world's birds, this gull also manages to survive the bitterest Arctic winters. The Siberian Salamander (above) is the only land-hibernating amphibian to occur on the Arctic tundra.

inhospitable Arctic winter. Reindeer are migratory and retire inland to the northern edge of the taiga – the great northern coniferous forest – or into the sheltered regions in the lee of mountain ridges. The cold is less of a threat to them because their thick winter coats, consisting of hollow hairs, provide excellent insulation. Their chief concern is food, so they seek areas where the snow has been blown clear of the ground vegetation or lies in a layer thin enough for them to scrape it away with their hooves.

Lemmings and voles are too small to migrate and so lay up stores full of lichens and other nutritious plant material. These buried supplies enable them to carry on life as normal beneath the blanket of snow, where it is often considerably warmer than on the surface. Should they become too cold, these little creatures can increase their metabolic rates to keep warm.

Although many Willow Grouse (North American: Willow Ptarmigan) move south to the scrub tundra and taiga when the weather deteriorates, some stay put on the tundra and brave out the long Arctic winter. They live on the edge of an impending energy crisis because they must eke out an existence on coarse willow twigs of low calorific value, from which they can extract only about a third of the energy content at best.

At the height of winter, the grouse burrow into snow drifts which give them a measure of protection against the bitter cold, and here they spend up to twenty-one hours a day. Even when they come out to feed in the dim light, they are well camouflaged in their white winter plumage. If the snow is not deep enough for them to excavate good winter burrows, these otherwise hardy birds are unable to keep warm and maintain their health and many will die of starvation before spring returns. Many others are eaten by such predators as Arctic Foxes, Grey Wolves, Snowy Owls and Gyr Falcons.

The Polar Bear is warm-blooded and yet it is so well insulated by fat and fur that snow adhering to its fur fails to melt. Even the soles of its massive feet, consisting of thick, flexible pads of fat, are covered with roughened skin and tough hair.

The great white bear has other adaptations, too, for surviving the cold. Its white fur coat and black skin work together like a solar collector, absorbing the energy of the sun and preventing the precious heat from radiating into the cold air. The long outer hairs of the Polar Bear's fur are hollow – their white colour arises from light scattering within the empty shafts and not from any pigment. Being translucent, the hairs let through much of the sunlight, including the infra-red rays. These are absorbed by the bear's black skin which becomes warm in the process. The heat is not all radiated back into the atmosphere because the fleecy white hairs act like a greenhouse and retain some of it. The air trapped in the

A Willow Grouse, in its superbly camouflaged winter plumage,
emerges from its burrow in thick snow where it spends most of its
time sheltering from the icy blast of the Arctic winter.

underfur is thus warmed up by this recycled heat, and the insulating layer also prevents the
cold polar air from draining away the warmth by convection and conduction. The mechanism is so outstandingly efficient that, on a sunny day, the surface of the skin
may be warmer than the bear's deep body temperature, making the bear too warm for
comfort!

During August and September, Polar Bears begin to return to Wrangel after their
summer's hunting on the pack ice. Occasionally, the weather is so mild that the southern
edge of the pack ice may be 200 km (125 miles) away to the north, and the bears' arrival
coincides with the presence of up to 80,000 Walruses which concentrate at traditional
beaching sites. The Walruses do well in this part of the world, raking clams from the mud
that once lay on the land bridge of Beringia, which now forms the bottom of the shallow
Chukchi and Bering seas. The congregation of Walruses attracts gatherings of Polar Bears,

many of which are females with their cubs born earlier in the year. They are set on gorging themselves and becoming thoroughly obese in preparation for their long winter fast. Walruses, built like giant barrels of blubber, are a major source of food for the great bears.

The technique adopted by a bear hunting along the beaches of Wrangel Island is to amble alongside the heaving masses of resting Walruses, which snort in disgust at its temerity. Healthy adults have little to fear. Their great bulk, tough skin and lethal ivory tusks present the bear with too great a challenge. Instead, it tries to locate a young Walrus in the midst of the adults. As soon as one is momentarily exposed by the heaving mêlée of mother Walruses, the bear bounds in among them, seizes the youngster by its neck or a hind flipper and hauls it clear of the crowd. It drags the defenceless animal up the shore – an indication of the bear's immense strength, as the prey may be half its weight. Then, it immobilizes its victim by a series of savage shakes and bites. The hunts are not always successful, however. Sometimes, the bear emerges from the fray with its white coat bloodied, having sustained an injury from a slash by one of the adult Walruses' tusks.

As the days shorten and the weather deteriorates, the fattened and often pregnant Polar Bears head inland to the slopes where they will spend the next five months. Having found suitable sites, they make little attempt to excavate dens, simply waiting for the snow to cover their bodies. Once a reasonable depth has accumulated and drifted over them, they fashion out a chamber or two beneath the insulating white blanket which will protect them from the freezing wind. It is usually only the female bears that build dens and mothers with cubs of the year tend to make only temporary shelters. The males and mothers with older cubs mostly keep going all winter, returning to the sea ice to search for seals and occasionally lying down to sleep for short periods.

On Wrangel Island, the grim polar night begins on 18 November and the sun does not illuminate the sky again until 25 January. During this period, only the shimmering veils of the aurora borealis and the face of the moon cast their ghostly light upon the land. The snow that falls is often whipped by the icy wind into drifts as deep as 25 m (80 ft) and the

Preceding pages: Keeping a watchful eye on the formidable
tusks of the adults, a Wrangel Island Polar Bear sends the
nearest members of a group of Walruses splashing into the
sea in panic as it attempts to single out a vulnerable youngster.
The adults are more than a match for the bears if attacked.
Polar Bears are the most carnivorous of all the bears,
feeding mainly on Ringed Seals.

temperature regularly sinks to −50°C (−58°F). At this time, the mother bears are fast asleep beneath the snow.

The Arctic Fox is also a master of polar survival and is one of the few creatures to remain active throughout the year in these high latitudes. This amazing little mammal copes well with the severe cold, providing it can obtain enough food by scavenging from carcases killed by Polar Bears and other larger predators or by hunting rodents.

To prepare for the winter, the Arctic Fox grows a dense, white coat, and even its paws are furred on both sides. This layer of fine fleece insulates it so well that an Arctic Fox can apparently sleep on ice at −80°C (−112°F) for an hour before suffering the effects of exposure! If conditions become too severe, it can retreat into its den, which it digs out in the open tundra, often in a small hillock.

The Arctic Fox even begins its breeding cycle during the winter, before the Polar Bears have stirred from their dens. The vixens come into heat during March and engage the dog foxes in energetic courtship chases across the frozen ground, which may end in mating. Their sexual schedule ensures that the cubs arrive when the tundra is best able to support the foxes and their families.

Surprisingly, the realm of the great white bear and the Arctic Fox is not the coldest place in the northern hemisphere. During the winter, heat escapes from the icebound sea to ameliorate the harsh climate of the Arctic Frontier to some extent. The northern 'pole of cold' lies well away from the ocean's influence, and is situated south of the Arctic Circle, within the dense frozen forest of deepest Siberia.

SIBERIA:
THE FROZEN FOREST

SIBERIA IS RUSSIA'S frigid frontier. The great Russian writer Maxim Gorky called it 'the land of death and chains'. Certainly, the very name brings a shudder as it is easy to imagine the suffering of the millions who were exiled to Siberia, where they languished in slave camps, first under the Tsars, then under Stalin and his successors.

The Verkhoyansk Mountains, which rise to over 2,300 m (7,550 ft), lie to the east of the city of Yakutsk in north-eastern Siberia. Their river valleys trap cold Arctic air, producing winters of astonishing severity in which the temperature has plummeted to $-68°C$ ($-90.4°F$) – making this region, along with Oymyakon, 630 km (390 miles) to the south-east, the site of the lowest recorded temperature in the Northern Hemisphere. In summer, by contrast, the temperature often rises more than $100°C$ ($180°F$) to over $30°C$ ($86°F$). This is the greatest variation in temperature anywhere in the world, equivalent to the difference between the freezing and boiling points of water.

The largest of the former Soviet regions, Siberia sprawls across 10 million sq km (4 million sq miles) of marshy plains, desolate plateaus, rugged mountains and enormous coniferous forests. It is traversed by about 50,000 rivers, including some of the world's greatest, notably the Ob, Lena and Yenisei, each over 3,200 km (2,000 miles) long, while Lake Baikal sits like a blue jewel just within its boundary – the largest, oldest, and deepest body of fresh water in the world. Although Siberia covers nearly half the former USSR, today, less than one in ten of the Commonwealth of Independent States' people live in its vast area and endure its awesome climate.

Siberia is a colossal eldorado, formerly colonized by fur traders, but its modern wealth

Part of the great Russian coniferous forest, or taiga, in north-eastern Siberia,
seen here in the grip of winter. With water locked up as snow and ice, the
trees must cope with drought just like the plants in a desert.

is based on more than fur. So much gold is mined that Russia may take over from South Africa as the world's biggest producer of this precious metal. One of the largest sources of diamonds has been discovered in Yakutia, and now yields 12 million carats a year – nearly a quarter by weight of the world's total annual output.

Underlying parts of western Siberia are some 8.3 trillion (million million) cu m (27 trillion cu ft) of natural gas; according to the experts, this is the biggest reservoir in the world. And where there is gas, there is oil – an estimated 30 billion (thousand million) barrels of it. Siberia also has huge deposits of coal and minerals, and timber in immense quantity. However, these vast riches are difficult to exploit because the forbidding weather and harsh living conditions hinder efforts to extract them.

The Great Dark Carpet

The natural history of Siberia is largely the tale of the *taiga*, the vast carpet of coniferous trees that stretches across the continent immediately to the south of the tundra to form the greatest forest in the world. Underlying two thirds of Siberia is the permafrost. This is perennially frozen soil, of which only the surface layer – up to 30 cm (1 ft) in the north and 1.3 m ($4\frac{1}{4}$ ft) in the south – thaws during the summer months. Beneath this, the ground is like an iceberg, up to 400 m (1,300 ft) thick in the north and up to 1,200 m (3,900 ft) or more thick in mid-Yakutia, with a layer of vegetation covering the surface. The greatest known depth of permafrost is 1,450 m (4,750 ft) near Yakutsk.

Scientists believe that the iron-hard ground of northern Siberia and the Russian Arctic probably formed at least 70,000 years ago. At the height of the last great Ice Age, the permafrost region was covered with tundra plants, but when the climate ameliorated, trees spread northwards to blanket great areas of it. The steady shift of the tree line separating the taiga from the tundra shows that the process is still continuing, but it is balanced by an attrition of the southern edge of the forests as the steppes expand under the regime of a warm, dry climate.

The presence of ice beneath the soil is still very much in evidence. Drainage is poor, leading to boggy conditions during the warmer months of the year, and the plants cannot sink their roots far into the ground because of the ice barrier. Paradoxically, their presence helps to maintain the permafrost layer because their foliage shields the frigid ground from the warmth of the sun.

As in Scandinavia and North America, it is the coniferous trees that dominate the northern latitudes. They are more frost resistant than deciduous broadleaved trees, and can

The pale, slender trunks of birch trees mingle with the great serried
ranks of conifers in many places in the taiga.

probably start to grow earlier in the spring when the thaw sets in. Also, in winter, when
the sunlight is weak and of short duration, plants need to absorb as much light as possible
to manufacture their own food by photosynthesis. Coniferous foliage, which consists of
long, dark needles oriented at all angles, is a remarkably efficient arrangement for absorbing
light, as the gloom beneath a canopy of pine trees testifies.

In these austere forests, few green plants are able to grow in the permanent shade.
There are, however, numerous saprophytes which live without chlorophyll and instead of
producing food by photosynthesis survive on rotting vegetation. Lichens, intimate associ-
ations between fungi and simple algae, prosper in these conditions and many rodents and
deer, such as musk deer and forest-dwelling Reindeer, relish the encrusting growths. The
countless threads of many species of free-living fungi ramify the soil, and their pervading
presence is revealed during autumn when the spore-carrying parasols rise from the turf of
moss, and the edible varieties are harvested by local people as a welcome and important
addition to their diet.

The taiga is a rather monotonous habitat, with relatively few species, but each is present in huge numbers. Spruces dominate the western region, giving way to larches in the vast central region of Siberia. Towards the east and in the mountainous areas, such as the Altai, great Siberian Stone Pines take over. Russians call them 'cedars', although they are genuine pines and are not related to the true cedars, such as the Cedar of Lebanon. In the coastal region of the Russian Far East, where the cold, damp climate is associated with abundant snow, the Dwarf Japanese Stone Pine, a shrublike species, covers the ground with its prostrate branches.

Other kinds of trees, too, grow in the taiga. For instance, Scots Pines grow well where the soil is sandy. Birches are also very much in evidence in these high latitudes. They are essentially colonizers, with light seeds that are scattered by the wind, and become quickly established wherever the original conifers have been destroyed by fire or by logging. But they have short life-spans, and gradually give way to conifers. The mix of trees is richer in the south because of the warmer climate, and in low-lying river valleys willows, aspens and other broadleaved trees intrude into the domain of the conifers.

The trees of the taiga have evolved adaptations to withstand the rigours of the northern climate. When caked with fresh snow, spruces and firs present a picturesque sight, and yet the elegant, downward sweeping branches enable the mass of accumulated snow to slither off periodically before they break under its great weight. Larches avoid the problem entirely by shedding their needles in winter. They are by far the most numerous conifers in Russia, covering about 2.6 million sq km (1 million sq miles) in total. They dominate the landscape where the taiga meets the tundra, and in the central region of Siberia where the winter conditions are bleakest.

Being deciduous, larches effectively shut down during the winter months to resist the drought imposed by the severe frosts. Most of them grow above areas of permafrost. This means that their roots cannot penetrate to more than a few centimetres. However, the roots splay out very widely just beneath the thin carpet of vegetation, sometimes even breaking out onto the surface. Such a rambling root system enables the trees to tap moisture during the summer over as large an area as possible. The broad base gives support to the trunk when faced with gales, and prevents the trees from growing too close together.

Coping with Winter

The Siberian winter is fearsomely cold, and all creatures must prepare to endure its long, deep freeze. Snow and ice render most food supplies inaccessible, so many birds and mammals become frenetically active in August and September, laying up stores which will

The Siberian Jay (left) has especially soft, fluffy plumage, which helps to insulate
its body from the bitter cold of the taiga in winter. The powerful beak of the
Nutcracker (right) enables it to crush nuts and cones to release the seeds within.

guarantee their survival until the following spring. Siberian Tits remove insects from the outermost twigs of trees, where the snow would cover them, and place them on the central trunks that remain exposed. Siberian Jays use their sticky saliva to glue seeds as well as insects to the undersides of branches well above the height normally smothered by snow. During winter, the hungry birds rediscover their caches of food.

Conifer seeds are a crucial source of sustenance. For instance, 2.47 acres (a single hectare) of spruce – an area about $1\frac{1}{3}$ times that of a soccer pitch (about twice that of an American football pitch) – can yield an average of 1.8 tonnes (2 tons) of seed a year. Larch seeds are light and shed in the winter. They lie on the surface of the snow and can be eaten at a time when much else is covered up. The seeds of the Siberian Stone Pine are especially nutritious. Unlike the Scots Pine, which produces rather insubstantial, winged seeds, the Siberian Stone Pine makes large, wholesome 'nuts'.

Many creatures of the taiga depend on these seeds during the winter. Nutcrackers relentlessly hoard seeds during the short autumn period and transport them to higher altitudes where the snow lies less deeply. This may involve a great expenditure of effort. One of these dumpy, brown-speckled crows may hide 10,000 seeds before deep falls of snow put an end to this activity. Another bird was observed to make caches no less than 6 km ($3\frac{3}{4}$ miles) from the spot where it removed the seeds from the cones. The reward for this intense industry is survival through to the spring. But there are robbers about! Jays, both Eurasian and Siberian – also hoarders in their own right – watch where the Nutcrackers bury their winter stores and, given a chance, raid their relatives' hard-won supplies.

Cone Specialists

Nutcrackers, jays and various species of woodpecker use their strong, pointed beaks to hammer the cones apart and release the seeds. As their name suggests, crossbills have evolved highly specialized beaks to attack the armoured cones of conifers. The peasants of Central Europe claimed that the remarkable tip-twisted bills of these stout finches were a legacy of their attempts to wrench out the nails which impaled Christ to the cross and, as

The remarkable crossed mandibles that give the crossbills their name
can be seen clearly in this male Two-barred Crossbill.

a reward, God granted the birds the ability to nest in the middle of the winter. The males, so they maintained, still bore the stains of Christ's blood in their reddish plumage. In fact, the crossed mandibles allow the birds to extract seeds from tough cones. Indeed, so specialized are they at exploiting the bonanza of coniferous seeds that their ability to deal with other sorts of food is severely handicapped.

There are three species of crossbills in Russia, and each sports a bill neatly proportioned to tease open the cones of a particular species of conifer. The heavy-billed Parrot Crossbill is able to tackle the sturdy cones of pines; the Common Crossbill (North American: Red Crossbill), with its medium-sized bill, feeds primarily from the softer cones of spruce, and the Two-barred Crossbill (North American: White-winged Crossbill), with its tweezerlike beak, specializes in eating the seeds of larches, which are enclosed in relatively lightweight cones.

Resourceful Red Squirrels

Like Nutcrackers and jays, Red Squirrels are great exploiters of the taiga's seed bounty and make provision for the winter. The most widespread Siberian race is extremely beautiful, being rust red during the summer but changing to silvery grey before winter sets in. Those

This Red Squirrel, belonging to one of the Siberian races, has almost acquired its dark greyish winter coat.

from the far east of Russia tend to be a sooty colour. Almost all of the squirrel's life takes place in the trees. Sharp-clawed feet and prehensile front toes make it a sure and confident climber, and its great plume of a tail acts as a balancing device and rudder when the squirrel scampers across flimsy branches and leaps from one tree to another. The tail is also used like a duvet to keep the squirrel warm when it is curled up inside its treetop nest, or drey.

Although Red Squirrels thrive on a wide variety of foods, they are especially fond of the seeds of pines and spruces. These rodents are superbly evolved to relieve the cones of their seeds, cutting them from the outermost branches, manoeuvring them in their dextrous little forepaws and using their formidable incisor teeth to chisel away the scales. The nourishing seeds can then be extracted with the tongue.

A single squirrel can account for nearly 200 pine cones in a day; this means that it takes 1 hectare (2.47 acres) of conifers to support one of these industrious creatures. As winter approaches, they become busy 'squirrelling' away pine cones, nuts, mushrooms and other food items in the ground. When hoarding, their behaviour falls into a predictable routine of actions. The animal makes a little scrape in the ground with its forepaws into which it drops its prize. Next, it presses home the cone or nut with its incisors. The squirrel then collects some soil and a leaf or two with its forelegs and places these over the spot to hide the buried treasure, finishing off the action by packing down the ground with its forefeet.

Red Squirrels have various adaptations that help them survive the winter. Before the hard weather sets in, they store fat equivalent to 20 per cent of their body weight. Also, they possess an uncanny ability for locating their food caches, recovering their dispersed stockpile of food as needed during the winter. Although they do not hibernate properly, they spend up to 22 hours in their nests asleep, emerging when conditions are conducive to feasting on some of their hidden bounty of food. Even layers of snow are no hindrance, because the animals can apparently smell pine cones hidden beneath 30 cm (1 ft) of it. If the snow is really thick, they forage in the spaces underneath. Not all of the seeds are recovered. These eventually germinate and perhaps grow into new trees. The spread of forests may therefore depend in part upon the forgetfulness of squirrels and other animal hoarders.

The fortunes of Red Squirrels are intimately linked to the size of the taiga's seed crop. Spruces, larches and pines all undergo regular cycles that vary between the extremes of superabundance and total failure. The cropping depends partly on the natural rhythm of the trees and partly on the weather. Most of the trees that make up the great frozen forests of Russia require more than one season to accumulate sufficient reserves for making fruit; however, those that live in high latitudes, where the growing season is short, crop at long intervals.

Spruce trees, for instance, produce large yields of seed every two to three years in central Europe, only every three to four years in southern Sweden, and even less frequently further north. The weather can modify these cycles because a good crop of seeds follows a fine, warm autumn the previous year when the buds form, and a good spring when the flowers set. In any one area – which may be thousands or millions of square kilometres in extent – the trees are usually 'in phase' with one another because they have all experienced the same conditions.

Feast or Famine

For the creatures that depend upon the seeds the situation in the forests oscillates between feast and famine. During good years, squirrels and other seed-eaters produce several large broods, and this leads to dense populations which cannot be sustained during subsequent years. When the number of animals far exceeds the carrying capacity of the seed crop (the number which the crop will support), many die or move away in search of better areas. Birds such as jays, Nutcrackers, Great Spotted Woodpeckers, Eurasian Nuthatches and the three species of crossbills are the first to flee from the taiga.

Occasionally, the 'irruptions' may be felt as far away as the British Isles, as Siberian seed-eaters fly west in desperation to find food. Such mass movements were once considered

The most impressive of all the birds of the taiga
is the Great Grey Owl.

to be suicidal, but scientific bird ringing (banding) has confirmed that some individuals eventually return to the taiga. Moreover, some of the emigrants discover places where conifers are seeding and nest there as long as the cone crop permits.

Squirrels are, of course, less mobile than birds but may nevertheless migrate in large numbers a year after the birds have flown. The Kamchatkan Peninsula was colonized by these mammals after one such population explosion. During the 1940s, they moved round from the north-eastern taiga via the treeless isthmus of the Parapol Valley into the Kamchatkan forests, where they had previously not existed.

The fruiting cycles of the trees have repercussions for the forest predators, such as Lynx, Red Foxes, martens and birds of prey, including owls. Their numbers alternately build up and crash in response to the fluctuating fortunes of their rodent prey.

The Deep Sleep

Hibernating is another method of making it through the winter. This usually involves a period of gluttonous eating and becoming fat, and then assuming a torpid state with a lowered body temperature as cold weather approaches. Hibernation has an advantage insofar as it drastically reduces the demand for food – perhaps to as little as 1 per cent – at a time when there is precious little of it around. Even so, different rodents, for instance, have different hibernation strategies, depending on their body size.

Siberian Chipmunks are small, striped, squirrels with less bushy tails than their arboreal cousins. They are widely distributed throughout the taiga. Being small, they are unable to store enough fat in their bodies to see them through the winter, so they make caches of seeds up to 3 kg (6½ lb) in weight inside underground chambers dug specially for the purpose next to their nests. Periodically, they rouse themselves from their sleep and nibble away at their provisions, before once again sinking into a state of suspended animation.

Susliks are ground squirrels that are a little larger than chipmunks; there are several species in the former USSR. That found in the Siberian taiga, the Long-tailed Siberian Suslik, must emerge from its hibernation every two weeks, not to feed but to urinate and so excrete the waste products of its metabolism, which ticks over just sufficiently to prevent it from freezing.

The Black-capped Marmot is about the size of a small rabbit. It is a relict from glacial times and now inhabits the alpine areas of the Yakutian and Kamchatkan mountains. It rates as one of the world's greatest sleepers, hibernating for between eight and nine months of each year. Before the long lie-in begins in mid September, each marmot is bloated with fat and weighs about 5 kg (11 lb). It then retires underground, perhaps huddling with up to eight members of its family group, and curls into a ball, its head tucked between its paws and tail furled over them. The body temperature sinks to 4–8°C (39–46°F) and can fall to just below freezing. Signs of life are not easy to detect in this deepest of sleepers. Its heart beats only every two or three minutes and it breathes only once every ten minutes. However, the flickering fire of life accumulates unwanted wastes and so, every three weeks, the marmot's

Peering round the trunk of a tree, a Siberian Chipmunk checks for
danger before scampering off in search of food.

metabolism quickens under hormonal control and the creature warms, wakes and urinates.

Even when it is hibernating so deeply, the marmot is not oblivious of its surroundings because if the temperature of its nest falls dangerously low, the animal will wake up to prevent itself from freezing to death. In May, the marmots emerge from their burrows a sleek 2.5 kg (5½ lb) and the females are pregnant, showing that they must engage in sexual romps during their brief interludes of wakefulness inside their chilly nests.

By contrast, the Russian Flying Squirrel does not hibernate at all. This attractive little animal is found throughout most of the great coniferous and mixed forest belt of northern Eurasia, from Finland to Japan. Its name is misleading, for it is a glider, and not capable of powered flight. It can extend a squirrel's leap into a 50 m (165 ft) glide, using the patagium, the thin membrane of skin that joins its wrists and ankles. It uses its flattened tail for steering

during its long, shallow descent. On touch-down, the membranes are folded up, allowing the little animal to scamper up the tree to its next take-off point without the risk of their becoming snagged on branches. The membranes also store fat to help the squirrel survive the long northern winter.

Turning to the other end of the mammalian size scale, Brown Bears are big enough to carry large amounts of fat and barely need to hibernate properly. During autumn, they gorge themselves on the fruits of the forest – the wild strawberries, bilberries and other delicious berries that ripen at this time of year. By the time winter arrives, they are corpulent and have settled down in dens located beneath fallen trees or in the shelter of rocks – or sometimes in open places in the forest, where they build a nestlike mound of moss and other vegetation. Here, they become drowsy and sleep away the cold months for 75-195 days, depending on the region.

The bears' slumber is not a true hibernation. While sleeping, their body temperature falls only slightly to 34°C (93°F), with a consequential saving on energy reserves. However, they are tolerably alert and, if woken, are capable of bursting out of their hiding place fit to fight or flee. Nevertheless, their body chemistry does change subtly. Somehow, it seems, they are able to suppress their protein metabolism. Normally, when these compounds are broken down, urea and other nitrogenous wastes are produced, and these need to be flushed out of the bloodstream by the kidneys. The change is not due simply to enforced starvation because bears prevented from feeding during the summer produce plenty of urea. But during the winter, a sleepy bear produces virtually none.

Like Polar Bears, female Brown Bears give birth to rat-sized cubs around Christmas when most of the dens are covered with a thick layer of snow. They both produce a single tiny offspring for the same reason. As bears cannot feed in the depths of winter, the cubs enter the world small enough so as not to tax the internal resources of their mothers, who have to suckle them for several months before they can go foraging.

How Forest Plants survive the Cold

Plants, too, must prepare themselves for the formidable Siberian winter. On the eastern seaboard of the taiga, the dwarf Japanese Stone Pines form an almost impenetrable mat of horizontal branches only a metre or so above the ground. This mat of flattened vegetation

A Russian Flying Squirrel begins a long glide that will carry it to the base of the next tree trunk. This is a shy, strictly nocturnal and almost entirely arboreal creature, so its dramatic leaps are rarely witnessed in the wild.

is called *stlanik*. The branches are so resinous that the low winter temperatures would freeze the sticky fluid and greatly damage the plants. As the temperature sinks to −3°C (26·6°F), the branches 'wilt' even further to hug the ground. When it snows, most of the dwarf pines become covered with an insulating blanket which protects them from freezing. Beneath the low, arching branches and the vaults of snow, mice, voles and lemmings continue to thrive on a diet of pine seeds and lichens. They may be followed there, however, by small predators, such as weasels, which mete out sudden death.

Ice formation within living tissues is also a killer. The crystals are sharp and disrupt the delicate membranes inside cells, causing death. The problem faced by plants is that they have no way of keeping warm, and so they are in danger of becoming lethally frozen. But conifers are superior to hardwood trees in limiting ice damage, especially in the water-conducting tissues – or *xylem* – inside their trunks.

In flowering plants, including broadleaved trees, water is transported from the roots to the leaves in long, tubular cells forming a pipelike plumbing system. Should the contents freeze, the 'pipes' are often subsequently blocked by bubbles after they thaw out, and are therefore rendered useless. The plants must, therefore, grow new water-conducting cells in spring before they can begin to function properly.

The plumbing of needle-leafed trees differs. Their xylem is composed of smaller individual cells called *tracheids* which pass water from one to another through microscopic perforations called 'bordered pits'. The advantage of this system is that air embolisms caused by ice can be locally contained without impairing the working of the xylem as a whole. This ability to function earlier than hardwoods may account for the competitive advantage of conifers in very frosty areas and explain their predominance in the taiga. But that is not the whole story.

Some plants prepare for the approach of winter by manufacturing sugars and alcohols which deter the formation of ice. They also actively pump water from their cells so that if ice crystals do form they do so in the spaces between the cell walls, where they cause comparatively little harm. The salts and other compounds remain inside the cell vacuole (the fluid-filled, membrane-bound space within the cell), lowering its freezing point. Frost resistance may also depend upon the physical properties of water.

Under certain circumstances, water can remain a liquid – that is, become supercooled – down to −39°C (−38°F). Supercooling may account for the survival of the shoots of hardy species such as Siberian Larch. However, should ice form in the bud scales, the process draws water from the living cells which makes them denser in salts and possibly in 'antifreeze' chemicals. In this state, the trees of the frozen forest can probably withstand temperatures down to −70°C (−94°F).

Supercooled Caterpillars

A similar process to that described for plants occurs in insects such as Siberian silk moths. The caterpillars feed on larch and take two years to mature. At the end of summer, they go underground, dehydrate and synthesize glycerol, a natural anti-freeze, and allow themselves to become supercooled to the ambient temperature of their surroundings. The adults of some butterflies such as Camberwell Beauties and Small Tortoiseshells tuck themselves into nooks and crannies and presumably survive freezing in the same way.

The caterpillars of the Black-veined White Butterfly shelter in the curled, dry leaves of hawthorns. They feed upon the foliage but, as summer draws to an end, each caterpillar attaches the leaf of its choice to a twig by strong silk from its silk glands. It then uses more silk to bind the edges of the leaf together so that they enclose it, hiding it from the prying eyes of hungry birds. Sometimes, several caterpillars create such a shelter within a single leaf, when they appear more conspicuous.

Keeping Warm

When winter arrives, it settles in with an uncompromising grip, especially in the region of the Verkhoyansk Mountains. The biting polar winds whistle across the taiga, whipping up blizzards that smother the landscape with snow. Glacial temperatures of below −50°C (−58°F) are often accompanied by suffocating, claustrophobia-inducing frozen fog that shields the ground from the mean warmth that issues from the sun at this time of year.

By February, an anti-cyclonic high-pressure cell becomes established over Siberia. Dawn is transformed into a magic time when the sun edges above the veils of mist in a lemon-yellow haze to reveal a dazzling white Disneyland of sculptured snowdrifts and sparkling snow crystals, glinting in the still, crisp air. Six hours later, the day is over, sometimes marked by a blaze of heavenly fire in the western sky. What little heat the sun radiates is immediately reflected into space by the glistening cover of snow and, at night, the absence of clouds does nothing to hinder the loss of yet more residual heat from the frozen land.

Nevertheless, Siberian people take all kinds of difficulties and discomforts in their stride. When it is really cold (−60°C (−76°F)), car engines are kept running continuously and most places of work close down; water is stored outside, next to the wood pile, as blocks

Although some Arctic Redpolls remain on the tundra all year, many
others wander south in winter to the taiga.

of ice. Exposed fingers numb within seconds, the nose freezes, and moisture in the breath
settles as a thick rime of hoar frost around the face. It is a marvel that any warm-blooded
creatures can remain active in this bitter cold. And yet many do.

Keeping warm is crucial. It is astonishing how birds such as Arctic Redpolls (North
American: Hoary Redpoll) and Siberian Tits manage to maintain the temperature of their
minute bodies at 41°C (106°F) in the bitter Siberian winter. Dense plumage is the key to
their success; one square mm ($\frac{1}{600}$ in) of skin supports 100 down feathers – the best insulation
in the animal kingdom. The feathers trap a layer of air next to the body; the colder it is,
the more the feathers are erected and the greater the thickness of insulation to keep the
icy air at bay.

When it becomes seriously cold, at below −30°C (−22°F), the birds reduce activity to
a minimum and become silent, barely flicking their wings, and sit hunched up for much
of the day like fluffy balls to conserve their energy. At still lower temperatures, they are
loath to leave their sheltered roosting places and huddle in groups for warmth. This saves
up to almost half of their energy consumption. At night, they allow their bodies to cool
down to about 38°C (100°F), and this conserves yet more fuel.

214

The luxuriant fur of the Sable, much sought after for high-fashion
garments, nearly proved the animal's downfall.

The Silky Sable

The intense cold of Siberia is responsible for the soft, thick pelt of many kinds of valuable fur-bearing animals that inhabit the taiga, such as Red Fox, Grey Wolf, Wolverine, European Mink, Stoat, Siberian Weasel, Least Weasel, Pine Marten and Beech Marten. But of all of those creatures enveloped in warm fur, the Sable has the most luxurious coat. It is a Russian speciality, virtually confined to the forests of Siberia and Kamchatka, and belongs to the group of carnivores called martens, a family of fierce super-ferrets.

Martens are medium-sized carnivores, elongated in shape, with furry feet and bushy tails. Most of them, like Pine Martens, are arboreal and catch squirrels with astonishing success. Although sables are perfectly competent climbers, they spend most of their time on the forest floor. Here, these wiry predators search out Northern Red-backed Voles, mice, and other small mammals with boundless energy, killing them by delivering furious bites to the back of their heads. They supplement their rodent diet with nestlings and eggs, slugs – which they are said to roll on the ground with their paws to remove the slime – fish scooped from streams, pine nuts, and honey from wild bees.

Sable fur varies from lustrous black to bright yellow, although brown is by far the most common colour. The animals are active throughout the winter months and are 'double wrapped' against the bitter cold. Unlike the smaller Stoats and weasels, which turn white in winter, and are then known as ermine, Sable retain their dark coloration, and moult into their thick coat during autumn in preparation for the cold months ahead. Next to the skin, the fur is soft and dense, trapping a layer of warm air, and this is overlain by long, lustrous guard hairs.

Since ancient times, people have prized the Sable's winter coats. In the past, as now, these have been a source of considerable commerce for Russia and were a major inducement for the exploration of Siberia. With the escalating demand, the price of the pelts spiralled upwards, and the population of Sable steadily declined until they had been eliminated from much of their range.

After the Russian revolution, hunting was controlled and conservation measures were taken to restore the valuable Sable to areas where it had formerly lived. Barguzin, an area of just over 2,590 sq km (1,000 sq miles) along the north-east shore of Lake Baikal, had already been declared a nature reserve in 1916 to protect Sable which had escaped the attentions of the fur-trappers.

Each Sable needs several square kilometres of spruce or pine forest to provide it with the necessary pool of prey. Within this area, the den is located – it is usually in a hollow stump, a hole in the ground, or an old squirrel's drey. During April or early May, the females give birth to between three and five blind and naked young, called kits. After a month or more, their eyes are open and their bodies fully clad in fine fur.

By midsummer, the mother Sable are ready to mate again. They engage in wanton affairs, copulating up to thirty times, during which they may remain intimately linked to their mates for 18 hours or so before returning to a solitary existence. The fertilized eggs delay embedding into the womb until the following winter, to give an apparent gestation period of 250–300 days. This ensures that the females are not burdened with families during the period of the year when food is scarcest. This phenomenon of delayed implantation is found in many other mammals, too, including weasels, badgers and seals.

Once the technique of persuading Sable to breed regularly in captivity had been developed, commercial production became feasible from about 1933. The first captive-bred animals were not sacrificed for their skins but were released into many suitable parts of Russia. By the middle of the twentieth century, Sable enjoyed the same status as they did three hundred years ago.

Sable are still big business. Many wild individuals are trapped or hunted during the winter. Before the snow becomes too deep, dogs are sometimes employed to track them down and send them up trees where they can be shot. However, the majority of the furs now come from animals kept in breeding farms. Today, one huge warehouse in Irkutsk handles 160,000 Sable furs annually. Most go abroad and eventually cloak wealthy women in New York and Tokyo.

The Biggest Deer

Other mammals, too, are exploited by humans in the Siberian forests. These include the Elk and the Maral. The Elk (North American: Moose) is the most common species of large mammal in the taiga. It is also the largest of all deer: a large bull can stand as high as 2.3 m ($7\frac{1}{2}$ ft) at the shoulders and weigh over 800 kg (over $\frac{3}{4}$ ton) and its massive flattened antlers can span as much as 2 m ($6\frac{1}{2}$ ft). Elk have long played an important role in feeding people in Siberia – there are many towns to this day that rely heavily on their meat, much of it supplied by poachers. Elk have also been domesticated in Russia for the production of meat and milk, and even for use as a draught animal on farms.

Another large deer is the Maral, the Siberian race of the Red Deer (*maral* is a Siberian word for 'deer'). Found in southern Siberia, Maral are related to the North American races of Red Deer (sometimes regarded as a separate species, called Wapiti or, confusingly, Elk). Stags grow up to 1.5 m (5 ft) high at the shoulders, weigh up to 460 kg (almost $\frac{1}{2}$ ton) and have antlers up to 1 m ($3\frac{1}{4}$ ft) long. The velvet (soft hairy skin, that covers the growing bone of the antlers and supplies it with food and oxygen via a rich supply of blood vessels) contains a substance called pantocrine, regarded in the Far East as a vital constituent of various medicines. There are many farms in the southern taiga where herds of semi-wild Maral are rounded up and herded into paddocks when the time comes to saw off their antlers and extract the pantocrine. Experienced deer breeders ensure good reproduction and hay and other food is supplied to the deer in winter, when they find it difficult to dig through the snow to reach vegetation.

Living Beneath the Snow

As in the Arctic, many creatures take advantage of the fact that it is warmer *underneath* the snow. The small mammals of the taiga, such as Northern Red-backed Voles and shrews, are incapable of generating sufficient warmth to survive on the frozen surface during the coldest periods. However, they need a reasonable depth of snow to insulate themselves from the worst of the frosts.

When there are only a few centimetres of snow cover, these little mammals scurry across the surface, leaving their tracks everywhere. However, when 15-20 cm (6-8 in) of snow has accumulated, their trails, along with the creatures that made them, disappear beneath the thick white blanket, which is sufficient to protect the little creatures from the effects of very low air temperatures. For this reason, they avoid the bowl-like depressions under trees where the ground cover is thin because the falling snow has clung to the branches above.

The voles and lemmings seek the spaces that often form between the ground and the base of the snow cover. In this relatively snug environment, it may be a comparatively warm −5°C (23°F). Here, the little mammals busily carry on eating, the rodents on plant food such as lichens and larch twigs, and the shrews on insects and other invertebrates, and providing the food supply holds out, life can carry on much as usual. However, it has its problems. The spaces beneath the snow are often warm enough to allow bacteria and fungi to continue their work of breaking down the vegetation. This results in the accumulation of noxious carbon dioxide. When this happens, the voles and lemmings excavate ventilation shafts to the surface from which they can poke their noses into the cold, refreshing air. For much of the year, voles tend to be rather intolerant of each other and stake out territories

A Willow Grouse in autumn plumage perches
in a willow tree in the taiga.

for themselves. But the winter's chill forces them to become more friendly towards each other, and they often huddle together for warmth in their nests, with a consequential energy saving of up to 40 per cent.

Rock Ptarmigan, Willow Grouse (North American: Willow Ptarmigan), Hazel Grouse, Siberian Spruce Grouse and Western and Black-billed Capercaillies also tunnel into the snow for shelter. Their burrows are inclined at a fairly shallow angle, sometimes with a couple of ventilation shafts, terminating in an enlarged living chamber set off to one side. When it is very cold – around −55°C (−67°F) – the birds may emerge to feed for only half an hour or so at dawn and dusk.

The fibre-rich winter diet of Willow Grouse – chiefly willow and birch twigs – requires special processing, and these birds possess an intestine evolved for the purpose. The tough wood passes straight through the gut and is excreted as dry droppings, usually inside the snow burrow, about once every fifteen minutes. However, the protein-rich part of the diet is shunted into blind alleys (diverticula) of the intestine where a workforce of microbes renders the material digestible and liberates the nourishment.

The need for young, protein-rich shoots is at the root of the Black-billed Capercaillie's remarkable 'gardening' behaviour. These birds concentrate their feeding in patches of larch forest, where their regular plucking of leading shoots stunts the trees into bushlike forms. This regular pruning by the birds causes a prolific growth of tender, fresh buds on which the capercaillies depend.

Throughout the course of the winter, the weight of accumulated snow may cause branches to sag, and this brings more of the foliage and the encrustation of lichens to within reach of animals such as Arctic Hares and various species of deer. Siberian Musk Deer, for example, can extend their reach by standing on their hind legs to browse 2 m (6½ ft) above ground level on the bowed branches.

Spring comes to the Frozen Forest

As the hours of daylight increase, the strength of the sun helps to banish the winter. One of the first birds to nest is the Siberian Jay. It lays its eggs during April when the temperature can still be only −30°C (−22°F) at night. They are incubated for 22–24 days by the female, who covers them tightly with her body because the embryos would quickly die if the eggs were exposed to the bitterly cold air. Her mate provides her with food during her vigil on the nest.

These wily birds gain a head start over other species in the race to breed so that they are able to take advantage of the insects and spiders that appear when the snow thaws during the early part of May. By the end of the month, when the young jays are fledging, other birds are just beginning to lay, and the young jays, which like their parents relish birds' eggs, can therefore benefit from this new source of food.

The spring snow-melt spreads northwards across the taiga. Suddenly moisture becomes available, and persuades buds to unfurl into foliage which glows green in the strong sunshine. Birds migrating from warm wintering quarters add their voices to those of the hardy Siberian residents. As the weather warms, the taiga can support large populations of insectivorous species. Some, such as Red-flanked Bluetails and Siberian Rubythroats, are exotic birds for western naturalists. Bluethroats range into the tundra, but those that settle in the northern Siberian taiga rear the largest families of all.

Several species of leaf warblers – Willow, Greenish, Yellow-browed, and Arctic – take up territories in various regions of the taiga; they are most easily distinguished from one another by the details of their songs. Berry and worm-eating thrushes add their flutelike notes to the spring chorus. Redwings and Fieldfares are the common species in the northern forests, but the variety increases towards the south where the woods are richer in berry-bearing plants. Here, Siberian, White's, and Naumann's Thrushes survive alongside the more familiar Blackbirds and Mistle Thrushes.

The spring awakening is helped along in the valleys by the huge rivers that flow northwards through them. It is warmer towards the south, and the surge of water from those regions helps to break up and flush out the ice. It also brings enough heat to warm the air and accelerate the growth of birches, alders and willows that grow along many of the river banks. In these valleys, there are some beautiful flowers, such as the orange Martagon Lily, the most northerly lily in the world, and *Chamaenerion angustifolium*, with its high, slender candles of rosy-violet blooms.

The Yenisei is one of the great rivers that flows through the taiga – indeed, it is among the longest of all rivers in the former Soviet Union. One of its tributaries, the Angara, acts as the overflow from Lake Baikal – one of the biological wonders of the world.

The Blue Eye of Siberia

Set in the southern taiga 1,500 km (930 miles) inland, Lake Baikal runs in a crescent, 636 km (400 miles) long and up to 80 km (50 miles) wide, amid the mountains on the north-eastern border of Central Asia. In typical romantic, poetic fashion, it has been called by the Russians 'the blue eye of Siberia'.

A view of the Brown Bear Coast at the Baikal nature reserve.

To the south of Baikal stretch the boundless Mongolian steppes. The indigenous people called Buryats, who have Buddhist leanings, revere it as a sacred sea. It is not difficult to understand why, because the lake and its surroundings have a serenity unsurpassed by any other place in the realms of the Russian bear. The air is often astonishingly transparent and the jagged, snow-capped peaks which form the backdrop to the lake are then perfectly mirrored in the cool, clear, waters. The mountains which skirt the western shore of the lake form the watershed between the Lena and Yenisei – two of the mightiest rivers in Asia, which ultimately deliver their water to the Arctic Ocean.

During the summer, the taiga around Baikal is decorated with an understorey of flamboyant mauve and purple rhododendrons and azaleas and scented honeysuckles. Later in the season, the first frosts of winter transform the tree canopies into a collage of vivid colours as stunning as the famous maples of New England. The slanting autumnal light picks out the silver-barked birches among the conifers around the edge and gives the lake

221

a unique enchantment. But Baikal is not just a beautiful place. It is in a class of its own among the world's lakes.

Lake Baikal sits in the biggest, steepest continental trough on the surface of our planet. The presence of hot water springs testifies to the fact that the fault in the Earth's crust is still active; indeed, it is widening the lake at the rate of 2 cm ($\frac{3}{4}$ in) a year. Although the surface of the lake is 455.6 m (1,495 ft) above sea level, in its great depth Baikal has no equal. The mountainous rim plunges so precipitously into the lake, that almost anywhere beyond a few kilometres from the shore, there is enough water to cover Ben Nevis, at 1,340 m (4,406 ft) the highest mountain in the British Isles.

The steepness of its sides has fortunately prevented the margins of the lake from becoming heavily settled by people. At its deepest, the muddy floor of the lake lies just over 1.6 km (1 mile) beneath the surface. At this bone-crushing depth, no sunlight penetrates and the temperature hardly varies from 4°C (39°F). And yet there are sponges, small crustaceans and bizarrely shaped fish living in these pitch-black waters. Furthermore, tracks in the soft mud also betray the presence of worms and molluscs on the lake bed. However, the surface of the sludge is merely the top of a great layer of sediment, perhaps as much as 5 km (3 miles) thick, accumulated over 26 million years of the lake's existence.

With a surface area of 31,500 sq km (12,160 sq miles), Baikal is the world's seventh largest lake by area but, because of its huge depth, it easily rates as the greatest volume of freshwater in the world. Indeed, its 22,900 cu km (5,500 cu miles) is reckoned to contain about one-fifth of the world's total stock of freshwater. If the lake could miraculously be drained and all of the rivers in the world be re-routed to empty into the vast rift, it would take a whole year to fill up. In purely practical terms, Baikal could supply humanity's need for drinking water for nearly half a century.

This huge lake is naturally replenished by summer rain and by some 336 streams and rivers that tumble down the surrounding mountains, and bring nourishment from the taiga in the form of pollen and decaying vegetation. However, only two of this multitude of rivers are of any great size. Half of the 60 cu km ($14\frac{1}{2}$ cu miles) of water added to the lake each year is carried by the Selenga, a large river which has its origins 1,480 km (920 miles) away in the Khingan Range in Mongolia and flows into the east side of the lake.

The sediment carried by this river has produced a delta 40 km (25 miles) across. It is one of the few shallow situations in the region where wildfowl and other water birds can dive and dabble, and herons can stalk their prey. During the summer, it is a haven for rare Asiatic Dowitchers, snipelike waders (North American: shorebirds) with warm brown

Lichens flourish among autumn leaves in the taiga surrounding Lake Baikal.
Over 5,000 species of lichens occur in the former Soviet Union.

plumage and long beaks, while graceful White-winged Black Terns build their floating nests among its reed-fringed lagoons. During August and September, the marshes are an important refuge for thousands of wildfowl which have nested to the north and are travelling south for the winter.

Only one river flows out of Lake Baikal. This is the Angara, which exits at the extreme south-western corner. It is a powerful river up to 1 km ($\frac{2}{3}$ mile) wide, which cuts through the Primorsky Range. After 1,853 km (1,151 miles), it merges with the 4,130 km (2,565 mile) long Yenisei River to form the longest river system in the former Soviet Union and one of the longest in the world.

One of the marvels of Lake Baikal is that its slightly alkaline water is inherently very pure and exceptionally well oxygenated. Indeed, during the summer, the surface waters are often supersaturated with oxygen because of the photosynthetic activity of phytoplankton.

Gales blast across the lake, often without warning, whipping the surface into angry, foaming crests which gleam in the sun. Although the storms are a serious and even life-threatening hazard to the Baikal fishermen, they have their beneficial side, too. The turbulence they create, especially during the autumn months, churns up the waters of the lake, transporting oxygen far into the depths, where it may reach a level of 80 per cent saturation.

Threats to Lake Baikal

Unfortunately, the purity of this great lake is currently imperilled. Many of its original problems stemmed from the lumber industry, set up to exploit the seemingly inexhaustible supply of timber in the neighbouring taiga. Without the protective grip of trees on the soil, much silt was carried into the lake from areas cleared of forest, and a huge tonnage of sunken wood clogged the rivers and spoilt places used by fish for spawning. Furthermore, bacteria feeding on the rotting timber built up in Baikal, depriving parts of it of oxygen.

The air and water pollution from this wood pulp mill at Baikalsk, on the southern side of Lake Baikal, is one of the chief threats to the lake.

But effluents are the most insidious threat to Baikal's purity. Over 100 factories are now situated by the side of the lake. Every year, they dump millions of tonnes of filthy material, including poisonous heavy metals, into the lake's crystal waters. The most notorious sources of pollution are two pulp and cellulose mills, one on the southern shore at Baikalsk, and the other on the Selenga River. Farms around the lake also foul it with agrochemicals and slurry. The Selenga itself is also a major source of pollution, bringing effluent from Mongolia and Ulan Ude, the capital of the Buryat Autonomous Republic. The city annually adds partially treated sewage containing 635 tonnes (625 tons) of nitrates to the Selenga. So far, the desecration seems to be local, but if the growing international campaign to protect the lake comes to nothing, Baikal's beauty will be tarnished forever.

Solid Ice and Swarming Caddis

Because of its great mass of water, Lake Baikal substantially modifies the local climate, making it less warm during the early summer, and conversely less cold during the early part of the winter. As it is so deep, the lake takes time to cool down and does not freeze over until the first half of January. At first, the ice is as transparent as glass and anyone standing on it can see into the crystal depths. As it thickens, the ice becomes more opaque, and by the end of February, it reaches 80-120 cm (about a yard) thick, sufficient to bear the weight of cars and heavy lorries which can then use the lake as a thoroughfare – arguably the best in Russia! In the early days of the Trans-Siberian Railway, the trains crossed Lake Baikal in winter via a single track laid across the ice.

Then, at the beginning of May, the frozen surface begins to break up in a symphony of sound, starting at the southern end of the lake. As the great slabs of ice fracture and fragment, the wind and water shunt them into hummocks, and the friction between adjacent plates makes them squeak and groan. The breaking up of the ice is the cue for one of the lake's most remarkable zoological phenomena.

From between the cracks in the pressure ridges close to the shore emerge small, black insects. These are the immature stages of a caddis fly called *Radema*, the first of a succession of species to appear. At this freezing temperature, most cold-blooded creatures would be utterly immobile, but this insect has evolved a cellular chemistry capable of operating within such a chill environment. After casting off their pupal skins, the caddis clamber over the ice towards the land and inflate their tightly folded wings. As the ice thaws, it releases many dead, frozen pupae which failed to reach the surface. Together with the living individuals, these are greedily devoured by dapper little Citrine and White Wagtails.

Above: Winter locks Lake Baikal in its icy grip, with spectacular icicles
forming a curtain along the overhanging rocks.
Opposite: Caddis flies swarm in dense clouds on a Baikal shoreline.

Baikalian caddis flies have extended larval lives due to the cold environment in which they live. When they eventually metamorphose into adults, they resemble moths, with rather large membranous wings covered with hairs rather than scales. Their existence as adults is brief; they are not built for feeding, since their mouthparts are poorly developed, and their sole purpose is to perpetuate their kind. After mating, the females lay their eggs very close to the shore – the only part of the lake where it is comparatively shallow and suitable for the aquatic larvae.

Many species of caddis flies have evolved in Lake Baikal, including some very unusual ones. At the beginning of June, before the ice has disappeared, stretches of the shore teem with the adults of *Thamastes dipterus* and *Baicalina reducta*. They make no attempt to fly but skitter about on the surface like pond skaters. The hind wings are rudimentary and the

middle pair of legs are modified for swimming. Both the wings and the body are covered with water-repellent hairs to help the insects from sinking through the water film.

The flightless caddis swim ashore at dusk and shelter in the lee of rocks and pieces of driftwood, appearing like a black scum. At dawn, they take to the water again and mate on the surface. Sometimes, these insects can be present in such numbers that, by day, it appears as though the inshore waters are covered with an oil slick. The loss of flight in these species may have been evolved because, over the years, those that flew very actively may have been blown out into the centre of the lake where it is too deep for larval caddis to survive, and hence flying adults died out.

The most spectacular mass emergence of caddis occurs at the beginning of June, and includes a large species called *Baicalina bellicosa*. The branches of the larches often turn black with seething masses of the adults. On calm days, the pupae rise to the surface, float about for some time and then change into adults. In the evening the air over the shore is filled with a myriad of these insects, but at the slightest hint of wind, they drop to the ground and smother the stones and driftwood, where they form a tasty and nutritious snack for shorebound animals.

The swarming hordes of caddis entice Brown Bears out of the woods. After waking up, they forage around in the forest looking for freshly germinated herbs and berries that have survived the winter, and pine nuts left over from caches made by chipmunks. Now, the caddis flies give them a welcome bonus of insect protein. During the evenings, the bears – many of them females with small cubs in attendance – wander along the water's edge, deftly turning over stones with their great forepaws and quickly licking up the insects clinging to them. When they have eaten their fill, the sated bears shuffle off into the forest until the following day.

A Unique Fauna

Baikal is one of the biological wonders of the world, with about 1,800 species of animals living in it, of which no less than 1,200 are exclusive to the lake. Many of them, such as the caddis flies which need several seasons to mature in the cool water, are adapted to the bitter cold of Siberia. Forests of freshwater sponges flourish in Baikal like nowhere else in the world. Some grow like fingers, others like vases and Greek amphorae. Giant flatworms, or planarians, glide over the bottom at moderate depths. Elsewhere, most planarians reach a maximum length of only 1–2 cm ($\frac{1}{2}$–$\frac{3}{4}$ in) but in Baikal, one unique species grows to nearly half a metre (over $1\frac{1}{2}$ ft) long.

The reason for Baikal's singular fauna lies partly in both its long history and its great size. Lakes tend to be ephemeral features, at least on a geological time-scale, and so the animals and plants that live in them do not usually have enough time to evolve their own unique characteristics. However, Lake Baikal is exceptional. It has existed for at least 25 million years, making it the oldest lake in the world.

Lake Baikal contains a wealth of endemic animals, including these golden crustaceans, seen here on a vivid green sponge.

Many of Baikal's original inhabitants, such as the ancestors of the sponges and the bristleworm *Manayunka baicalensis*, came from the ancient northern ocean which extended southwards into the heart of Siberia. Some, including some primitive crustaceans that still live in Baikal, have barely changed in all that time. For them, this great lake has been a refuge, protecting them from the cut and thrust of outside competition.

The antiquity of Baikal is not the only reason for its unique aquatic animals. After the sea had retreated, the basin in which the lake sat was quite shallow. But as it deepened (and has continued to deepen to this day) and the volume of water has increased, so the average temperature of the lake fell to such an extent that its coolness acted as a deterrent to settlement by many animals that were swept in by the rivers and streams, or blown in from the surrounding taiga.

Those that did manage to settle evolved a tolerance to the low temperatures. They were then unable to invade neighbouring lakes which were shallow enough to warm up significantly in the short, hot Siberian summers. Within various animal groups, such as caddis flies, molluscs, gammarid shrimps and cottid fish, the crucible of evolution has worked its creative magic, and resulted in a diversity of unique forms.

Remarkable Crustaceans

The crustaceans of Lake Baikal are especially interesting. Bathynellids, small, virtually transparent planktonic creatures, are living fossils. Although related to shrimps, these primitive animals have wormlike bodies with tiny appendages and swim at great depths.

Gammarid shrimps are particularly well represented in Lake Baikal. These laterally flattened crustaceans have evolved there into a large number of species of diverse shapes

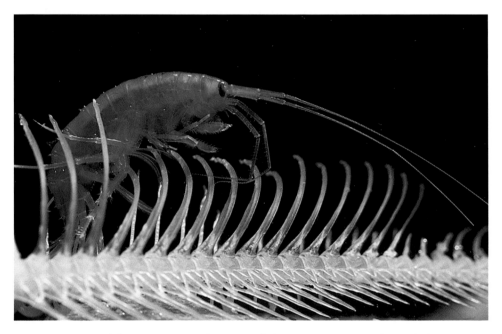

One of the 255 species of gammarid shrimps unique to Lake Baikal
scavenges the last morsels of flesh from the skeleton of a dead fish.

and sizes – one-third of all known species live there and nowhere else. Some, such as *Acanthogammarus maximus* at 7 cm ($2\frac{3}{4}$ in) long, are big and ponderous, and bear a resemblance to the armoured gammarids that crawl around on the sea-bed in Antarctica. Others are decorated with cutaneous outgrowths that give them a positively antediluvian appearance.

Certain gammarid species, such as *Macrohectopus branckii*, have taken to a pelagic way of life in which they consume plankton, and have evolved a more orthodox shrimplike structure, with long legs and antennae. Gammarids have even penetrated Baikal's great abyss. The species that live there are very pale, with red or pink eyes, and possess long sensory antennae for reaching out into the black void of the deep.

Gammarid shrimps occasionally occur in astronomical numbers – as many as 30,000 per sq m (25,200 per sq yd). They graze upon weeds and decaying matter. One rather strange species is called 'the Baikal Horse'. It is barely the size of a grain of rice and lives on the stony lake bed close to the shore. When observed with the aid of a lens, this little crustacean can be seen grasping a pair of stones in its middle and hind legs which are modified for the purpose. Exactly why it should do this is a mystery. Perhaps the habit makes it look unappetizing to fish.

Other gammarids are predators and are in turn feasted upon by fish such as graylings and Omul. This is particularly true, too, of another type of crustacean called *Epischura baicalensis*. This tiny species is important in the lake's web of life because it is the chief consumer of plankton and bacteria. During August, the upper layer of the lake is full of *Epischura*, which are avidly devoured by the pelagic fish.

A Variety of Fish

Baikal boasts over fifty species of fish, some of which are very special to the lake. By far the most fascinating are the cottids, or bullheads. With but little competition, they have diversified into over twenty-five different species, probably from a single stock of ancestral marine fish, and become physiologically attuned to Baikal's fresh water.

One of the most easily seen and prettiest is the Yellow-winged Cottid, appropriately named because the males possess enormously developed pectoral fins which are saffron yellow during the summer courtship period, giving them the appearance of exotic but-terflies. At this time, they swim in shoals into the shallow water at the edge of the lake where it is warmest and set up territories among the sponges. Each male has a stone shelter and attempts to lure a drably marked female or two inside to lay their eggs. If he is successful, he guards the clutch until the pin-headed fry appear. His job completed, he then disappears into deeper water and dies.

Other kinds of fish inhabit the abyssal depths. A fish called the Golomyanka is one of two related species unique to Baikal. It is the commonest of all the lake's fishes. The Golomyanka grows to about 25 cm (10 in) in length and is translucent and scaleless. Although the ventral fins are absent, the pectoral fins are very long – reaching half the length of the body.

Like deep-sea fish, Golomyanka are adapted to survive in the near-freezing, dark

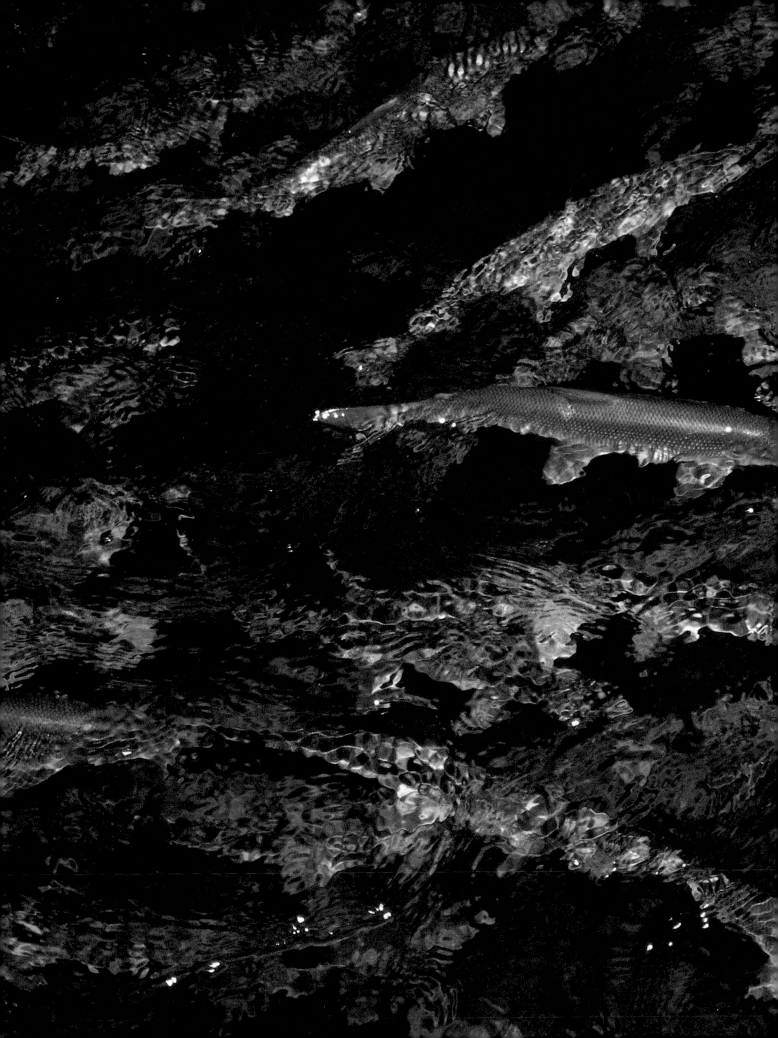

time of the year to whelp, perhaps betraying their Arctic ancestry. Between the end of February and the beginning of April, the females pop up through gaps in the pressure ridges and give birth beneath igloos of drifted snow or ice, so that the newborn pups are protected to some extent from the bitter winds.

Just after they have given birth, the females are ready to mate beneath the ice. The mothers maintain bolt-holes into the water should danger threaten from marauding wolves – or humans. Up to 6,000 seals, both adults and fleecy young, are slaughtered each year mainly for their skins. The hunt is part of the Buryat tradition, although nowadays settlers from other parts of the former Soviet Union join in. The seals are captured by nets placed across their breathing holes, and shot by white-clothed hunters who stalk them using boats and special sledges equipped with white screens to camouflage both the sledges and the hunters. Dogs are also employed to sniff out the ice caves where the pups cower.

By the time the ice starts to disperse, the pups are able to take to the water and learn to sustain themselves on cottids and Golomyanka. Not long afterwards, the seals start their moult and retire to traditional boulder-strewn beaches, where they doze and groom for much of the day. One such rookery is on the Ushkani Islands, where up to 4,000 of these appealing little mammals spend much of the summer.

Deer with a Price on their Bellies

In the forests that surround Lake Baikal lives another Russian speciality – Siberian Musk Deer. Musk deer are primarily forest animals, and three species range across the Himalayas, East Asia and southern Siberia. The Siberian Musk Deer is the largest, the bucks being about the size of a Labrador dog.

Every mature male carries a fortune in musk within a pouch beneath its belly. Unfortunately, this has been their downfall because the musk, a pungent, red jelly, is used not only as a base for expensive perfumes, but is also employed in the Far East as an elixir to cure all manner of ailments, both real and imagined.

With musk occasionally fetching more than its weight in gold, the demand has resulted in the relentless hunting of these diminutive deer. Each year, 320 kg (700 lb) of musk reaches the world markets, mainly in Japan, where it sells for as much as $64,000 a kilo ($28,800 a pound). This represents the deaths of nearly 13,000 musk deer. It is little wonder that these animals are now comparatively rare over much of their range.

Musk deer are unusual because the bucks do not grow antlers, but instead are equipped with a set of sabrelike tusks which gives them a rather doleful countenance. Zoologists

believe that they represent the kind of ancestral stock from which the more familiar antlered deer evolved. These stocky little animals are built for bounding, using their longer hind-legs for leaping along through the undergrowth like bouncing balls. Thanks to their well developed lateral toes, musk deer can also cross snowfields and climb trees and rock faces if forced to.

Siberian Musk Deer live in the more southerly parts of the taiga, often keeping to steeper areas which are comparatively free of snow during winter. At this time of year, they scrape away the snow to reveal the vegetation upon which they depend for their survival, and if the cover is too deep, they resort to mounting inclined trees to reach the foliage. During summer, they move into the valleys to graze.

Unlike most deer, musk deer are rarely seen in groups, but disperse themselves in widely spaced home ranges. Each territory is about 2.6 sq km (1 sq mile) in area, traversed by well-worn trails which connect the feeding locations with the resting places and toilets. These latrines are often quite large, despite the fact that the deer attempt to cover up their droppings by scraping soil over them. The animals distribute their own personal body odour throughout their territories by smearing an oily scent from their anal glands onto trees and twigs. The bucks' musk may serve to excite the females during the rutting season.

Breeding starts in November in the frozen forest and lasts for about a month. At this time, the bucks become very quarrelsome, chasing each other and occasionally fighting, their long canine teeth often inflicting serious wounds from which the vanquished animal will not recover. Courtship, too, is a far from gentle affair, the dominant bucks harrying the does into submission. If mating is successful, the dappled fawns appear in April and May, to coincide with the flush of tender spring vegetation.

One of the first naturalists to explore the taiga and Lake Baikal was Georg Wilhelm Steller, a Prussian doctor and a member of the Imperial Academy of Sciences. In 1739, Steller and some companions embarked on a voyage up Lake Baikal, where they discovered some of the remarkable gammarid shrimps, noted the seals, or 'sea dogs' as he called them, and described many plants new to science. However, his visit to this enchanting lake was ancillary to Steller's main purpose, which was to reach Kamchatka in the Russian far east, and enlist on Vitus Bering's second expedition to the New World.

Amid the deep snows of the Altai region of southern Siberia, a male
Siberian Musk Deer stretches up on his hind legs to nibble at lichens
growing on the slender branches of a tree.

CHAPTER SEVEN

THE FAR EAST
OF RUSSIA–
BORN OF FIRE

ALF A WORLD away from Europe and North America, on Russia's eastern flank, are some of the world's most dramatic landscapes. This is a region of contrasts, firmly under the chilling influence of the Arctic at its northern end and, in summer, blessed by the monsoonal lushness of South-east Asia at its other extremity. Much of this remote terrain was conceived by the forces that expanded and are still expanding the Pacific Ocean; these spewed forth fire and magma from the belly of the earth, and built ranks of rugged mountains along the edge of Asia. Some, such as the Kolyma and Sikhote-Alin mountains, are the eroded ramparts erected along an ancient line of volcanism. But on Kamchatka, the great peninsula which hangs from the eastern tip of Siberia, the process continues apace, with young and boisterous volcanoes which are among the most active in the world.

Kamchatka is a 1,200 km (745 mile) long wilderness, containing no less than thirty-three smouldering volcanoes, innumerable tumbling streams, and large expanses of swampy tundra. Although it has almost the same area as Japan, only 250,000 people inhabit the region and most are located around the capital, Petropavlovsk-Kamchatsky. Its remoteness is enhanced by the Sea of Okhotsk which isolates the peninsula from the Asian mainland.

To the south, the Kuril Islands descend south-westwards, like stepping stones, all the way to Japan. The jagged east coast faces the Pacific, but here, the ocean is rarely as calm as its name suggests. For days on end, the alchemy between sea and air generates swirling

In winter, great plumes of steam issue hundreds of metres into the air
from the gaping crater of the snow-covered Mytnovsky volcano, one
of the thirty-three active cones on the Kamchatkan peninsula that
form part of the great Pacific 'ring of fire'.

fogs and layers of low cloud, bestowing upon Kamchatka one of the gloomiest of climates. During the extended winter, Arctic storms buffet the land and smother it with snow; even the warmth of summer does little to disperse the constant mists and drizzle until August and September, which are marginally the finest months of the year.

The Ring of Fire

The rocky foundations of the Kamchatkan peninsula are at least 600 million years old, but much of what can be seen on the surface is the result of recent intense phases of volcanic activity. Both Kamchatka and the Kuril Islands form a part of the 'ring of fire' – the chain of volcanoes that encircles the Pacific. The section between Kamchatka and Japan is particularly vigorous and includes seventy active cones, which constitute 12 per cent of all terrestrial volcanoes; these are responsible for betweeen 16 and 18 per cent of the world's annual volcanic emissions.

The underlying cause of the volcanism is the slow-paced movement of tectonic plates – enormous segments of the earth's thin crust. In the process known as continental drift, these plates are driven by powerful convective forces within the molten mantle of the planet, generating earthquakes and volcanoes in the zones where they meet and grind against each other.

The boundary between the Eurasian and Pacific plates runs down the spine of Kamchatka and continues south, all the way to New Zealand via the Kuril Islands and Japan. Each year, the huge Pacific plate moves several centimetres in a north-westerly direction, and where it collides with the Eurasian landmass, its leading edge is driven obliquely downwards at an angle of about 50 degrees beneath the continental plate, producing a deep submarine canyon – the Kuril Trench – and a line of undersea volcanoes. The descending plate also generates tremendous friction, causing some of the material to melt. This molten magma rises along the fault line, and erupts onto the surface as volcanoes.

The most spectacular volcanism of Kamchatka – second only to Java's – can be traced to a 'hot spot' beneath the peninsula. This is where the Kamchatka-Kuril Fault intersects the fault that underlies the Aleutian Islands. The latter follows the curve of the Aleutian Islands westwards across the Pacific Ocean towards Asia. At the intersection of the two faults, beneath the very centre of Kamchatka, lies an impressive cluster of young and very active volcanoes. Twelve great cones rise from a plateau of ash and larva so resembling the surface of the moon that it was used for testing the Soviet lunar vehicles or *lunokhods*.

Collectively known as the Klyuchevskaya Complex, most of the volcanoes are tall enough to dwarf Vesuvius (1,277 m/4,190 ft), Etna (3,323 m/10,902 ft) and Fujiyama (3,776 m/12,389 ft) – the world's best known volcanoes. Indeed, three of the Klyuchevskaya volcanoes are over 4,000 m (13,123 ft) high – Blizhny Plosky (4,030 m/13,222 ft), Kaman (4,617 m/15,148 ft), and Klyuchevskaya Sopka, the highest volcano in Eurasia. This magnificent volcano is no more than 7,000 years old, so it has reached its 4,750 m (15,584 ft) since the days when the first pyramids were built in the fifth millennium BC.

Like many of Kamchatka's volcanoes, the snow-covered cones of Klyuchevskaya Sopka rise with exquisite symmetry, and, in clear conditions, can be seen 130 km (81 miles) away. There are over fifty secondary fissures and craters on Klyuchevskaya Sopka's slopes, but most of the major eruptions take place from the summit, and with great frequency. Since records began in 1697, this mighty volcano has erupted over seventy times – the last in 1990 – making it second only to Etna as the most active volcano in the world.

Many of the Klyuchevskaya Complex eruptions are comparatively gentle outpourings of liquid lava or fountains of ash and smoke, but some have been cataclysmic explosions. In 1907, Shtubelya, a small volcano, awakened with great vigour and produced so much ash that visibility to the north was reduced to just a few metres. When the debris settled on the snow, sledge travel across much of the Kamchatkan peninsula was prevented by the layer of sharp grit.

An eruption comparable in violence to the famous 1980 eruption of Mount St Helens in Washington State, USA, took place on Kamchatka in 1956, when Bezymianny, one of the Klyuchevskaya group, exploded. This was a little known volcano – Bezymianny means 'no name'. Long considered to be extinct, the 3,102 m (10,177 ft) high conical peak started generating earth tremors of increasing severity in September 1955, and then erupted on 22 October. For several months, there was intermittent volcanic activity, which died down somewhat by early 1956. Then, on 30 March 1956, there was a colossal explosion that blasted away the top 200 m (660 ft) of the mountain, and projected some 4 cu km (1 cu mile) of black cinders at a speed of about 500 m per second (1,640 ft per second) up to 38 km (24 miles) high into the stratosphere; lightning flickered and deafening cracks of thunder rumbled around the billowing clouds.

Such was the scale of the blast that bushes and trees situated 25–30 km (15–19 miles) away from the volcano were stripped of their foliage; at twice this distance, huge rocks fell like bombs from the sky and the pall of glowing ash turned night into day. The eruption was accompanied by a glowing avalanche of incandescent ash and scalding gas that roared down the volcano's slopes at hurricane speed, and smothered the landscape for many

and the men were weakened by scurvy, the plague of mariners at that time. A short stop to revictual the ship at the Shumagin Islands, at the westerly tip of Alaska, did little to help as contaminated water was taken aboard, and many of the crew subsequently died. On 4 November, land loomed out of the stormy seas, but the rejoicing soon ceased when Bering realized that this was not Kamchatka, but an uncharted island well to the east of Siberia that is now known as Bering Island, one of the Komandor group.

With most of his remaining crew incapacitated, Bering decided to settle on the island for the winter, and he miraculously managed to manoeuvre his stricken ship over the rocky reefs into a sheltered bay, allowing the few able-bodied crew to go ashore. But disaster struck again a few weeks later, when the ship was smashed by gale force winds. Exhausted by his endeavour and dispirited by this turn of events, Bering's health steadily declined. He was ravaged by scurvy, complicated by other diseases, and he eventually died on 8 December. His two surviving officers were too ill to take command, and so Steller himself assumed the responsibility for leadership.

Although uninhabited by people, Bering Island was well provisioned with creatures suited to the needs of half-starved castaways. Even in the depths of winter, many marine mammals swam in the coastal waters; there were large numbers of Sea Otters bobbing and diving among the kelp beds, and sea lions, too, to which Steller gave his name; whales occasionally became stranded, providing the shipwrecked sailors with a surfeit of meat and blubber. As the business of survival became less pressing, Steller turned his attention to the natural history of the island, and discovered creatures new to science.

A Wealth of New Animals

The most remarkable of Steller's finds was a monstrous sea cow that lived by browsing on the great beds of kelp that flourished along the shore. This sea mammal had a superficial resemblance to a seal, but was furnished with tail flukes like its only surviving relatives, the three species of manatees and single species of dugong, which are confined to the tropics. The sea cow, dugong and manatees are grouped in the Order Sirenia and are collectively known as sirenians. Their nearest relatives are, surprisingly, the elephants, with which they share a common ancestor. They are the only mammals that are fully aquatic herbivores.

The sea cows of Bering Island were colossal, growing to at least 8 m (26 ft) long and weighing 6 tonnes (5.9 tons) — many times larger than their tropical cousins. Sadly, Steller was the only trained naturalist ever to watch these great, wrinkled sirenians in action, so his observations are especially poignant. He noted that they were so fat and buoyant that much of their body appeared to float above the surface. Feeding was their chief preoccupation, the animals making their way across the beds of giant seaweed, tearing the fronds from the rocks with their feet and chewing them ceaselessly. This they did with much snorting 'after the manner of horses'. To assist them with feeding on the slippery kelp, their large lips were furnished with strong bristles, those on the lower jaw being like the quills of 'fowls'. They had no teeth. The skin was remarkably thick as well as creased and, according to Steller, resembled 'the bark of an old oak'. For those of such large beasts, the eyes were small, and they were lidless. The external ear openings were hidden among the grooves of skin.

Like cattle, sea cows were sociable, the members of both sexes and their young living in herds. Predictably, these great placid creatures were valued as floating supplies of meat by the Russians. Steller reported that an adult would yield 3 tonnes (3 tons) of fat and of flesh, which tasted rather like beef.

Steller's Sea Cow did not long survive its discovery by the man whose name it came to bear. Steller was not privy to what we now know from the evidence of fossils, namely that two million years ago, the species was widely dispersed around the northern shores of the Pacific, from Japan to Mexico. However, the sea cows' gentle disposition made the herds extremely vulnerable to human hunters who slowly but surely exterminated them in prehistoric times. The sea cow population that Steller chanced upon in 1741 had been isolated on its island refuge from the harsh realities of the world at large. But that was to change for the last 1,500 or so animals that survived on Bering Island. Steller and his companions sowed the seeds of the sea cow's destruction.

Over the next twenty-five years, Bering Island became the ideal port of call for the early Russian hunters to kill and butcher sea cows for the ships' larders. Despite their bulk, the great beasts were utterly defenceless, and when one animal was attacked, its companions mustered around it instead of fleeing, so exposing themselves to the hunters' deadly harpoons. In 1755, a Russian geologist visited the island and, realizing the perilous state of the sea cow population, petitioned the Kamchatkan authorities to pass a law protecting the species. Tragically, though, no action was taken and by 1768 the last Steller's Sea Cow had been slaughtered.

On Bering Island, Steller also discovered a new species of cormorant. It was a big bird, the size of a goose, with rather stubby wings that rendered it virtually flightless. The plumage on its body was bottle green with a metallic sheen, and it had bronze wing feathers. The males sported a jaunty double crest decorated with long, pale yellow wisps of hairlike feathers hanging down the neck. There were white markings around the eyes reminiscent of spectacles, from which the species acquired its name, Spectacled Cormorant.

The Spectacled Cormorants met the same fate as Steller's Sea Cow. Steller noted that the flesh of one of these plump seabirds would satisfy the hunger of three men. At the time of his enforced stay on Bering Island, they were numerous and were later found living on the neighbouring island of Medny. Over the course of the next century, the birds were systematically hunted to extinction by visiting sealers and indigenous Aleuts. Their confiding nature and their inability to move fast on land did nothing to help these seabirds elude their human pursuers, and by about 1850, the species was gone forever.

As spring came to Bering Island, the place was enlivened by the arrival of huge numbers of seabirds. Guillemots (North American: murres) and Black-legged Kittiwakes settled on

The smallest of the eiders, Steller's Eider breeds on the tundra of
north-eastern Siberia and winters mainly in the southern Bering Sea.

the cliffs, while Black Guillemots fluttered around the rocky shores displaying their vermilion legs and white forewings. Skeins of geese wove patterns in the sky and bayed like packs of hounds as they swept overhead towards their Arctic nesting grounds. Ducks joined in the throng, especially dramatic looking eiders which bobbed in immense rafts just out to sea. The drakes of one species of sea-duck were black and white above, with a largely white head, but 'stained' reddish orange underneath as though they had skidded through mud. Later, in 1769, Pallas christened this new species Steller's Eider. In contrast to the Spectacled Cormorants, Steller's Eiders still thrive around Bering Island as well as along the coasts of eastern Siberia and Alaska.

During the second half of May, the resident coastal sea lions gathered on the beaches of Bering Island to breed, and a month later, the ocean-going fur seals arrived *en masse*. The great breeding colonies, or rookeries, of these two seal species throbbed with the deafening chorus of bleating babies, whinnying mothers and roaring males. Steller noted that the places where they assembled were so crowded that it was impossible to pass through the undulating mass of bodies without endangering life and limb. These great rookeries had never been disturbed and so Steller had the privilege of studying them in their primeval condition, unsullied by humans. His observations have never been bettered.

Steller's Sea Lions and the Northern Fur Seal, as they became known, share many characteristics. Both belong to the family of 'eared' seals, which are more closely related to the walrus than to the 'true' seals like the Harp, Caspian and Baikal Seals. The males are much heavier than their mates, with heavy, scruffy manes, which tend to exaggerate

A top male, or 'beachmaster', is surrounded by females at this colony of
Northern Fur Seals. Each female is only about one-fifth of his weight.

the size differences. The biggest, most dominant and aggressive males, called beachmasters, mate with the most females. At about 250 kg (550 lb), full-grown bull Northern Fur Seals are five times the weight of the lithe-bodied females — a sexual disparity in size rivalled among mammals only by the Southern Elephant Seal.

Steller's Sea Lion is the larger of the two species, and the beachmasters are gross, weighing over a tonne. Sexual competition has resulted in the evolution of these big, bullying males. They are the first to arrive at the rookeries and fight each other for the possession of a stretch of shore suitable for holding a harem of females. When the cows emerge from the sea ready to give birth and mate, the competition becomes intense as the beachmasters try to herd and retain the new arrivals on their own pieces of beach, while fending off the attentions of neighbouring bulls. The advantage of size, strength, and stamina for a beachmaster is self-apparent during the bloody battles, and triumph in these engagements is rewarded by success in fathering more of the next season's pups than the vanquished males.

As in Steller's day, both these seal species occur today around the northern region of the Pacific, although their numbers have been greatly reduced since the naturalist-explorer studied them. The Northern Fur Seal suffered greatly at the hands of seal hunters, and its magnificent rookeries were decimated. The largest population was in the Pribilof Islands, now part of Alaska, USA: in 1870, it was estimated to stand at 4.5 million, but by 1914 it had been reduced to only 200,000 animals.

In 1911 Russia became a signatory to an international agreement to restore the fortunes of the fur seals. Today, there are about 1.3 million in the Pribilofs and a further 350,000 or so are based on Russian territory, chiefly where Steller found them, in the Komandor Islands. For instance, there are four rookeries on Medny Island, the outermost island of the Komandor group, which total 40,000 adults, and these produce 20,000 pups every year. Other populations of Northern Fur Seals breed in the Sea of Okhotsk and in the Kuril Islands, and most of them winter off the coast of Japan.

Steller's Sea Lions are scarcer than fur seals, and at present are suffering from a catastrophic failure in their breeding success. About 250,000 are scattered in rookeries in the Kuril Islands, along the coasts of the Sea of Okhotsk and Kamchatka, and on Medny Island. On Medny, there are between 6,000 and 8,000 sea lions, producing only 200 or so pups a year. Just two decades ago, it was possible to find 10,000 animals in one rookery alone. Why this large sea mammal is suffering such a dramatic decline is a mystery.

Among the expedition's trophies were pelts of Sea Otters. They are the only sea

A Sea Otter floats lazily on its back among the great waving fronds of
an offshore kelp bed. Their fondness for eating sea-urchins accounts
for the purple hue of the skeletons of some Sea Otters – the colour
comes from a dye in the urchins' shells.

mammals that are not endowed with layers of blubber beneath the skin, depending instead
upon their dense, water-repellent fur coat for both buoyancy and warmth. This is why they
spend such a long time grooming themselves to fluff up their fur and enable them to bob
high in the choppy seas like corks. Baby Sea Otters are so fluffy that they do not sink.
Predictably, these luxurious coats proved to be their downfall, and the Russian fur traders
saw a source of rich profits in the newly discovered mammal. Within a year or two, ships
were plying up and down the Bering Sea searching for Sea Otters.

Sea Otters were once very common around the northern shores of the Pacific, and
were originally exploited only by the sparse population of native people who used their
fur for making warm clothes. As soon as the Russian pioneers discovered their value,
though, the killing escalated dramatically; tens of thousands of Sea Otters were slaughtered
at a time. Such was the commercial demand for otter pelts, especially from the lucrative
Chinese market, that this motivated the Russian expansion into the Far East and Alaska.
The quest for Sea Otters was so ruthless that the species had been brought to the brink of
extinction by the end of the nineteenth century. Only strict protective measures taken by

both the former Soviet authorities and the USA allowed these charming creatures to recover. Today, the total world population numbers about 120,000.

There are some 20,000 Sea Otters in Russian waters, 12,000 of which live at the southern tip of the Kamchatkan peninsula and on Shumshu, the most northerly of the Kuril Islands. They spend much of their time afloat, and dive for their food. An analysis of the otters' droppings, or spraints, reveals that they derive much of their nourishment from sea-urchins (60 per cent), and supplement this with molluscs (23 per cent), crabs (10 per cent) and fish (7 per cent). Like their North American counterparts, Russian Sea Otters use stones held on their bellies as they float along on their backs as tools to crack open the hard shells of much of their prey.

With the return of better weather, the marooned mariners focused their energies on getting back to the mainland. They managed to salvage parts of their shattered ship and built a new vessel which they stocked with sea cow meat. In August 1742, they hoisted the sails and by the end of the month, the remnants of the original expedition disembarked at Petropavlovsk. Nevertheless, despite their ordeal, they had discovered Alaska, and Steller brought back a wealth of new information about the natural world. By the end of 1746, though, Steller was dead. After wandering through Siberia for four years, being mercilessly hounded for a bad debt and enduring a period of wrongful imprisonment, he died of a fever in Tyumen, Siberia, at the age of thirty-seven, but not before he had described many more new animals and plants in Kamchatka. He had achieved an immense amount in his short life; perhaps his crowning glory is his most famous work, *De Bestiis Marinis*, a book of observations on the marine mammals he studied, which he wrote in a hut on Bering Island under appalling conditions. This was published posthumously in 1751 and includes his unique observations, description and dissection of the sea cows which bear his name. It is still a classic of zoology.

Steller's researches on his epic journey and later in Kamchatka confirmed the importance of the bountiful sea in sustaining the rich animal communities in this part of the Far East. The connection is sometimes very obvious, as in the case of sea mammals and marine birds. Over two-thirds of the total seabird population of the former USSR — $4\frac{1}{2}$ million pairs — occurs in the Bering Sea and Sea of Okhotsk. In the Bering Sea, the most important colonies are on the Komandor Islands (500,000 pairs, including 1,000 pairs of Red-legged Kittiwakes, found only in the Bering Sea and adjacent waters of the North Pacific), Karaginsky Island on the east coast of Kamchatka (200,000 pairs), and Verkhoturova Island in the Karaginsky Gulf (50,000 pairs). The Sea of Okhotsk is by far the richest of the

Russian seas in terms of seabird numbers, accounting for an estimated 3,285,000 pairs. The biggest colonies are situated on the northern and central islands of the Kuril Island chain, especially Ushishir and Broughton.

This huge concentration of seabirds is sustained on the seemingly inexhaustible supplies of small fish, squid, and shrimplike krill in the cool but fertile waters of these latitudes. Some of the birds are familiar species, such as Black-legged Kittiwakes, Common and Brünnich's Guillemots (North America: Common and Thick-billed Murres) and Razor-bills, which also occur on the North Atlantic seaboard. Others are specialities of the North Pacific, including three species of cormorants (the Red-faced, Pelagic and Japanese, or Temminck's, Cormorant), the Spectacled Guillemot, a pair of puffins (Tufted and Horned), and a bevy of eight plankton-feeding auklets and murrelets that range in size from that of a sparrow to a small duck. All except the kittiwakes and cormorants belong to the auk family, a small group of twenty-two seabird species found only in the northern hemisphere that are the ecological counterpart of the totally unrelated penguins of the southern oceans. Like penguins, they pursue their prey underwater using their short wings to swim, but, unlike them, they can fly, with a whirring action.

One of the most abundant of the auklets and murrelets is the Crested Auklet, which is thrush-sized. It is a jaunty grey bird with piercing white eyes and a crest curling forwards over its stout, stubby scarlet bill. Like most auks, Crested Auklets are intensely gregarious, and the stupendous numbers that swirl around the nesting cliffs bear witness to the abundance of the planktonic crustaceans on which they feed. These aerial manoeuvres are especially exciting during spring, when the birds return from the sea at dawn and towards dusk to prospect their nesting burrows. The snow may still be on their nesting slopes at the end of May, but this does not deflect the auklets from the vital business of breeding. Every now and again, parties of them precipitate from the blizzard of birds onto slabs of rock, where they jostle for space, before once again dispersing into the air with a blur of wings. As the breeding season progresses, these aerial displays become less intense.

Each female lays a single egg which she incubates in shifts with her mate. When the chick arrives, both parents help to look after it, changing shifts during the early morning and at dusk. The off-duty partner joins the skeins of birds flying low over the water towards the feeding areas, perhaps 65 km (40 miles) away. There, they will dive for krill and larval fish. The birds released by their partners from incubation duty to feed at night must be able to intercept their prey in very low light conditions, because they return at dawn with their throat pouches bulging with plankton.

Two of the five species of auklets that breed along the coasts of the Russian Far East: Parakeet Auklets (left) and Crested Auklets (right). Auklets are members of the exclusively northern hemisphere auk family; out of a total of 22 species, no less than 16 occur in the Bering Sea region, and 12 of these are found nowhere else.

In some years, there is a drastic slump in the sea's natural productivity. When this happens, the Crested Auklets fail to hatch many of their eggs – only 35 per cent of them produce chicks. If food is scarce, the parents stay away from the nests for longer periods, and the chicks then become torpid to extend their ability to survive without being fed. Occasionally, some seabirds have a catastrophic breeding season and completely fail to rear any young.

Ancient Murrelets are unusual auks in that the females lay two eggs rather than the single one of most species, and their activity on land always takes place at the very dead of night. Birds intending to relieve their mates begin to assemble at dusk. Rafts of the smart black-and-white murrelets drift close inshore to the accompaniment of a bewitching chorus of tinkling whistles. When the night is at its darkest – at around one o'clock in the morning in these latitudes – the birds patter along the surface of the sea into the air and, despite the apparently dismal visibility, fly with supreme confidence to their own burrows, guided by the voices of their mates. After a short while, the off-duty bird departs. The tiny chicks also leave the safety of the nests under the cover of darkness.

Crested Auklets feed their offspring for several weeks until they are very fat, whereupon they are abandoned to make their own way down to the sea. Ancient Murrelets, on the other hand, have no throat pouch for transporting food in bulk to their chicks and so they have a very much curtailed nestling stage – shorter than that of any other seabird. The chicks hatch in early August, and leave their parents' burrows when they are fluffy mites, only a day or two old and highly vulnerable. Their chance of survival is enhanced by their instinct for making the perilous journey to the sea at night.

The chicks soon appear above ground, often joining up with others. They waste no time scurrying along gaps between the tussocks of vegetation and tumbling over rocks in their headlong rush for the sea. They finally cross the pebbly beaches and take to the water where their parents await them. But there are other, less welcome, birds eager to intercept the chicks – hungry Slaty-backed Gulls. The gulls stand little chance of catching them if it is dark, but as dawn approaches, they can see their quarry and swallow many of the stragglers head first, their little legs kicking vainly in the corner of the gulls' gapes before disappearing into their gullets. Those baby murrelets that successfully evade the killers paddle out to sea, accompanied by their parents.

With so many different species competing for the riches of the sea, each particular seabird has carved out its own niche. Among the auks, the large species tend towards a diet of fish, the Ancient Murrelet, with its tweezer-like beak, probably opts for small planktonic fish, and the broad-billed auklets take planktonic crustaceans. Feeding habits,

A Tufted Puffin shows off the colourful plate-like structures that adorn
its great triangular bill during the breeding season, along with
the tufts that give the species its name.

too, differ in detail. For instance, both of the two Pacific species of puffins live on fish, bringing them back to their nests in beakfuls, often neatly arrayed crosswise in their great triangular bills. However, Tufted Puffins commute for long distances out to sea and prefer to catch ocean-going herrings, while Horned Puffins tend to capture sand eels relatively close inshore.

During the hours of daylight, the shoals of shrimplike krill migrate away from the surface, so the smaller auks that prey on them must dive to depths of 30 m (100 ft) or more to intercept them. Many kittiwakes likewise live on krill, but these ocean-going gulls are surface feeders, and pick up only those prey dropped or injured by the deep-diving species as they come up for air. At dusk, when the krill move towards the surface, they become more accessible to Crested Auklets which can feed in dim light.

When they have finished breeding, many of the birds disappear from the land and spend the rest of the year on the heaving surface of the open sea. But even when the ice advances around the coastal waters of Kamchatka, there are fish- and krill-eating mammals to be seen. One of them is the Ribbon Seal, the most strikingly coloured of all marine mammals. The adult has a black body with four gleaming white bands, one encircling the head, another encircling the trunk at or behind the level of the navel, and one on each side of the body, circling the 'shoulders'. About 90,000 of these handsome seals are confined to the icebound region of the Bering Sea and North Pacific, and many of them whelp on the ice in Karaginsky Bay.

The King of the Fish

The seas bathing the eastern shores of Russia are rich feeding grounds for hundreds of millions of migratory salmon, many of which are ultimately eaten by terrestrial creatures on Kamchatka, and on the Siberian mainland bordering the Sea of Okhotsk. The fish spend most of their lives fattening themselves up in the North Pacific and Bering Sea and when they mature, they return to the rivers of their birth, resplendent in their nuptial colours, where they spawn and die.

Krashenninikov was impressed by the great salmon runs in Kamchatka, and recorded that the fish swam in such numbers that they blocked the rivers, causing them to overflow their banks. He elucidated in considerable detail the different species of these magnificent fishes that he encountered. Five of them occur in and around Kamchatka. Foremost among them are the Sockeye Salmon, the Pink or Humpbacked Salmon and the Chum Salmon. The largest is the King Salmon, which can reach 1.9 m (6¼ ft) long. It is also the tastiest

259

Above: A Brown Bear prepares to eat a fish she has just caught, watched
intently by her two cubs. Salmon form a major part of the diet of Kamchatka's
large Brown Bear population in winter.

Preceding pages: Sockeye Salmon, resplendent in their breeding colours, gather
together to spawn. These magnificent fish are also known as Red Salmon.

and yields the best red 'caviare'. The fifth species is the Silver Salmon, also known as the
Jack or Coho Salmon.

As the ripe salmon make their way in from the sea, they run the gauntlet of predators,
eager for their flesh. Some are intercepted by Common, or Harbour, Seals. At the end of
the summer, when the salmon migration reaches its peak, thousands of these seals laze
around on sandbars in the mouths of rivers, such as the Kamchatka River. When they feel
hungry, the seals simply heave themselves into the water and snatch a passing salmon. Local
fishermen also net the salmon in the estuaries. Even in Krashenninikov's day, the native
people were heavily dependent upon harvesting them, and used nets and woven baskets to
catch the fish as they migrated towards their spawning beds. Such was the value of the east
coast fisheries that the rights to exploit the annual influxes of salmon were disputed by
Japan, and even led to territorial claims against Tsarist Russia. Nowadays, salmon fishing
is big business in Kamchatka, Sakhalin Island, in the northern Sea of Okhotsk, and in the

Anadyr and Amur rivers, and the stocks are managed by a programme of rearing and releasing young fish.

The spawning salmon provide a bonanza of nutrients, derived from the sea, which helps to nourish the animal and plant communities that live on Kamchatka's raw volcanic soil. Even in death, salmon bequeath the goodness in their exhausted bodies to the rivers in which they breed. The flush of fertilizing minerals from the putrefying fish stimulates the growth of aquatic invertebrates on which the newly hatched salmon depend. The dead and dying fish are also consumed by terrestrial animals – indeed, they are crucial to their survival during the winter. Large numbers of Northern Ravens and Slaty-backed Gulls assemble to peck at the carcases. They are joined by some of Russia's – and the world's – biggest Brown Bears. About 9,000 of these great bears live on Kamchatka; when rearing up on their hind legs, the largest males stand nearly 3 m (9 feet) tall and weigh up to 800 kg ($\frac{3}{4}$ ton), rivalling their equally well-fed cousins, the Grizzly Bears of Kodiak Island, Alaska.

The Kamchatka peninsula is one of the richest realms for these outsize Brown Bears, with a profusion of wild berries and oil-rich salmon available just before they settle down for their winter's sleep. When putting on fat at this time of the year, a hungry Kamchatkan bear can eat up to 20,000 berries or nearly 50 kg (110 lb) of fish in a day! In Alaska, Grizzly Bears often gather in impressive groups to feast on the glut of fish, but in Kamchatka, the bears appear to keep their distance from each other, tolerating only other scavengers, such as Steller's Sea Eagle.

The Ultimate Eagle

Originally discovered by Steller on Bering Island, Steller's Sea Eagle is one of the world's most impressive birds of prey. With piercing eyes and a massive, yellow hook for a beak, this huge bird epitomizes everything an eagle should be – fearsome, magisterial and powerful. This spectacular sea eagle is larger than the sea eagle of North America, the Bald Eagle, and larger, too, than the Golden Eagle. As with most birds of prey, the females are the larger sex. Those of Steller's Sea Eagle reach just over 1 m ($3\frac{1}{4}$ ft) in length, and have great, broad carpets of wings that stretch almost 2.5 m ($8\frac{1}{4}$ ft) from tip to tip. The adults have striking white forewings, from which the bird derives its Russian name of *beloplechy orlan* – 'white-shouldered eagle'. The long, wedge-shaped tail, rump, vent and thigh feathers are also white and there is a white blaze on the forehead as well.

Like the world's eight other species of sea eagles, Steller's Sea Eagle is largely a fish

The world's largest and most impressive sea eagle, Steller's Sea Eagle
breeds and winters in the Far East of Russia.

catcher and a scavenger. Although these magnificent birds kill such prey as hares, Arctic Foxes, geese and capercaillie, most of their food is obtained on the shores and rivers of the Far East. While hunting, the great eagles sit patiently for hours at vantage points watching for living or dead fish. They catch their prey by stooping down, often from the direction of the sun if it is shining, and grasping the slippery fish in their powerful talons. If the water is shallow, they simply wade in and gaff their prey.

A different hunting method is used by Steller's Sea Eagles that spend the summer months on seabird islands, where they often prey on seabirds and their young. The birds regularly patrol the high nesting cliffs, their great pinions straining to extract every ounce of lift from the air as it rises against the edifices of rock. The eagles use surprise tactics, panicking the auks and kittiwakes by swooping close to their nesting ledges and either snatching a terrified parent from the air or grabbing a temporarily abandoned chick from the cliff-face. Steller's Sea Eagles are also capable of killing young seals.

This superb bird of prey is a comparatively rare species. Today, there are an estimated 7,500 individuals, breeding only in the far east of Russia and North Korea and wintering in Kamchatka, Ussuriland, Korea and northern Japan, notably off the northern island of

Japan, Hokkaido, where more than 2,000 of the eagles have been recorded in February. Russia has the lion's share of the population, with approximately 2,200 nesting pairs. These are found in the coastal regions and river basins around the Sea of Okhotsk and Kamchatka. Over one-half of the nesting pairs (about 1,200 pairs) occur at the northern end of the Sea of Okhotsk, around Penzhinskaya Bay, with some 320 pairs breeding on Kamchatka. However, the highest recorded *density* of nests is found around the perimeter of Lake Udyl, in Ussuriland.

The eagles' breeding territories are always located near good fishing areas, usually in river valleys, where the birds build their bulky nests of branches at the tops of very tall trees. They usually use the same nest year after year, and an old nest may measure 2.4 m (8 ft) across and 3.6 m (12 ft) deep. Coastal eagles build their nests on cliff ledges. The birds start breeding at the end of February and in early March. As in most birds of prey, courtship takes the form of dramatic displays of aerobatics, with much soaring and calling. The pairs then set about repairing their nests with fresh branches in readiness for the eggs, which are laid in late April or early May.

Normally, each female lays a clutch of two white eggs, which she incubates for almost 6 weeks. The chicks are offered a diet of fish, supplemented by birds and a little mammal flesh, which their parents bring to the eyrie between two and three times daily. During early August, they are ready to fledge but, by then, only one-third of the nests still contain two young; a few eaglets fall victim to Sable and possibly Stoats, some die of disease, and others are killed when their nests collapse. On average, a pair of eagles can expect to fledge only one youngster every other year, at least on Kamchatka.

Kamchatka is a particularly important winter refuge for Steller's Sea Eagles because the number soars to between 4,300 and 4,500 birds, equivalent to 57–60 per cent of the world population. Salmon are the attraction. In autumn, after the major spawning period, there is a surfeit of dying and dead fish upon which the eagles gorge themselves. This is especially true of Lake Kurilsky, at the southern end of Kamchatka, which hosts one of the greatest aggregations of Steller's Sea Eagles in the world. In August, millions of vermilion Sockeye Salmon enter the lake to spawn around its edges, attracting large numbers of hungry bears.

Such is the severity of the competition among the fish for the favoured sites that many of the Sockeyes are still courting and laying their orange eggs well into the winter season. By this time, the shallow margins of the lake may well have frozen over, except for certain stretches of water where the salmon can still be caught. This is where up to 700 Steller's Sea Eagles gather to feed during the bitterly cold months of the year, along with Whooper

Swans, Goosanders (North American: Common Mergansers) and Common Goldeneyes, which take advantage of the channels in the ice.

During winter, many of the northerly nesting sea eagles migrate south along the Kuril Islands to Unishir and northern Japan, while others make their way to the coast and river basins of Ussuriland where they join up with those that reside in that bountiful region. Some even winter in the busy harbour of Vladivostok, along with many of their smaller relatives, White-tailed Eagles.

A Land of Contrasts

Ussuriland is a unique region of Russia because animals and plants of northern Siberian origin mix with those from South-east Asia to create a remarkably rich and diverse wildlife community. It embraces an area running southwards from the Amur estuary to the border of China and Korea, and westwards to the bank of the great Ussuri River, within the administrative region of Primorsky Kray (Maritime Territory). Much of Ussuriland is mountainous, due to the presence of the Sikhote-Alin range, which runs from north to south. Built on formerly active fault lines of the 'ring of fire', this range of comparatively low mountains averages 1,000 m (3,300 ft) in height, with some of its summits reaching double this figure, and runs for 1,000 kms (620 miles) from the mouth of the Amur River to the southern coast of the Sea of Japan. To the south-west lies the vast Khanka lowland, an area of meadows, marshes, rice paddies and expanses of open water. Three rare species of cranes nest in the region of the Khanka Lake – the Hooded Crane, the White-naped Crane, and the lovely Japanese Crane.

The history of this part of the Russian landscape has helped to shape the remarkably varied fauna of Ussuriland. This region never experienced the devastating effects of glaciers. During the glacial advances of the last great Ice Age, when the creeping tongues of ice were clearing everything before them in other areas, many animals and plants were able to survive in Ussuriland. This may account for the varied forests and the accompanying flora.

The north-south alignment of the mountains enabled them to act as conduits, facilitating both the northerly infiltration of Chinese and Indo-Malayan species and the southerly penetration of northern ones. The broad valleys etched out by the Ussuri and Amur rivers likewise behaved like corridors for the spread of animals and plants into the area. This is presumably how Russia's only soft-shelled turtle, the Chinese Soft-shelled Turtle, managed to reach Ussuriland. It has a shell which grows to 30 cm (1 ft) across, a long, snakelike neck and pointed nostrils which can pierce the surface of the water like a snorkel.

Autumn colours tint the taiga along the River Bikin in Ussuriland,
one of Russia's richest environments for wildlife.

In the north of Ussuriland, parts of the landscape are dominated by birch, spruce and stands of creeping stone pine. Other areas are covered with great Korean pines. Each of their enormous cones contain up to 200 'nuts' which are saturated with oil. These are shed between autumn and spring, and sustain numerous birds, such as Nutcrackers, Hawfinches, and various species of woodpeckers, as well as a variety of mammals, from squirrels and chipmunks to Wild Boars and several species of deer. This is also the realm of Brown Bears, albeit rather smaller ones than those on Kamchatka. Lynx and Wolverine live in these woods, too, as well as Siberian Flying Squirrels, whose range extends as far west as Finland.

Further south, where summer typhoons occasionally sweep in from the sea and boost

A wealth of beautiful wildflowers bloom in the lush mixed forests of
Ussuriland: these include the flame-coloured campion *Lychnis fulgens* (top left);
various species of iris, such as *Iris pennsylvanicum* (top right)
and *Iris ensata* (above right); and the day-lilies, such as
Hemerocallis minor (above left).

the annual rainfall to 1,000 mm (39 in), the forests take on an almost subtropical character. One of the most southerly woodlands in Ussuriland is at Kedrovaya Pad, a nature reserve of 180 sq km (70 sq miles) a few kilometres from the North Korean and Chinese borders. As in the rest of Ussuriland, the forest contains a mixture of conifers, but these are infiltrated by a variety of beautiful deciduous oaks, spiky-leafed maples, hornbeams and ash. In spring, rhododendrons decorate the forest with delicate pink blooms, and the scent of Amur Lilac pervades the air. In summer, the place exudes a semi-tropical lushness, with lianas – including magnolia vines – festooning the branches, ferns sprouting in explosions of green fronds from the rocky ground, and a wealth of beautiful flowers decorating the glades, including Scarlet Campions and various peonies, lilies and orchids. Even the famous Ginseng plant, the 'root of life' in Chinese medicine, grows in the shaded parts of these Ussuri forests.

Here and there, the great arching canopies give way to chattering streams of cool, clear water. In the heat of the day, insects hum, cicadas sing, and butterflies flit in and out of

Its wings spread in all their iridescent glory, a Maack's Swallowtail
butterfly brightens a woodland glade in Ussuriland.

There are many species of moths in the Ussuri forests, such as this ghostly green moon moth, photographed in the Lazo nature reserve in the southern Sikhote-Alin Mountains.

Ussuriland is home to a variety of amphibians, including exotic-looking tree frogs (above left) and fire-bellied toads (above right).

the sunbeams. Some of the butterflies are large and colourful, including the enormous Maack's Swallowtail, shot like the finest silk with shimmering velvety greens and electric blues, with a row of black eyespots on its hind wings; there are also yellow Ussurian Swallowtails, as well as Purple Emperors and a lively selection of satyrs and apollos. At night, their place is taken by exquisite-looking giant moths, including pallid green moon moths with trailing 'tails' on their hind wings.

This is also the realm of reptiles and amphibians — of snakes, tree frogs, and pretty fire-bellied toads. The latter, when threatened by a predator such as the black-and-red Tiger Snake, perform bizarre contortions to expose as much of their strikingly patterned under-sides as possible as a warning that they taste unpleasant.

The Siberian Salamander, which ranges as far north as the Arctic region (see page 191), making it one of the most northerly of all amphibians, also lives as far south as Ussuriland, where it breeds in forest pools. Mating in this species is a most remarkable affair. The males gather in the best egg-laying sites and, their mouths gaping, waft pheromones — chemical attractants — into the water with their tails. The females soon appear and lay two egg masses (one from each oviduct), over which the males shed their sperm. When the egg masses emerge, the transparent purple membrane that covers each egg mass expands and assumes the appearance of a crinkled, purple sea-gooseberry, suspended from submerged vegetation or a twig.

Birdwatcher's Paradise

Ussuriland is a birdwatcher's paradise. Over half of the former Soviet Union's 796 species of breeding birds have been recorded in this corner of the continent. Many are familiar taiga species — such as Arctic and Greenish Warblers, Coal Tits, crossbills, Nutcrackers and Siberian Spruce Grouse. The latter are tame, confiding birds, the size of a crow and inhabiting the dense forests of larch and spruce in the south-eastern region of Russia. They are most closely related to the North American Spruce Grouse, and may have entered Asia when the Beringian land bridge was open (see page 163).

Other birds, such as white-eyes, drongos, and minivets, are representatives of tropical families, which do not occur elsewhere in the former USSR. No less than seven species of flycatchers breed in Ussuriland; the males of several species, including the beautiful, long-tailed Asian Paradise-Flycatcher (see page 89), bring a touch of the tropics to the dark canopies where they sit, watch, and sally forth from their perches to snap up insects. Here, there are also sweet choristers, such as Black-naped Orioles, Daurian Redstarts, Grey-backed Thrushes and Siberian Blue Robins to delight the ear, and five species of cuckoos. And Ussuriland has a wealth of other birdlife, too.

The Ussuriland rivers have an interesting mixture of wildfowl, including Harlequin Ducks, which are normally associated with rocky coasts and turbulent mountain streams in the arctic and subarctic regions, ranging around the northern Pacific, and across parts of the far north of Canada to Greenland and Iceland. The drakes are boldly plumaged birds, largely slate-blue with chestnut flanks, and decorated with odd white patches and spots. Harlequins are diving ducks, but there are also exotic dabbling ducks in Ussuriland, such as the beautiful Baikal and Falcated Teal. However, the most flamboyant of all the ducks is the Mandarin Duck.

The Mandarin Duck is an exquisite little duck that is often associated with China because it is such a popular subject for Chinese artists. It belongs to the group known as perching ducks, which, unlike most ducks, are quite at home among the branches of trees. Although it breeds sparsely in north-eastern China and Korea, the Mandarin's main stronghold is northern Japan; it also breeds in the Amur and Ussuri regions of Russia. There is an important feral population in Britain, too, derived from captive birds accidentally and deliberately released – about 7,000 individuals now live wild there, about the same number as live in the species' native habitats in the Far East.

The Mandarin drake is among the most beautiful of all wildfowl. He is a colourful, exotic looking bird, with elaborate head plumage, including a bold white crest edged in green, bronze and purple and a long ruff of orange-red feathers decorating the side of the head. Some of his wing feathers are fashioned like bright orange sails, which he can raise over his back and display to dramatic effect during courtship.

The Ussuriland Mandarin Ducks winter in Japan and China, returning north in spring to breed alongside fast-flowing streams, where they settle at a density of about one pair per square kilometre (three pairs per square mile). The soberly plumaged females lay their eggs in tree holes up to 20 m (65 ft) above the ground. When the ducklings hatch, they are called from their tree-top nursery by their mothers, and tumble into the water or onto the forest floor far below without suffering any injuries.

Young Scaly-sided (or Chinese) Mergansers also make their entrance into the world in this spectacular, death-defying fashion. There are only about 1,000 pairs of these fish-eating sawbilled ducks in the world and, of these, 350 pairs breed along the fast-flowing rivers that course through the mountainous taiga forests of the Russian Far East; the rest breed along mountain rivers in northern Heilongjiang in north-eastern China. The drakes are

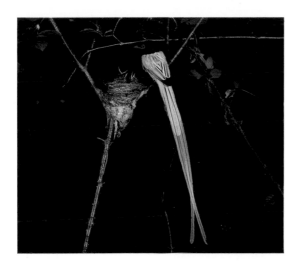

Birds breeding in Ussuriland include the stunning Asian Paradise Flycatcher (white phase male, top left); the Blue-and-White Flycatcher (male, top right); the Black-naped Oriole (female, centre); and the gorgeous Mandarin Duck (male, above left); the exquisite and increasingly rare Baikal Teal (male, above right) breeds in Kamchatka and Sakhalin.

very handsome birds, their glossy bottle green heads sporting a double crest, and their salmon pink underparts boldly marked on the flanks to produce the scaly effect that gives them one of their names. After they have finished nesting, these rare mergansers disappear into China, and no-one knows for sure their winter destination.

One of the largest owls in the world, Blakiston's Fish Owl, lives beside the relatively slow-moving rivers west of the Sikhote-Alin Range, such as the 500 km (300 mile) long Bikin, which is a tributary of the Ussuri. It is a magnificent, loose-feathered bird, with streaked and barred brown plumage and great blazing orange eyes, and measures up to 72 cm ($2\frac{1}{2}$ ft) long, with a wingspan of almost 2 m ($6\frac{1}{2}$ ft).

Like other fishing owls, sea and fish eagles and the osprey, Blakiston's Fish Owl is well adapted for getting its feet wet. The legs have small feathers that dry quickly, and the toes

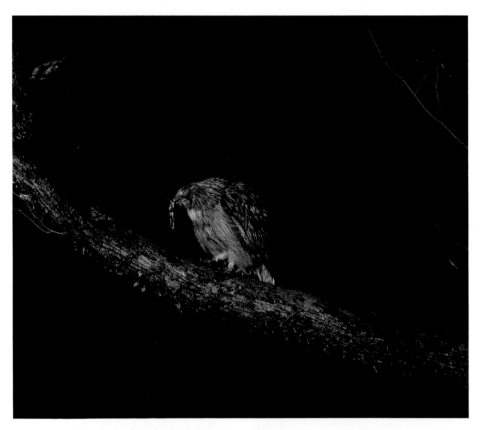

Above: One of the most exciting – and enigmatic – birds of Ussuriland is the huge Blakiston's Fish Owl, seen here with a frog it has just plucked from the Bikin River.
Opposite: A pair of stately Japanese Cranes perform their ecstatic courtship dance in the snow. This is one of three rare species of crane that breed in the marshes of Ussuriland.

are almost naked. The undersides of the feet are covered with spiky scales which doubtless work with the long, curved claws and their sharp lower cutting edge to help the owl to keep a secure grip on its slippery, wriggling prey. These great owls hunt mainly for fish, including large salmon, Amur Pike and catfish, snatching them at night from the water in flurries of spray. They also eat frogs and crayfish. During the winter, when the rivers are iced over, the birds turn to more orthodox owl fare, and hunt for voles, flying squirrels, martens and sometimes small birds.

This splendid owl takes its name from the British businessman and consul Captain Thomas Wright Blakiston, who discovered them when exploring Hokkaido, the north-ernmost island of Japan, in 1883. The deep hoots of the owls were familiar to the Ainu people who lived on the banks of Hokkaido's rivers; they believed them to be the voice of the god, *Kotan koru kamui*, who protected their villages. Along with the Brown Bear and salmon, the great fish owl was one of the Ainu's most important deities. Sadly, those that occur in Russia have never been regarded with such reverence.

Blakiston's Fish Owl is a rare and elusive bird throughout its limited range in South-east Asia – there are only twenty breeding pairs in Hokkaido, and very few on the Bikin River in Ussuriland. Elsewhere, it occurs sparsely in Sakhalin, the southern Kuril islands and north-east China. Each pair commands a stretch of river which is defended from other fish owls. The two white eggs are laid in a hollow during March, often when snow still lies on the ground. The female is responsible for incubating them while her mate supplies her with food, up to five times a night. The eggs hatch at the end of April, but the mother takes no time off from brooding her owlets to hunt until May when the nights get warmer. Being the larger of the two sexes, the female often returns with fish while her mate tends to deliver frogs caught in the neighbourhood of the nest. After fledging, the young remain in their parents' territories for up to two years. A pair of these owls may stay together for perhaps twenty years, attempting to nest only every other year.

Remarkable Mammals

Some of Russia's most interesting and spectacular mammals occur in the Far East. The Grey Goral lives in the Sikhote-Alin Mountains and on the steep coastal cliffs of northern Ussuriland. This is a member of the goat-antelope family, which includes not only ibex and various wild sheep but also Musk Ox and Chamois. The Grey Goral is one of the smallest members of the family and its distribution covers northern Burma and Kashmir, the mountain ranges of China and Korea, and Ussuriland. The males stand barely 60 cm

(2 ft) at the shoulder and weigh about 25 kg (55 lb). The legs are short and powerful for climbing, and the horns are short and straight, like daggers.

The ewes and juveniles live in groups of up to a dozen animals, whereas the mature rams are loners. They come together only during the autumn rut, after which the rams return to their solitary way of life. The calves are born in June and, to begin with, lie hidden among rocks while their mothers scale the cliffs to graze. They are weaned after three or four months but accompany their mothers until the following spring.

Ussuriland is well endowed with predatory mammals. One of the most intriguing is the Yellow-throated Marten, a South-east Asian species whose range nudges into this part of Russia. It is the largest and most spectacular of the marten family, with a combined body and tail length of up to 1.3 m ($4\frac{1}{4}$ ft). Although it is basically a brown animal, the head is black, the back often golden and, as the name suggests, it has a yellow bib. Like its cousin, the Sable, the Yellow-throated Marten is an energetic beast, capable of hunting on the ground or bounding along branches with great agility, thanks to its semi-retractile claws.

These martens are unique in often hunting *en famille*. When the young are strong enough, they apparently accompany their parents on their hunting forays at dusk. By the end of summer, the offspring are nearly fully grown, so a family party forms a formidable team, capable of killing not only birds and hares but also larger prey, including Siberian Musk Deer. The deer are territorial and therefore tend to run in circles, and are quickly out-manoeuvred by the relentless martens.

Another interesting mammal of the Ussuri forests is the Asian Black Bear, a small species with a longish black mane and a distinctive white crescent on its chest, from which it derives its other name of 'Moon Bear'. Its range extends from Iran to Japan.

Several members of the dog family are found in the far east of Russia, including Grey Wolves, Dholes (Asian Wild Dogs) and Raccoon Dogs. The latter are very unusual because they are the only member of the dog family to hibernate during the winter. At first sight, Raccoon Dogs, with their striking 'bandit masks' and squat shapes, bear a superficial resemblance to the North American Raccoons from which they acquired their name. However, they are not very closely related to them — they are true dogs. Raccoon Dogs occur naturally in China, Japan, and Ussuriland, but their range has been greatly extended this century by human intervention.

Raccoon Dog fur was commercially important in the Russian Far East, where it was known as 'Ussuri Raccoon'. In the 1920s, Raccoon Dogs were introduced to western

Looking more like a raccoon than a member of the dog family to which it
belongs, the aptly named Raccoon Dog is one of the oddest of all Ussuriland
animals. Its introduction to western Russia and subsequent invasion of Europe
has not helped the control of rabies, for it is a carrier of this disease.

Russia and, especially, to the Ukraine. Some were kept on fur farms, but others were
liberated into the countryside, and quickly established themselves and spread across Europe.
The first wild Raccoon Dogs were spotted in Finland in 1931, and in succeeding years,
the aliens from the east occupied Romania, Poland, Czechoslovakia, Hungary and East
Germany. Recently, they have spread into Western Europe.

Raccoon Dogs live in pairs, the bitches producing their pups between March and May.
When they are about three weeks old, the youngsters emerge from their den just before
dusk to play and bask in what remains of the sunlight. Their father tends to guard them at
this stage of their development, and leads them back into the den before both he and his
mate go off searching for food. Raccoon Dogs tend to be nocturnal, using their keen sense
of smell to root out rodents, reptiles and insects. Like Raccoons, they take readily to water,

and will even dive for fish and frogs. At dawn, the adults return to their den, often wet and grubby from their night-time forays, in order to feed the pups, groom, and sleep for the rest of the day.

At night, Far-eastern Wild Cats pad silently through the forests hunting for rodents. Also known as Amur Forest Cats, these animals are very closely related to the Leopard Cat, or Bengal Cat, of South-east Asia and resemble very large tabbies, weighing up to 8 kg (17 lb). However, there are also really big cats in Ussuriland.

The Great Cats of Ussuriland

Amur Leopards are confined to a narrow band of country bordering China and North Korea. They belong to the most northerly of the 30 or so different races (subspecies) of the Leopard (experts disagree as to the precise number). Adapted to the bitter winters, these Leopards grow thick, pale coats during autumn, to keep out the cold. During summer, the long hairs are moulted and the animals revert to the typical lithe form so characteristic of the species. Unfortunately, the beautiful Amur Leopard is in the gravest danger of extinction, with only twenty to twenty-five of them on Russian territory, and perhaps a few more in China.

A pair or two of these great spotted cats have taken refuge in the Kedrovaya Pad nature reserve, using rocky outcrops and overhangs as lairs where they lie up and rear their cubs. At night, they creep around the forested slopes, stalking Roe Deer, Raccoon Dogs and badgers. Like their African counterparts, these Russian Leopards often take their prey to a ledge and may cover the remains with leaves or snow to keep it hidden from scavengers such as crows.

During the hot, monsoonal summers, the Leopards probably live quite well, but the frosty winters, when the snow is lying deep, are a challenging period for these great cats. If a Leopard manages to kill a Roe Deer, the flesh may have to last it for over three weeks. But at this time of year, deer may be scarce, and the badgers and Raccoon Dogs will have hidden themselves away inside their holes. Even hares are hard to come by, and are hardly a mouthful for a hungry leopard. In the end, hunger may force the cats to turn to scavenging, or to eating domestic dogs.

All Russian Leopards are strictly protected. Luckily, there are many Amur Leopards in captivity, and plans are afoot to reintroduce captive-bred animals into areas once occupied by the species.

Siberian Tigers, the largest and most powerful of all the big cats, are also native to the

Above: A Siberian tiger – greatest of all the big cats – takes a siesta in the dappled light of an Ussuriland wood.

Preceding pages: One of the world's few remaining Amur Leopards strides across a fallen tree to avoid getting its feet wet in a river at the Kedrovaya Pad (Cedar Ravine) nature reserve, in the extreme south of Ussuriland.

forests of Ussuriland. Males grow to 4 m (13 ft) in length and weigh over 380 kg (840 lb). Despite their size, there is little evidence that they pose any threat to people, even when they lurk in the vicinity of remote villages and farms. Although probably between 200 and 300 of these superb creatures survive on Russian territory, they or their huge pug-marks are regularly discovered, sometimes even on the outskirts of the city of Vladivostok!

Large predators need a great deal of space in which to find enough food, and tigers are no exception. They are solitary hunters, and each adult requires an area of about 400 sq km (150 sq miles) to provide it with the necessary supply of prey. Most Siberian Tigers are confined to the fairly thick forests and river systems of the Sikhote-Alin Mountains, where they feed upon Wild Boar and various species of deer. Only if these are in short supply will the big cats divert their attentions to domestic cattle and dogs.

In this region, the tigers need to be tough because of the cold winters. Being large, with thick, furry coats, they are better able to withstand the cold than their smaller tropical cousins. Indeed, there is evidence that the modern tiger evolved in the cooler parts of northern Asia, and only in comparatively recent times did the species spread southwards into the subtropical and tropical lands where it is now mainly found. Certainly, the inclement weather does not seem to affect the Ussuri tigers, and the tigresses produce their cubs – usually four at a time – throughout the year.

In historical times, tigers were widespread in the former USSR. Members of the small, dark Caspian race lived around the southern shores of the Caspian in Turkmenistan, and were observed as far north as Lake Balkhash in Kazakhstan. A few Caspian Tigers may have lingered on Soviet soil until just after the Second World War. The causes of their extinction were over-hunting and the conversion of their habitat into cotton fields.

The shaggy-coated Siberian Tigers have fared a little better than their Caspian relatives. They used to roam the taiga, westwards to Lake Baikal and northwards into the upper reaches of the Lena River; during the early years of this century, tigers were shot not far from Yakutsk. However, they are now rigorously protected, and these magnificent cats are possibly even increasing in their Ussuriland refuges. Unfortunately, the tiger's propensity to wander great distances renders it difficult to guarantee the animals complete safety from illegal shooting.

The forests of Ussuriland, at the very south-eastern corner of Russia, are a long way from the shores of the Baltic. And yet, despite the distance and the differences between them, these woodlands overlooking the Pacific Ocean are still part of the Realms of the Russian Bear – a kingdom full of fascination with so much yet to be discovered.

BIBLIOGRAPHY

The following books are recommended for further information on many of the topics covered in this book. All titles were originally published in English unless otherwise indicated.

Bannikov, A. G. *Nature Reserves of the USSR,* English translation of Russian edition of 1966, Israel Program for Scientific Translations, Jerusalem, 1966

Bannikov, A. G., Darevskiy, I. S., & Rustamov, A. K., *Zemnovodnye 1 Presmykaytushchiesya SSSR: Spravochnik-Opredelite'* (Amphibians & Reptiles of the USSR: Handbook & Identification Guide), in Russian, Mysl', Moscow 1971.

Borodin, A. M., *Krasnaya Kniga SSSR* (Red Data Book of the USSR, Lesnay promyshlennost', Moscow, 2nd revised and enlarged edition, 1984–

Borodin, A. M. & Syroechkovskiy, E. E. (eds.), *Zapovedniki SSSR: Spravochnik* (Nature Reserves of the USSR: A Guide), in Russian, Mysl', Moscow 1983

Chernov, Yu. I., *The Living Tundra: Studies in Polar Research,* Cambridge University Press, Cambridge, 1985

Davydova, M. & Koshevoi, V., *Nature Reserves in the USSR,* English translation of Russian edition, Progress Publishers, Moscow, 1989

Dementiev, G. P. & Gladkov, N. A., *The Birds of the Soviet Union,* 6 volumes, English translation of 1951–4 Russian edition, Israel Program for Scientific Translations, Jerusalem, 1966–70

Durrell, G. & Durrell, L., *Durrell in Russia,* Macdonald, London, 1986

Flint, V. E., Boehme, R. L., Kostin, Y. V. & Kuznetsov, A. A., *A Field Guide to the Birds of the USSR,* English translation of 1968 Russian edition, Princeton University Press, Princeton and Guildford, 1989

Flint, V. E., Chugunov, Y. D. & Smirin, V. M., *Mlekopitayushchie SSSR: Spravochnik-Opredelitel'* (Mammals of the USSR: Handbook & Identification Guide), in Russian, Mysl', Moscow, 1965

Geptner, V. G. *et al, Mlekopitayushchie Sovetskogo Soyuza* (Mammals of the Soviet Union), in Russian, in 4 volumes, Vysshaya Shkola, Moscow, 1961–76

Ilychev, V. D. & Flint, V. E. (general eds.), *Ptitsy SSSR* (The Birds of the USSR), in Russian, in 12 volumes, Nauka, Leningrad, 1982–

Ilychev, V. D. & Flint, V. E. (general eds.), *Handbuch der Vögel der Sowietunion,* German translation of the above series, in 12 volumes, A. Ziemsen Verlag, Wittenberg Lutherstadt, Germany, 1985–

Komarov, V. L. (ed.), *Flora SSSR* (The Flora of the USSR), in Russian, in 30 volumes, Nauka, Leningrad, 1936–60

Kovshar, A. F., *The Bird World of Kazakhstan,* in Russian, Mektep, Alma-Ata, 1988

Kozhov, M., *Lake Baikal and its Life,* English translation, Junk Publishers, The Hague, 1963

Knystautas, A. & Liutkus, A., *In the World of Birds,* in English, Lithuanian and Russian, Vilnius, Lithuania, 1982

Knystautas, A. & Shibnev, Yu., *Die Vögelwelt Ussuriens* (*The Bird World of Ussuriland,*) in German, A Ziemsen Verlag, Wittenberg Lutherstadt, 1986

Knystautas, A. & Januškis, V., *Nature of the Soviet Union: Landscapes, Flora and Fauna,* in English, Lithuanian and Russian, Mosklas Publishers, Vilnius, 1987

Knystautas, A., *The Natural History of the USSR,* Century, London, 1987

Knystautas, A., *The Birds of the USSR,* Harper-Collins, London, 1992

Lobkov, E. G., *The Breeding Birds of Kamchatka,* in Russian, Vladivostok, 1986

Mearns, B., & Mearns, R., *Biographies for Birdwatchers,* Academic Press, New York and London 1988

Ognev, S. I., *Animals of the USSR & Adjoining Countries* (first three volumes entitled *Animals of Eastern Europe & Northern Asia*), in English, translated from original Russian edition, 1928–50, in 7 volumes, Israel Program for Scientific Translation, Jerusalem, 1960–4

Potapov, R. L. (ed.), *Our Rare Native Animals,* in Russian, Nauka, Leningrad, 1989

Pride, P. R., *Conservation in the Soviet Union,* Cambridge University Press, Cambridge, 1972

Sage, B., *The Arctic & Its Wildlife,* Croom Helm, Beckenham, 1986

St. George, G., *Soviet Deserts & Mountains* (*The World's Wild Places* series), Time-Life Books, Amsterdam, 1974

Vaughan, R., *In Search of Arctic Birds,* Poyser/Academic Press, London and New York 1991

Sokolov, V. E. & Syraechkovskii (general eds.), *Zapovedniki SSSR Nature Reserves of the USSR),* 10-volume series, in Russian, Mysl', Moscow 1985–

A Field Guide to the Birds of Japan (for birds of the Far East of Russia), Wildlife Society of Japan, 1982

Sound recordings of birds of the former USSR can be heard on:
Soviet Bird Songs, featuring 122 species, with announcements in English, two C-90 cassettes recorded by Krister Mild, Mild Bioacoustics, Stockholm, 1987

INDEX

Figures in italics refer to illustrations

Abies gracilis, 246
Adams' Oxytrope, 172
agama lizards, 117–18; *117*
Alatau Range, 76, 78
alder, 246
Alpine Chough, 84
Alpine Swift, 84
Alatai Mountains, 78
Amu Darya River, 114, 124, 144–6
Amur Forest Cat (Far-eastern Wild Cat), 279
Amur Leopard, 279; *280–1*
Ancient Murrelets, 256–8
Angara River, 223
ant, desert (*Phaeton*), 123
Antelope, Pronghorn, 152
  Tibetan (Chiru), 152
Anthia mannerheimi, beetle, 123
aphids, 143
Aral Sea, 35–7; *36*
Arctic
  climate, 163, 166, 190, 196–7
  fish, 186–8
  temperatures, 154, 160, 197
  vegetation, 22–3, 163, 169–70, 172–4
Arctic Buttercup, 163
Arctic Char, 187
Arctic Forget-me-not, *171*
Arctic Fox, 163, 184, 188–90, 197; *183*
Arctic Hare, 219
Arctic Jaeger (Arctic Skua), 180
Arctic Poppy, 246; *171*
Arctic Redpoll (Hoary Redpoll), 167, 169, 214; *214*
Arctic Skua (Arctic Jaeger), 180
Arctic Tern, 162, 180
Arctic Warbler, 220, 271
Arctic Willow, 172–3; *173*
Arkhar Sheep, 142; *142*
Asian Black Bear, 277
Asian Paradise-Flycatcher, 89, 271; *273*
Asiatic Dowitcher, 222–3
Asiatic Wild Ass (Kulan), 140, 142; *111*
Asian Wild Dog (Dhole), 277
Atlantic Sturgeon, 62
auklets, 256–7, 259; *257*
auks, 162, 256–9
Azov, Sea of, 34–5
Azure Tit, 89

Bactrian Camel, 135–6
Badkhyz, 136–40, 142; *111, 112, 137*
Baikal, Lake, 31, 198, 220–6, 228–31, 234–7; *221, 224, 226*
Baikal Seal, 235–7; *236*
Baikal Teal, 272; *273*
Banded Agrion damselfly, 47
barkhans, 112
bar-headed goose, 19, 79, 95, 98–9; *98*
Bar-tailed Godwit, 70
Barguzin, 216
bathynellids (crustaceans), 230
Bay-backed Shrike, 141
Bean Goose, 174
Bearded Vulture (Lammergeier), 84–5
bears
  Asian Black, 277

Brown (Grizzly), 26–8, 30–1, 92, 102, 211, 228, 263, 267; *27, 29, 262*
  Isabelline (White-clawed), Brown, 31, 91–2; *30*
  Polar, 154, 156–7, 163, 192–3, 196; *155, 194–5*
  Syrian Brown, 28
Beech Marten, 215
beetles, 123
Beluga (sturgeon), 62–3
Bering, Vitus, 247
Bering Island, 249–52
Beringia, 163–4
Bester (sturgeon), 62
Betpakdala desert, 113
Bezymianny, 243
Bikin River, 274
birches, 170, 202, 246; *201*
birds
  desert, 119–20
  forest, 124
  seabirds, 255–9
  Siberia, 214
  steppe, 152–3
  taiga, 271–2, 274, 276
  tundra, 166–7, 169
  Ussuriland, 271–2
  Volga Delta, 52, 55, 57
  and see name of bird
bison, 25, 163
Black Guillemots, 251
Black Lark, 152
Black Saxaul, 121–3; *122*
Black Sea, 24, 34–5, 37
Black-billed Capercaillie, 219
Black-billed Desert Finch, 124
Black-capped Marmot, 208–9
Black-crested Tit (Simla or Rufous-naped), 89
Black-crowned Night Heron, 56
Black-legged Kittiwake, 162, 251, 256
Black-naped Oriole, 271; *273*
Black-veined White butterfly, 213
Blackbird, 220
Blackfish, 188
Blakiston's Fish Owl, 274, 276; *274*
Blizhny Plosky, (volcano), 243
Blue (Himalayan) Whistling Thrush, *88*
Blue-and-white Flycatcher, *273*
Bluetail, Red-flanked, 220
Bluethroat, 167, 185
Boar, Wild, 34, 89–90, 267
Boa, Sand, 129; *129*
Brent (Brants) Goose, 162
bristleworms, 229
broomrape, giant (*cistanche*) 123; *123*
Brown Bear (Grizzly Bear), 26–8, 30–1, 92, 102, 211, 228, 263, 267; *27, 29, 262*
Brown Trout, 39
Brown-headed Gull, 99; *96–7*
Brunnich's Guillemot (Thick-billed Murre), 162, 256
Buckthorn, Siberian, 102
Bukhara Deer, 124
Bukhara Tit, 118, 141
bullheads, 231
bumblebees, 172
Bunting
  Lapland (Lapland Longspur), 167, 169

Little, 167
  Red-headed, 87
  Rock, 143
  Snow, 162, 167, 169; *169*
Bustard, Houbara, 152–3; *153*
Buttercup, Arctic, 163
butterflies, 87, 185, 213, 271; *269*
Buturlin, Sergei Alexandrovitch, 178
buzgunch, 143
Buzzard
  Long-legged, 138
  Rough-legged (Rough-legged Hawk), 182, 188–9

caddis flies, 225–8; *227*
Camberwell Beauty butterfly, 213
camels, 135–6; *135*
campions, 269, *268*
Capercaillie
  Black-billed, 219
  Western, 219
Caribou, 163, 174–5, 191; *175*
carp, 48, 52
Caspian Sea, 34, 37–41, 43, 46; *33*
Caspian Seal, 39–40; *40*
Caspian Sturgeon, 62–3
Caspian Tern, 69–70, 99; *68, 69*
Caspian Tiger, 283
caterpillars, 191, 213
catfish, 60
cats, 279 *and see* cheetahs, leopards, lynx, tigers
Cattle Egret, 73
Caucasus, 34, 76
caviare, 66–7
Central Asian Cobra, 127
Chamaenerion angustifolium, 220
Char, Arctic, 187
Cheetah, 139
chernozem, 147
Chinese Merganser, 272, 274
Chinese Soft-shelled Turtle, 266
chipmunks, 208, 267; *209*
chironomid midges, 185
Chiru (Tibetan Antelope), 152
Chough, Alpine, 84
Chukar Partridge, 143
chukchi people, 174, 176
Chukot Mountains, 78
Chum Salmon, 259
Citrine Wagtail, 226
Cladonia (lichens), 175
climate, 19, 36, 79, 83–4, 114
  Aral Sea, 36
  Arctic, 163, 166, 190, 196–7
  deserts, 110, 112–14, 116
  Pamir, 79, 82
  Siberia, 198, 213–14
  Tien Shan, 83–4, 100
  Ussuriland, 267, 269, 271
  and see rainfall, temperatures
Coal Tit, 271
Cobra, Central Asian, 127
Coho Salmon, 262
Common Crossbill (Red Crossbill), 205, 207
Common Goldeneye 39, 266
Common Greenshank, 70

Common Guillemot (Common Murre), 256
Common Merganser, 266
Common Murre, 256
Common Seal, 262
Common Tern, 99
conifers, 200–1, 203, 212; *201*
conservation, 55, 253
Coot, 52, 57–8
Cormorant, Great, 59–61, 250–1, 256; *61*
Corsac fox, 142
Cottids (bullheads), 231
Cottid, Yellow-winged, 231; *235*
cotton, 145–6; *145*
cotton grass, 170
Cow Parsley, 246
Crane
  Hooded, 266
  Japanese, 266; *275*
  Sandbill, 164, 167
  Siberian White, 164, 176; *177*
  White-naped, 266
Crested Auklet, 256–7, 259; *257*
Crested Lark, 143
Crossbill
  Common (Red), 205
  Parrot, 205
  Two-barrel (White-winged), 205; *204*
crossbills, 204–5, 207, 271; *204*
Crow, Hooded, 60
cuckoo, 272
cuckoo, Eurasian, 70
Curlew, Eurasian, 70

Dalmatian Pelican, 59
damselflies, *47*
Daurian Redstart, 271
deer, 25, 124, 217, 267 *and see* musk deer
desert candles (fox-tailed lilies), 85; *86*
Desert Monitor, 118–19; *118*
Desert Sparrow, 119–20
deserts, *15*, 113, *115*
  birds, 119–20
  climate, 110, 112–14, 116
  forests, 121–3
  rainfall, 114, 116, 137
  temperatures, 116, 124
  vegetation, 120–4
Desman, Russian, 41–3; *42*
Dhole (Asian Wild Dog), 277
divers (loons), 162; *162*
Djemchusny, 67–9
Djeran (Guitred Gazelle), 139–40, 143–4; *139*
dogs, 277–9; *278*
Dovekie (Little Auk), 162
dowitchers, 164, 222–3
Dromedary Camel, 135–6; *135*
ducks
  Goldeneye, Common, 39, 266
  Harlequin Duck, 272
  King Eider, *186*
  Long-tailed Duck (Oldsquaw), 167, 185–6
  Mandarin Duck, 272; *273*
  Smew, 39
  Steller's Eider, 251–2; *251*
  Velvet Scoter, 39

· INDEX ·

Dwarf Birch, 170
Dwarf Japanese Stone Pine, 202, 211–12

Eagle Owl, Northern, 133; *134, 137*
Eagle
  Golden, 57, 84, 138
  Short-toed, 138
  Steller's Sea, 263–6
  White-tailed, 57–9, 74, 266; *58*
Eastern Rock Nuthatch, 143
Egret
  Cattle, 73
  Great White, 55; *52*
  Little, 52, 55
egrets, 37, 52, 55, 73; *53*
Elk (Moose), 25, 217
Emperor Goose, 164
Epischura baicalensis (crustacean), 231
ermine, 216
Eurasian Black Vulture, 84, 141
Eurasian Cuckoo, 124
Eurasian Curlew, 70
Eurasian Nuthatch, 207
Eurasian Wigeon, 167
European Bison (Wisent), 25
European Mink, 215

Falcated Teal, 272
Falcon
  Gyr, 186
  Peregrine, 181–2
Far-eastern Wild Cat, (Amur Forest Cat), 279
feather grasses, 146; *147*
Fedchenko Glacier, 78–9, 82
fennel, giant (ferula), 92, 138; *138*
Fieldfare, 220
Finch, Black-billed Desert, 124
Finsche's Wheatear, 138
fire-bellied toad, 271; *270*
fish, 48, 52
  Arctic, 186–8
  Caspian Sea, 40–1
  Lake Baikal, 231, 234
  Ussuriland, 276
  Volga, 48, 52
  and see name of fish
Fish Owl, Blakiston's, 274, 276; *274*
Flag, Yellow, 48; *49*
Flamingo, Greater, 72–3
flatworms, 228
Flycatcher
  Asian Paradise, 89, 271; *273*
  Blue-and-white, *273*
Forda hirsuta (aphid), 143
forests, 24–5
  birds, 124
  desert, 121–3
  Siberia, 200–2
  Tien Shan, 83–4
  Ussuriland, 269
  and see vegetation
Forget-me-not, Arctic, *171*
fox-tailed lilies (desert candles), 85; *86*
Fox
  Arctic, 163, 184, 188–90, 197; *183*
  Corsac, 142
  Red, 208, 215
Franz Josef Land, 161

Frog
  Marsh, 48
  Tree, *270*
frogs, *48*
Fulmar, Northern, 162

Gadwall, 70
Gallinule, Purple, 73
gammarid shrimp, 230–1; *230*
Gazelle, Goitred (Djeran), 139–40, 143–4; *139*
geckos, 132–3; *132*
Gerald Island, 156–7, 160
Gerbil, Great, 124–6, 142–3; *125*
geysers, 245; *246*
glaciers, 78–9, 82, *77*
Glaucous Gull, 162, 180
Glossy Ibis, 57, 70
goats, 103–5; *105*
Godwit, Bar-tailed, 70
Goitred Gazelle (Djeran), 139–40, 143–4; *139*
Golden Eagle, 57, 84, 138
Goldeneye, Common, 39, 265
Golomyanka, 231, 234; *234*
Goosander (Common Merganser), 265–6
Goose
  Bar-headed, 19, 79, 95, 98–9; *98*
  bean, 174
  Brent (Brant), 162
  Emperor, 164
  Greylag, 52, 70, 72
  Red-breasted, 180–2, 190; *181*
  Snow, 167, 184, 190; *182*
Goral, Grey, 276–7
Grass Snake, 48
grasses, 146, 170; *147*
Grayling, Pallas's Arctic, 188
Great Black-headed Gull, 67–9, 99; *67, 69*
Great Cormorant, 60; *61*
Great Gerbil, 124–6, 142–3; *125*
Great Grey Owl, 207
Great Spotted Woodpecker, 207
Great White Egret, 52, 55; *53*
Greater Flamingo, 72–3
Greater Rosefinch, 89
Greater Scaup, 185–6
Green-winged Teal, 70, 167
Greenish Warbler, 220, 271
Greenshank, Common, 70
Grey Coral, 276–7
Grey Heron, 55
Grey Wolf, 25, 215, 277
Grey-backed Thrush, 271
Greylag Goose, 52, 70, 72
Grieg's Tulip, 85; *86*
griffon vultures, 84–5
Grizzly Bear, 26–8, 30–1, 92, 102, 211, 228, 263, 267; *27, 29, 262*
Grouse
  Hazel, 219
  Siberian Spruce, 219, 271
  Willow (Willow Ptarmigan), 173, 185, 192, 219; *193, 218*
guillemots (murres), 162, 251, 256
Güldenstädt's Redstart, 90–1, 100, 102
Gull-billed Tern, 99
gull
  Brown-Headed, 99; *96–7*

Glaucous, 162, 180
Great Black-headed, 67–9, 99; *67, 69*
  herring, 180, 182, 184
  Ivory, 162; *190*
  Relict, 99–100; *101*
  Ross's, 164, 176–8, 180, 186–8, 190–1; *179*
  Sabine's, 162
  Slaty-backed, 258, 263
Gyr Falcon, 186

Harbour Seal, 262
Hare, Arctic, 219
Harlequin Duck, 272
Hawfinch, 267
Hawk, Rough-legged, 182, 188–9
Hazel Grouse, 219
Hedgehog, Long-eared, 131–2; *131*
herons, 52, 55–7, 73; *54*
Herring Gull, 180, 182, 184
Himalayan Griffon, 84
Himalayan Rubythroat, 89; *88*
Himalayan Snowcock, 79, 100; *101*
Himalayan Whistling Thrush, *88*
Hoary Redpoll, 167, 169, 214; *214*
Hooded Crane, 266
Hooded Crow, 60
Horned Puffin, 256, 259
horses, 93–4, 163
Horsfield's Tortoise, 116–17
Houbara Bustard, 152–3; *153*
Humpbacked Salmon, 259
Hyena, Striped, 131, 142; *130*

Ibex, Siberian, 89, 104
Ibis, Glossy, 57, 70
Ibisbill, 82–3; *83*
insects, 172, 184–5
Inylchek Glacier, 79; *77*
iris (flag), 48; *49, 268*
irrigation, 144–6
Isabelline (White-clawed) Brown Bear, 31, 92; *30*
Isabelline Wheatear, 126
Issyk-Kul Lake, 94–5
Ivory Gull, 162; *190*

Jack Salmon, 262
jaegers, 180, 188
Japanese Cormorant, 256
Japanese Crane, 266; *275*
Jay, 207
  Pander's Ground, 124
  Siberian, 203–4, 219–20; *203*
  Steller's, 248
jerboas, 128–9; *128*
juniper, 83–4

Kaman, (volcano), 243
Kamchatka, 31, 78, 208, 240, 242–3, 245–9, 255, 265
Kamchatkan Alder, 246
Kamchatkan Nettle, 246
Kara Bogaz Gol, 34
Karaginsky Island, 255
Kara-Kul Lake, 95; *96–7*
Karakum, 110, 112, 116, 120–1
Kayak Island, 248

Kazakh people, 92–4
Kedrovaya Pad, 269
Khan Tengri, 78
khangul, 124
King Eider duck, *186*
King Salmon, 259, 262
Kirov Bay, 73
Kittiwake, 259
  Black-legged, 162, 251, 256
  Red-legged, 255
Klyuchevskaya Complex (volcanoes), 242–3
Klyuchevskaya Sopka (volcano), 243
Kolyma Mountains, 78
Komandor Islands, 253, 255
Kopet-Dag Mountains, 76
Korean Pine, 267
Koryak Mountains, 78
Krasnovodsk, 72–3
Krashenninikov, Stepan Petrovich, 247, 259
Kronotskiy State Nature Reserve, 245
Kulan (Asiatic Wild Ass), 140, 142; *111*
Kuril Islands, 240, 242, 253, 255–6
Kurilsky Lake, 265
Kyzyl-Agach, 73
Kyzylkum, 112

Lammergeier (Bearded Vulture), 84–5
Lapland Bunting (Lapland Longspur), 167, 169
larches, 202–3, 212–13
Large-eared Pika, 102–3
Lark
  Black, 152
  Crested, 143
  Short-toed, 152
leaf warblers, 220 *and see* warblers
Least Weasel, 215
lemmings, 173–4, 184, 188–9, 192, 218
Lenin Peak, 79
Leopard
  Iranian race, 139
  Amur race, 279; *280–1*
  Snow, 108–9; *106–7*
lichens, 175–6; *223*
lilies, 85, 220; *86, 286*
Little Auk (Dovekie), 162
Little Bunting, 167
Little Egret, 52, 55
Little Owl, 133
lizards, 117–19, 132–3; *117 and see* monitors
Long-billed Dowitcher, 164
Long-eared Hedgehog, 131–2; *131*
Long-eared Toad-headed Agama Lizard, 117–18; *117*
Long-tailed Duck (Oldsquaw), 167, 185–6
Long-tailed Jaeger, 180, 188
Long-tailed Marmot, 90; *91*
Long-tailed Siberian Suslik, 208
Long-tailed Skua (Long-tailed Jaeger), 180, 188
Longspur, Lapland, 167, 169
loons, 162; *162*
lotus, 70, 72; *71*
louseworts, 170, 172; *171*
Lynx, 25, 208, 267

286

Maack's Swallowtail Butterfly, 271; *269*
Mallard, 70
mammoths, 163–4
Mandarin Duck, 272; *273*
Maral, 217
Marco Polo Sheep, 79, 89, 105, 108
Markhor Goat, 104–5; *105*
Marmot
  Black-capped, 208–9
  Long-tailed, 90
  Red, 90, *91*
marmots, 90, 100; *91*
Marsh Frog, 48
Martagon Lily, 85, 220
Marten
  Beech, 215
  Pine, 215
  Yellow-throated, 277
martens, 208, 215–17, 277
Meadow Sweet, 246
Medny Island, 251, 253
Merganser
  Chinese, 272
  Common, 265–6
  Red-breasted, 90
  Scaly-sided, 272, 274
Middendorf's Oxytrope, 172
midges, 185–6, 191
Mink, European, 215
Mistle Thrush, 220
Monitor, Desert, 118–19; *118 and see* lizards
Moose, 25, 217
mosquitoes, 185–6, 191
moths, 213, 271; *270*
Mount Belukha, 78
Mount Elbrus, 17, 76
Mountain Primula, 87
Murgab River, 114, 144–5
murrelets, 256–8
murres, 162, 251, 256
musk deer, 103, 237 *and see* deer
Musk Deer, Siberian, 219, 237, 239, 277; *239*
Musk Ox, 163–6; *165*
Mute Swan, 52
Mytnovsky volcano, *241*

Naumann's Thrush, 220
nematode worms, 184
nettles, 246
New Siberian Islands, 162
nightjars, 133
Northern Eagle Owl, 133
Northern Fulmar, 162
Northern Fur Seal, 252–3; *252*
Northern Pike, 188
Northern Pintail, 70, 167
Northern Raven, 263
Northern Red-backed Vole, 217–18
Novaya Zemlya, 161
nutcracker, 203–4, 207, 267, 271; *203*
Nuthatch
  Eastern Rock, 143
  Eurasian, 207

Okhotsk, Sea of, 255–6
Oldsquaw, 167, 185–6
Omul, 234–5; *232–3*
onions, wild, 85, 87; *86*

Orioles, Black-naped, 271; *273*
Otter, sea, 253–5; *254*
Owl
  Blakiston's Fish, 274, 276; *274*
  Great Grey, *207*
  Little, 133
  Northern Eagle, 133; *134, 137*
  Snowy, 163, 188–91; *189*
owls, 133, 208
oxytropes, 172

Pacific Golden Plover, *168*
Pallas's Arctic Grayling, 188
Pamir Mountains, 32, 79, 82; *18, 80–1*
Pamir-Alai Mountains, 78
Pander's Ground Jay, 124
Paradise-flycatcher, Asian, 89, 271; *273*
Parakeet Auklet, 257
Parrot Crossbill, 205, 207
Partridge, Chukar, 143
Pechora-Ilych Nature Reserve, *23*
Pectoral Sandpiper, 164, 169
Pelagic Cormorant, 256
Pelican, Dalmatian, 59
Peregrine Falcon, 181–2
permafrost, 23, 170, 200
Persian robin, 87, 89; *88*
Phaeton (desert ant), 123
phalaropes, 185
Pheasant, Common, 124
Piebald Shrew, 133
Pik Kommunisma (Communism Peak), 79
Pik Pobeda (Victory Peak), 78
Pika
  Altai, *102*
  Large-eared, 102
  Red, 103
pikas, 102–3
Pike, Northern, 188
Pin-tailed Snipe, 169
Pine Marten, 215
pines, 202–3, 211–12, 267
Pink Salmon, 259
Pintail, Northern, 70, 167
pipefish, 39; *38*
Pipit, Red-throated, 167
Pistachio tree, 140–3; *121, 141*
planarians, 228
Plover, Pacific Golden, *168*
Podyapolsky, Nicolai, 55
Polar Bear, 154, 156–7, 163, 192–3, 196; *155, 194–5*
pollution, 36–7, 145–6, 224–5; *224*
Pomarine Skua (Pomarine Jaeger), 180, 188
poppies, 121, 246; *121, 171*
population, 16–17
Porcupine, White-tailed, 142
Primorska Nizmennost, 164
Primula, Mountain, *87*
Pronghorn Antelope, 152
ptarmigan
  Rock, 219
  Willow, 173, 185, 192, 219; *193, 218*
ptarmigans, 173, 185, 192, 219; *193, 218*
Puffin
  Horned, 256, 259
  Tufted, 256, 259; *258*

Purple Emperor butterfly, 271
Purple Gallinule, 73
Purple Heron, 55; *54*
Purple Sandpiper, 162
Purple Saxifrage, *171*

Raccoon Dog, 277–9; *278*
racer snakes, 127
Racerunner, Reticulate, 119
Rainbow Trout, 95
rainfall, 19, 22, 24
  deserts, 114, 116, 137
  Pamir, 79
  steppe, 147
  Ussuriland, 269
  and see climate, temperatures
Ran-Kul Lake, 98–9
Raven, Northern, 263
Razorbill, 256
Red Crossbill, 205, 207
Red Deer, 25, 217
Red Fox, 208, 215
Red Marmot, 90; *91*
Red Pika, 102–3
Red Squirrel, 205–6; *205*
Red Salmon, 259, 265; *260–1*
Red-breasted Goose, 180–2, 190; *181*
Red-breasted Merganser, 90
Red-faced Cormorant, 256
Red-flanked Bluetail, 220
Red-fronted Serin, 89
Red-headed Bunting, 87
Red-legged Kittiwake, 255
Red-throated Pipit, 167
Redpoll, Arctic (Hoary Redpoll), 167, 169, 214; *214*
Redshank, Spotted, 70, 169; *168*
Redstart
  Daurian, 271
  Güldenstädt's, 90–1, 100, 102
Redwing, 220
Reindeer (Caribou), 163, 174–5, 191; *175*
reindeer moss, 175
Relict Gull, 99–100; *101*
Repetek, 114, 116
Reticulate Racerunner, 119
rhododendrons, 246–7; *25*
rhubarb, 120–1
Ribbon Seal, 259
Ringed Seal, 39
Robin
  Persian, 87, 89; *88*
  Siberian Blue, 272
Rock Bunting, 143
Rock Ptarmigan, 219
Rosefinch, Greater, 89
Ross, Sir James Clark, 178
Ross's Gull, 164, 176–8, 180, 186–8, 190–1; *179*
Rough-legged Buzzard (Rough-legged Hawk), 182, 188–9
Rubythroat, 89, 220; *88*
Ruddy Shelduck, 90
Ruff, 70, 169; *168*
Rufous-naped tit, 89
Russian Desman, 41–3; *42*

Russian Flying Squirrel, 209, 211; *210*
Russian Sturgeon, 62

Sabine's Gull, 162
sable, 215–17, 265; *215*
Sacred Lotus, 70, 72; *71*
Saiga, 150–2, 163; *148–9*
Salamander, Siberian, 191, 271; *191*
salmon, 259, 262–3, 265
Salmon
  chum, 259
  Coho, 262
  Humpbacked, 259
  Jack, 262
  King, 259
  Pink, 259
  Silver, 262
  Sockeye, 259; *260–1*
Sand Boa, 129; *129*
Sand Tarantula, 127
Sand Toad-headed Agama, 118
sandgrouse, 120
  Tibetan, 79
Sandhill Crane, 164, 167
Sandpiper
  Pectoral, 164, 169
  Purple, 164
  Sharp-tailed, 167, 169
  Spoon-billed, 176
Saw-scaled Viper, 126–7, 132
Saxaul
  Black, 121–3; *122*
  White, 121
saxifrages, 170; *171*
Sayan Mountains, 78
Scaly-sided Merganser, 272, 274
Scarlet Campion, 269; *268*
Scaup, Greater, 185–6
scorpions, 127–8
Scots Pine, 202
Sea Cow, Steller's, 249–50
Sea Eagle, Steller's, 263–6; *264*
Sea Lion, Steller's, 252–3
Sea Otter, 253–5; *254*
Seal
  Baikal, 235–7; *236*
  Caspian, 39–40; *40*
  Common or Harbour, 262
  Northern Fur, 252–3; *252*
  Ribbon, 259
  Ringed, 39
Selenga River, 222, 225
Serin, Red-fronted, 89
Sevruga (or Caspian) Sturgeon, 62–3
Sharp-tailed Sandpiper, 164, 167
sheep, 103–5, 108
  Arkhar, 142; *142*
  Marco Polo, 79, 89, 105, 108
Shelduck, Ruddy, 90
Short-eared Owl, 188
Short-toed Eagle, 138
Short-toed Lark, 152
Shrew, Piebald, 133
Shrike, Bay-backed, 141
shrimps, gammarid, 230–1; *230*
Siberia
  birds, 214
  climate and temperatures, 19, 198, 213–14

Siberia—*contd*
vegetation, 200–2, 206–7, 211–13, 220
Siberian Blue Robin, 272
Siberian Buckthorn, 102
Siberian Chipmunk, 208; *209*
Siberian Flying Squirrel, 267
Siberian Ibex, 89, 104
Siberian Jay, 203–4, 219–20; *203*
Siberian Larch, 212–13
Siberian Musk Deer, 219, 237, 239, 277; *238*
Siberian Rubythroat, 220
Siberian Salamander, 191, 271; *191*
Siberian Snow Sheep, 108
Siberian Spruce Grouse, 219, 271
Siberian Stone Pine, 202–3
Siberian Thrush, 220
Siberian Tiger, 279, 283; *282*
Siberian Tit, 203, 214
Siberian Weasel, 215
Siberian White Crane, 164, 176; *177*
Siberinauta snails, 186
Sikhote-Alin Mountains, 78, 266
Silver Salmon, 262
Simla Tit, 89
Sirenians, 249
skuas (jaegers), 180, 188
Slaty-backed Gull, 258, 263
Slavum lentiscoides (aphid), 143
Small Tortoiseshell butterfly, 213
Smew, 39
snakes, 126–7, 129, 132, 271; *48, 129*
Snipe, Pin-tailed, 169
Snow Bunting, 162, 167, 169; *169*
Snow Goose, 167, 184, 190; *182*
Snow Leopard, 108–9; *106–7*
Snowcock, 100, 102
Himalayan, 79, 100; *101*
Tibetan, 79, 100
Snowy Owl, 163, 188–9; *189*
Sockeye Salmon, 259, 265; *260–1*
solifugids (sun spiders), 128
Solonchak desert, 113
Spanish Sparrow, 141
Sparrow
Desert, 119–20
Spanish, 141
Tree, 59
Spectacled Cormorant, 250–1
Spectacled Guillemot, 256
spiders, 87, 127–8
sponges, 228; *229*
Spoon-billed Sandpiper, 176
Spoonbill, White, 57, 70
Spotted Redshank, 70, 169; *168*
springtails, 184–5
Spruce, Tien Shan, 83–4
Squacco Heron, 55
Squirrel
Red, 205–8; *205*
Russian Flying, 209, 211, 267; *210*
Siberian flying, 267
Stanovoy Mountains, 78
Steller, Georg Wilhelm, 239, 247–55
Steller's Eider, 251–2; *251*
Steller's Jay, 248

Steller's Sea Cow, 249–50
Steller's Sea Eagle, 263–6; *264*
Steller's Sea Lion, 252–3
steppes, 31, 146–7, 150
Sterlet, 62
Stickleback, Twelve-spined, 187–8
Stint, Temminck's, 169
stlanik, 211–12
Stoat, 215, 265
Striped Hyena, 131, 142; *130*
sturgeon, 61–3, 66–7; *64–5, 66*
sun spider, 128
susliks, 123–4, 208
Swan
Mute, 52
Whooper, 73–4, 265; *73*
Syr Darya Pheasant, 124

Taiga, 200; *199*
birds, 271–2, 274, 276
vegetation, 23–4, 206–7, 221
Taimyr Peninsula and Nature Reserve, 161, 165, 172; *161*
tarantulas, sand, 127
Teal
Baikal, 272; *273*
Falcated, 272
Green-winged, 70, 167
Tedjen River, 114, 144–5
Temminck's Cormorant, 256
Temminck's Stint, 169
temperatures, 19, 22
Arctic, 154, 160, 197
desert, 116, 124
Siberia, 19, 198, 213–14
Steppe, 147
Tien Shan, 83
and see climate, rainfall
Tern
Arctic, 162, 180
Caspian, 69–70, 99; *68, 69*
Common, 99
Gull-billed, 99
Whiskered, 56
White-winged Black, 223
Tethys Sea, 32, 34
Thick-billed Murre, 162, 256
thrift, 170
thrushes
Blackbird, 220
Blue Whistling Thrush, *88*
Fieldfare, 228
Grey-backed Thrush, 271
Mistle Thrush, 220
Naumann's Thrush, 220
Redwing, 220
Siberian Thrush, 220
Tibetan Sandgrouse, 79
Tibetan Snowcock, 79, 100
Tien Shan, 32, 78–9, 83–5, 87, 100
Tien Shan spruce, 83–4
tiger snake, 271
tiger, Siberian, 279, 283; *282*
Tit
Azure, 89
Black-crested (Simla or Rufous-naped), 89

Bukhara or Turkestan, 118, 141
Coal, 271
Siberian, 203, 214
Toad-headed Agama Lizard, *117*
toads, fire-bellied, 271; *270*
Tortoise, Horsfield's, 116–17
Trans-Siberian Railway, 16
Transbaikalian Mountains, 78
tree frog, *270*
Trout
Brown, 39
Rainbow, 95
Troytskovo, 245
Tschirr (fish), 187
Tufted Puffin, 256, 259; *258*
tugay, 124
Tulip, Greig's, 85; *86*
tulips, 85, 121; *86*
tundra, 160–1, 163–4; *160*
birds, 166–7, 169
vegetation, 22–3
Tungun (fish), 187
Turkestan Tit, 118, 141
Turtle
Chinese Soft-shelled, 266
freshwater, *50–1*
Twelve-spined Stickleback, 187–8
Two-barred Crossbill (White-winged Crossbill), 205, 207; *204*

Ural Mountains, 76
Ussurian Swallowtail butterfly, 271
Ussuriland, 266; *267*
birds, 271–2
climate, 267, 269, 271
fish, 276
rainfall, 269
vegetation, 267, 269, 271

vegetation, 22–5, 83–4
Arctic, 22–3, 163, 169–70, 172–4
desert, 120–4
Kamchatka, 245–6
Siberia, 200–2, 206–7, 211–13, 220
steppe, 146–7, 150
taiga, 23–4, 206–7, 221
Tien Shan, 85, 87
tundra, 22–3
Ussuriland, 267, 269, 271
Volga, 48
and see forests
Velikan geyser, 245
Velvet Scoter, 39
Verkhoturova Island, 255
Verkhoyansk Mountains, 78, 198; *20–1*
Viper, Saw-scaled, 126–7, 132
volcanoes, 31, 242–3, 245; *112, 241, 248*
voles, 188, 192, 217–19
Volga River, 41, 43, 46; *44–5, 75*
birds, 52, 55, 57
fish, 48, 52
vegetation, 48
Vulture
Bearded (Lammergeier), 84–5
Eurasian Black, 85, 141

Griffon, 84
Himalayan Griffon, 84–5

Wagtail
Citrine, 225
White, 225
Walrus, 193, 196; *194–5*
Wapiti, 217
warblers, 89, 271 *and see* leaf warblers
Weasel, Least, 215
Western Capercaillie, 219
wheatears, 185
Finsche's, 121
Isabelline, 126
Whimbrel, 70
Whiskered Tern, 56
White Saxaul, 121
White Spoonbill, 57
White Wagtail, 226
White-Billed Diver (Yellow-billed Loon), 162
White-clawed Bear, 31, 92; *30*
White-naped Crane, 266
White-tailed Eagle, 57–9, 74, 265; *58*
White-tailed Porcupine, 142
White-throated (or Persian) Robin, 87, 89; *88*
White-winged Black Tern, 223
White-winged Crossbill, 205, 207; *204*
White-winged Woodpecker, 118
whitefish, 39, 187, 234–5
White's Thrush, 220
Whooper Swan, 73–4, 265; *73*
Wigeon, Eurasian, 167
Wild Boar, 37, 89–90, 267
wild onions, 85, 87; *86*
Wildebeeste, 152
Willow Grouse (Willow Ptarmigan), 173, 185, 192, 219; *193, 218*
Willow Ptarmigan, 173, 185, 192, 219; *193, 218*
Willow Warbler, 167, 220
willows, 170, 172–3; *173*
Wisent (European Bison), 25
wolf spider, 87
Wolverine, 215, 267
Wolf, Grey, 25, 215, 277
Woodpecker
Great Spotted, 207
White-winged, 118
woodpeckers, 267
worms, 184, 229
Wrangel, Ferdinand Petrovich, 157
Wrangel Island, 156–7, 162, 165, 184, 190; *158–9*

yaks, 94; *93*
Yellow Flag (Yellow Iris), 48; *49*
Yellow-browed Warbler, 89, 220
Yellow-throated Marten, 277
Yellow-winged Cottid, 231; *235*
Yenisei River, 198, 223
Yer-Oilan-Duz, 136–8; *137*
yeti, 92
yurt, 92–3